THROUGH THESE MEN

BOOKS BY JOHN MASON BROWN

THROUGH THESE MEN

AS THEY APPEAR

DANIEL BOONE — THE OPENING OF THE WILDERNESS

STILL SEEING THINGS

MORNING FACES

SEEING MORE THINGS

SEEING THINGS

MANY A WATCHFUL NIGHT

TO ALL HANDS — AN AMPHIBIOUS ADVENTURE

INSIDES OUT

ACCUSTOMED AS I AM

BROADWAY IN REVIEW

TWO ON THE AISLE

THE ART OF PLAYGOING

LETTERS FROM GREENROOM GHOSTS

THE MODERN THEATRE IN REVOLT

UPSTAGE

THE AMERICAN THEATRE (1752–1934) AS SEEN
   BY ITS CRITICS (*edited with Montrose J. Moses*)

THROUGH
THESE MEN

Some Aspects of Our Passing History

by JOHN MASON BROWN

*. . . a little flesh, a little breath,
and the part which governs.*
MARCUS AURELIUS

HARPER & BROTHERS NEW YORK

For permission to reprint the following grateful acknowledgment is made to:
The Macmillan Company for a selection from *John Reed, The Making of a Revolutionary* by Granville Hicks and John Stuart, 1936.
Francis T. P. Plimpton for his verse read at the 25th anniversary of the Harvard Law School Class of 1925.
The Reporter for "Stag Dinners at the White House," from *The Reporter,* February 24, 1955.
Shawnee Press, Inc., for words from the song "Mamie" by Jimmie Dodd, Copyright MCMLII by Shawnee Press, Inc., Delaware Water Gap, Pa. Used by permission.
Estate of Jan Struther and Random House, Inc., for "Stevenson's Speech" by Jan Struther from *Major Campaign Speeches of Adlai E. Stevenson,* Copyright, 1953, by Randon House, Inc.

Library of Congress catalog card number: 56–6903

To NORMAN COUSINS
whose gift for abundant living
makes other lives the more abundant

CONTENTS

THROUGH THESE MEN

POINT OF ORDER
A Prefatory Note

In the course of a Fourth of July oration Artemus Ward once said, "I am not a politician, and my other habits are good." Skipping my other habits, let me explain at once that by profession I am not a political writer. As a critic of books and the theatre, I approach the field of government and politics, nervous in the knowledge that I am trespassing on the property of experts. I trust they will forgive me and not think that I mistake my interest for authority.

I know as a critic that "where life ends, art begins." I still recognize that art and life are imperatively different. But the Second World War changed my attitude toward both drastically. It snatched from my eyes the professional blinders I might otherwise have worn with contentment for the rest of my days. It widened my interests and outlook, and raised the ceiling of my hopes, sympathies, and caring. In the process it forced me to realize, as I had not before, that both the creation and the enjoyment of the arts depend upon conditions of living and thinking which governments make possible.

I am, therefore, grateful to Norman Cousins for giving me the opportunity to have a look into our own politics. Being grateful to him has been a habit of mine since I joined his staff on *The Saturday Review* more than eleven years ago. In a rash moment he asked me to cover the Republican and Democratic conventions in 1952. Once started with writing about figures on the national scene, I found it hard to stop, and this book is the result of my addiction.

In my innocence I first planned to write a rounded picture of the government at work in terms of the key men who make it work. I soon discovered, however, the impossibility of trying to impose an order on official and political Washington that it does not have. The more I observed Washington, the more frequently I visited it,

1

and the more people I interviewed there, the more I understood how prophetic L'Enfant was when he laid it out as a city that goes around in circles.

Although politics enters these pages, they are not really about politics. Certainly they do not deal with the day-to-day realities of the White House, the Hill, or the great government agencies. They do not tell the story of an administration, how it came to power, or used that power in the various departments. Nor do they appraise foreign policy, grapple with sociological problems, or analyze the economic changes which have resulted in the new morality of faith, hope, and deductibility.

Instead, I have written personally and in terms of personalities about certain events and contemporaries that in various ways have shaped our times and, in some instances, even our history. In doing this I no more pretend to write as a historian than I pretend to deal with politics as a professional observer. These sketches, without partisan bias I hope, are journalistic impressions, some gained first-hand, others by much reading and interviewing, but all the result of the passionate, though slightly autumnal, interest of a person accustomed to "seeing things" in one area now seeking to see them in another. Naturally I intrude on this new area, carrying with me old habits acquired from long employment as a critic. My endeavor has been to write not from prejudice but from what I have been able to perceive, and to re-create the image of what I have seen while appraising it.

I have left the accounts of specific events as I wrote them at the moment of their happenings, hoping in this way to retain a sense of immediacy impossible in writing done in retrospect. I offer them as snapshots, so to speak, in our family album to recall people as they once appeared or incidents perhaps already forgotten.

Like anyone else, I could have chosen others to serve as mirrors of our present. Two or three of my choices may seem capricious, if not downright evitable (to use a word I am delighted to find in the dictionary). But the list is mine, and I trust these sketches will themselves make clear my reasons for choosing as I did. Perhaps I should point out that the number of people I have written about is larger than the chapter headings indicate, just as the time spread is wider than the present. This is bound to be, since all of these men in their long careers have lived populous lives.

Even if my choices had been different, I would have approached them in the same way. I would have tried to root their present in their past, suggest the backgrounds against which they have moved, and trace the symptomatic changes in their thinking which our changing history has brought about. Above all, I would have written about them as individuals no less than forces, and as forces because of what they are as individuals. I would have done this because my abiding conviction is that, though history involves millions, it cannot escape from the personalities of those through whom in one way or another it happens to be funneled.

If I stress the individual, it is not because I am a subscriber to the "great man" theory of history. Its fallacies are so plain that the wonder is it ever gained acceptance. Quite aside from the trends which are larger than men and beyond the control of the greatest, or the ground swells in mass hopes and needs which the theory ignores, there has always been a scarcity of truly great men and never any guarantee that those whose gifts are great might not use them to do more harm than good.

It is easier to understand Carlyle, who championed the "great man" theory, when he defines history as "the essence of innumerable biographies." So it is to a degree, and so it might be as a whole, if it included the biographies of the faceless and forgotten who have been a part of it. For history is the record not only of its more important figures and what they have accomplished but of its anonymous millions and what they have been forced or willing to accept. Gaining this acceptance is the accomplishment or failure of those who govern, and the point of division between those who are leaders and those who are led.

In the long, or airplane, view which historians can achieve about the past, the panorama replaces persons, and individuals, if not lost from sight, are often reduced to a blurred swarm of bees. That is the cyclic vision made possible by the distance which is time, and rightly we describe it in terms of perspective. Such a view of the present is beyond most of us who walk in it.

We see the present, caught up in a crowd. Especially if those in front jostle us, it is hard to look over their heads and get a glimpse of the street's turning or the meadow's end. By obstructing the horizon, those we follow seem sometimes to replace it, since they are as far as we can see. The nearer they are to us, the greater our natural interest in them as individuals and personalities. If this is true of strangers in a crowd, it is no less true of those we may not know at all who touch our lives by holding positions of power or influence. The closer they are to us in time, the keener our concern with them as people, since we realize that what they do because of what they are will affect our well-being, modify our thinking, fulfill or fail our hopes, or give direction to our era.

Matthew Arnold, who recognized that "most of us, alas! are what we must be, not what we ought to be—not even what we know we ought to be," pointed out that greatness depends upon the man and the moment being in happy conjunction. The right man born at the wrong moment would be wrong because he would never have the chance to prove his greatness or have it recognized. In Arnold's phrase he would be "a man born out of date," or as we say ahead of or behind his times.

The nation that always had as its leaders the right men at the right moment, more than being fortunate, would be blessed. The only trouble is that such a nation has never existed. Our constant hope is for great men, but since we cannot count on their appearance at all the needed moments, it would seem more realistic to admit that all history, including our own, is the record of great challenges met or unmet because of the sufficiencies or insufficiencies of those so placed that they should meet them.

The mortal equation is always there, not only shadowing accomplishment but determining it. The public performance is based on the private self, and that is derived from the blend Marcus Aurelius had in mind when he wrote, "This being of mine, whatever it really is, consists of a little flesh, a little breath, and the part which governs." In sketching the following contemporaries my hope has been to suggest a little of their flesh, and a little of their breath, while dealing in the most literal sense with the part which governs, since we are affected by all three.

New York, N. Y., February, 1956   John Mason Brown

I

CIRCUS DRAMAS IN CHICAGO

1. The Younger Elephant Takes Over

Sense out of Madness

A national convention, as the Republicans and Democrats demonstrated in Chicago, is one of the oddest institutions known to men and women enjoying the right to vote. Although nowadays it can be attended in one's own home by means of television, it really has to be seen on the spot in order to be believed, and even then believing is sometimes difficult.

Unmentioned and unanticipated by the Constitution, a national convention is such a mountain of paradoxes that it must be described in images as mixed as its own contradictions. It is at once a decisive instrument of history and a rattle in the hands of grownups who are determined to outdo backward children in their behavior. It is a Mardi Gras carnival which, on the basis of appearances, deludes the novice into believing that a slaphappy Rex and his court have been granted the awesome responsibility of shaping the future.

A convention is a notion salesman's paradise, a huckster's heaven, an exhibitionist's dream world, and a windbag's delight. It stoops to many of the juvenile high jinks of a college reunion. Its outward temper is that of a Shriners' convention, a jamboree of the American Legion, and a mass meeting of the Salvation Army. Wherever one is being held, there for the moment is the center of the corn belt. And such corn! Not Country Gentleman, not Golden Bantam, not field corn, but the kind of corn so sheathed in bunting and buttered with patriotic and party bromides that soap operas would reject it and Fourth of July orators of a century back would have hesitated to dish it out.

The proceedings of a convention seem at first to have no other purpose than to waste time. Its program moves so slowly that it appears to be drawn up solely to torment the spectators, to test the endurance of the delegates, and to guarantee that the visitors who have crowded into the sponsoring city will remain there long enough to pay back the large sum that the city, its hotel men, its merchants, its restaurateurs, and its hot-spot operators have put up for the proud privilege of being hosts.

Does a national convention seem to reduce brains to buttons, wisdom to wind, and fairness to puerile invective? Does it appear to substitute noise for reason, careening parades for issues squarely met, and slogans for sense? All these things it does do, and against all such Mad Hatter aspects sober-minded citizens have railed ineffectually over the decades.

But do not be fooled by appearances. A convention, as the Republicans and the Democrats showed, can have its memorable features. What is confusing about it is that it reverses the practice of families cursed with daffy members. Instead of hiding, so to speak, its mentally backward indoors, it plants them in rocking chairs on the front porch and keeps its wise men and vital business secreted most of the time from the public gaze behind closed shutters.

If a convention can be the dullest of hippodromes, it can also be the most exciting of dramas. It may be an imperfect sounding board for the voice of the people. Yet the thunder of the people's voice in all its many regional accents has a way of making itself heard. It can drown out the noise of steamrollers and rise above the most sinister whirrings of a party machine.

In spite of its faults and lunacies a national convention is as American as hot dogs and hamburgers, blue jeans and baseball, or, for that matter, Walt Whitman, Eddie Guest, and Will Rogers. It is a patriotic charivari in which the oldest participants return to their own youth and America's, too. Although its boredom can be great, the encouragement—even the pride—it generates can be greater still, indeed as great as the tensions of its sudden moments of conflict or the awful suspense of the balloting.

The boos and howls, the cheers and chants, the insults and mass demonstrations of the Republicans in 1952 would have been frightening if, plainly, the love of party and country had not been so much stronger than the strongest devotion to particular candidates. Except for a few drunks and one psychopath, those in the hall did their fighting with speeches, banners, music, and jokes. They may have been as raucous as Hitler's Brown Shirts at Nuremberg. But there the similarity ended.

The men and women who composed this crowd had neither surrendered their freedom nor lost their sense of humor. They met as a free people who, though they had their heroes, did not have their *Führers*. They were partisans rather than zealots. Their violent faith in their candidates did not prevent them from being good losers. As their hopes dwindled, as their buttons and placards began to disappear, they may have been heartbroken at first, and bitterly antagonistic afterward. Their disappointment may have been followed by sullenness and gloom. Yet they resigned themselves to the majority's will and, at least for the time being, most seemed to forget the dissensions which only a few hours back had inflamed them.

Notwithstanding its expected Barnum and Bailey trimmings and its many tiresome hours, the Republican Convention had its moments which deserve to be remembered. It was a fight as well as a circus, and a circus in which the sideshow for a while stole the show. Spectators and delegates alike could not avoid the sense of being present at the making of history. The sharp cleavages in opinion and principle dividing the various contestants had long been known and stated with mounting acrimony. Rumors were everywhere; so were plots and counterplots, charges and countercharges.

MacArthur, Hoover, and McCarthy

The Elephant that invaded the cool and comfortable International Amphitheatre in the stockyard area of Chicago seemed at first to be very tired and venerable. Though still capable of trumpeting thunderous blasts, he showed the fondness of the aged for looking backward.

It soon became clear that this Elephant not only thought in the past but was living in the past, too. As the retired will, he resented what had happened since he had last closed his rolltop desk in public office. He had not occupied the White House for twenty years. The period intervening, which he had found interminable, had been so jet-paced in the race of events that most people, even the youngest and most agile-minded, had been unable to keep up with the mad succession of events and the ever-changing climate of their needs and thinking.

For the first day or so spectators must have been convinced that this elderly pachyderm was monarch of all he surveyed. The Old Guard was leading him and appeared to have him under complete control. The convention was Taft-rigged, and apparently under the invincible domination of a pro-Taft National Committee. This committee, sincere and ardent in its convictions, had apportioned the seats, controlled the assignment of hotel accommodations, and planned the program which was to sway, if not entertain, the delegates. Although Lot's wife was not listed among the party representatives, she must have been present as an alternate.

The first prominent evening speaker was the keynoter, General MacArthur, who had already declared himself for Taft. His appearance at the Monday night session was one of the electrifying events of the convention. A tingling sense of expectancy gripped the auditorium. A swarm of policemen supplemented the sergeants at arms in clearing the center aisle. Everyone was standing long before the general made his entrance. He did not need the committee appointed to accompany him to that jutting gray platform which, as it divided the press section and rose to a rostrum, bore a faint resemblance to a surfaced submarine.

MacArthur moved forward, escorted by the history he has made. Although he wore a blue suit, he was still in uniform to those gratefully aware of what they owe him. A proconsul returning to Rome in the glory of a triumph could not have received or deserved a greater ovation than greeted him as a general.

Then he spoke, a handsome bald eagle of a man. Yet among the twelve thousand in the auditorium there were many, not idolaters, who found their admiration mixed with apprehension. Knowing his special brand of eloquence and fearing the dynamite of his personality, they wondered if his speech would not ignite the convention and establish him as a runaway dark horse, should the well-laid plans of the Taft organization go astray. Their worries were groundless. Although MacArthur had the advantage of presenting the first major indictment of the Truman administration, within the first ten minutes his voice made clear that his was the speech of a tired man. By the time he had finished it was no less clear that an old general had faded away as a Presidential possibility, but by no means as a backstage threat at the convention.

The next evening Herbert Hoover was the speaker. Instead of striding down the center aisle like a conqueror, he edged his way civilian-wise to the rostrum from the rear of the platform. He stood there under the blinding lights, the party's elder statesman. He was manifestly touched by the ovation he received and touching as a figure long excoriated not for what he had done to history but for what history had done to him.

Looking very much like the ex-chairman of the board of a great corporation, he spoke mainly in term of "ex's." So far, at least in the big speeches heard in the hall, it must have seemed to many that the Elephant was an ancient of ancients, if not a museum specimen.

Matters were not helped from the liberal or progressive point of view when the Taft strategists, who ran the show, presented McCarthy the next afternoon. Nor did the standing and tumultuous ovation he received add to the Republicans' prestige or popular appeal. McCarthy's presence was a miscalculated risk, not because he had failed to render some needed services but because of the dangerous, undemocratic, and terrifying means he had employed to get them done. To most "McCarthyism" was scarcely a beckoning word.

The Contested Taft Delegation

Luckily, long before the convention met, everyone knew that the old Elephant was not the only Elephant to symbolize the Republican party in Chicago. Another one was in the arena, younger, quicker in his thinking, rejoicing in his strength, eager to do battle, and ready to fight to the finish. He was the aggressive representative of the younger Republicans, the men like Lodge, Brownell, and Dewey who wanted the Grand Old Party, which was no longer grand, to become the Grand New Party.

The methods, questionable when not malodorous, employed by Taft's lieutenants in deciding which of the delegates from Louisiana, Georgia, Florida, and Texas were to be seated handed the supporters of Eisenhower a formidable weapon. They used it brilliantly. A sign of weakening, a single concession, and their cause might have been lost.

For anyone in the Amphitheatre the most reliable signal that something exciting was about to happen always came from the press section. When dull speakers were proving how dull they could be, the newspapermen and women covering the convention were studies in boredom. They turned their backs on the rostrum. They talked among themselves, read newspapers, telephoned, pounded their typewriters, and in general displayed a lack of interest as monumental as it was justified. But let a threat of discord or action appear, or let the leaders of important groups emerge after caucusing in some unventilated cubbyhole behind the scenes, and all the reporters were standing up like exclamation points on the long planks which served them as desks.

The initial excitement came at the very first session with the so-called Langlie or "Fair Play" resolution that challenged the practices of Taftites in the South. On the firm moral ground that persons being tried should not be permitted to vote as jurors at their own trial, this resolution denied to the sixty-eight challenged Southern Taftites the right they would otherwise have had to vote on their own fitness to qualify as delegates. The introduction of the Brown amendment, which exempted seven of these delegates, served mainly to add to the confusion. Even so, the press realized at once that a conflict was at hand, and its expectancy communicated itself to the auditorium.

It was during this preliminary crisis that Senator Lodge, tall, handsome, and as swift-moving as a bloodhound on the scent, kept rushing up to the platform from the Massachusetts delegation, unmindful of boos or cheers, to make his demands for fair play. It was then, too, that Senator Saltonstall dashed up from the same group to wave an admonishing finger at the chairman.

In the heated public debate that followed, Governor John Lodge of Connecticut, the senator's younger brother, pleaded eloquently for the Republican party to prove to the country that it was uncorrupted from within before it charged the Truman administration with corruption. At the close of this same stormy session Representative Christian Herter of Massachusetts performed an act of mercy by explaining to the befuddled delegates what it was they were voting on.

The following roll call was Eisenhower's first triumph. It was an important victory, won on a moral issue by the decisive vote of 658 to 548. The Brown amendment, proposed by the Taft strategists, was in itself a confession of guilt. The refusal to accept this offer and the determination to put the whole matter to the test of a vote by the delegates were proofs of Senator Lodge's wisdom and courage.

Soon afterward the hearings on the contested delegates were held in the Gold Room of the Congress Hotel before the Taft-controlled Credentials Committee. Seldom have committeemen worked harder, longer, or with greater patience. Contrary to the desire of the Taft-ites and according to the wishes of Eisenhower's supporters, these meetings were not conducted behind closed doors but in public, with spectators and the press present, and with television cameras scrutinizing the scene.

Few climaxes in the convention were more absorbing. The position of the Southern diehards was hard to understand. They were among the few politicians on record who appeared to resent the addition of new voters to their party. They were unwilling to realize, as someone pointed out later that, when it comes to the recruiting of Republicans, the South is the party's last frontier, and that if its membership is to be increased there converts must be welcomed.

These hearings brought to light facts so sordid and disillusioning that at one point a cynical young man sitting next to me turned to his companion and said, "Gee, this *is* the place to learn politics!" That these sessions split the party temporarily no one can deny. Yet, though they were painful operations, they brought the party new health. On Thursday, with the seating of the contested delegates from Texas, Georgia, and Louisiana, they won the second victory for the Eisenhower forces. It was a victory so conclusive that it can be said that the first ballot by which the General captured the nomination was really the third ballot cast in his favor, all three of which had followed more or less the same pattern.

While, and even before, these hearings were in progress and the convention was in session, a thousand other things were happening downtown in a Chicago so changed by playing host to the convention that the city was almost unrecognizable. Candidates were holding incessant press conferences, appearing on radio or television programs, shaking hands with admirers, courting pivotal political figures, posing for photographs, and speaking to groups of all kinds.

Meanwhile, as long as their chances were good, their headquarters in the Conrad Hilton were besieged with workers, well-wishers, and those in search of free Cokes. Strategists were constantly on the telephone or hurrying from caucus to caucus and interview to interview, while their countless lesser henchmen were rushing around feverishly, doing whatever they were asked to do. The candidates' wives were no less overworked, forced as they were to maintain unbroken smiles, to give tactful answers to embarrassing questions, and to meet and shake hands with hordes of people.

Trivia and Clashes

Wearying yet stimulating, sleep-robbing yet eventful as the hectic days and nights were, they were not without their lighter side.

There was the paragraph, for example, on the front page of the *Chicago Tribune*, a pro-Taft paper if ever there was one, which in describing the arrival of its candidate reported, quite solemnly, that a "band made up of Taftites playing a strange but rhythmic instrument known as the bombast" was on hand to greet the senator.

There was the radio announcer who, toward three o'clock one morning, in exhausted tones confessed that his "feets were tired," adding he thought that sounded wrong but he was certain Kaltenborn would correct him.

There was the hilarious interlude, at least it sounded hilarious after what had gone before, when the names of the Puerto Rican delegates and an alternate caused a lot of confusion.

There were the cries demanding that the Virgin Islands delegation, consisting of one man, should be polled.

There was the time when Congressman Martin, understandably weary as the chairman, announced that General Eisenhower would meet senators and representatives in Room so-and-so at the Blackstone Hell.

There was the reception at the Palmer House at which Mrs. Eisenhower's well-wishers serenaded her with a song, the words of which, so help me, ran:

> Mamie, what a wonderful name is Mamie,
> In her heart burns a flame for the man that she loves,
>   and her family too.

> "Missus America" thru and thru is Mamie, with her
> style and her grace she's a lady oh so grand!
> Mamie what a wonderful name for the First Lady
> of our Land.

When the convention was over, the performance of John S. Fine, the governor of Pennsylvania, could be counted among its more ludicrous features. Until the decisive vote was in, no candidate or his staff would have dared to smile at the governor's ambivalent allegiances; his antics, peppery or Pickwickian; or his fogbound vocabulary, with its "buts" followed by "ifs" and its "ifs" somehow welded to "howevers." Fine's manners were nonexistent when he killed Martin's speech by grabbing Governors Dewey, Lodge, and Adams and insisting against their will that they be photographed together right under the rostrum.

Yet the Pennsylvania governor was Lord Chesterfield himself compared to Dirksen, when in the presence of the whole convention the senator from Illinois pointed at Dewey and cried, "We followed you before and you took us down the road to defeat." It was discourteous enough for the Republicans not to have invited their two-time candidate for the Presidency, and the titular head of their party, to address the convention, but for Dirksen, who is a vibrant and accomplished, if overelocutionary, speaker, to sink to such bathospheric levels of taste must have come as a shock even to those who know and admire him. The only comfort to be had from this uncomfortable incident came from the inherent sense of fair play in the spectators, which prompted them to follow their booing of Dewey with an ovation for him.

Fortunately, the delegates, already tardy in their schedule, were wise enough to devote only a few minutes to adopting the platform. This was hard on John Foster Dulles and the others who had toiled long and conscientiously to make it acceptable. They must have known, even while they slaved, that a party platform is a compromise achieved with anguish, written in sweat, and about as binding as a set of New Year's resolutions.

Victory for the General

Once the platform was out of the way, the convention got down to its real business—the selection of a candidate. Where there had been noise, there was only silence. Everyone knew that, after all the foolishness, the major maneuvering and minor skirmishing, the largesse of bromides, and the months of planning and hoping, the great moment had come. The roll call from Alabama to the Virgin Islands is always a drum beat no one can listen to without a quickening heart. As surely as it puts an end to past dreams and labors, it may change the future's course. History is in its mounting figures, history made by the slow accretion of four votes here or ninety-two there.

Nearly everyone in the auditorium recorded the balloting on a tally sheet, gratefully writing down the returns from the smaller states but waiting nervously to hear from the larger ones. Gradually it became clear that Eisenhower was ahead, even as he had been in the two preliminary tests of his strength. By the time the roll of the states and territories was completed, the score stood Eisenhower 595, Taft 500, Warren 81, Stassen 20, MacArthur 10. Eisenhower needed nine more votes to win.

Within seconds of each other Pennsylvania's and Minnesota's placards were lifted high to catch Martin's eye, and the leaders of these delegations were calling, "Mr. Chairman!" "Mr. Chairman!" If the chair chose to recognize Stassen's Minnesota, instead of Fine's Pennsylvania, and grant it the privilege of being the President-maker, Martin's personal reasons were understandable.

The bandwagon had started rolling. Delegates from state after state altered their allegiance and came to Eisenhower's banner. The shifting was so precipitous that, when this first and only ballot was declared closed, the General's 595 had risen to 845, and Taft's 500 had dwindled to 280. It was Senator Bricker of Ohio who, with great gallantry and genuine emotion, moved that Eisenhower's nomination be declared unanimous.

All the amenities were at once complied with. Eisenhower, upon hearing the news, slipped across the street from the Blackstone to the Hilton to have a friendly talk with Taft. Warren and Stassen sent wires. But, according to the most authentic reports, Eisenhower received no telegram from MacArthur reading, "Congratulations to my new commander in chief."

Late that afternoon thirty-nine-year-old Richard M. Nixon, junior senator from California, was nominated for the Vice-Presidency by acclamation. The young Elephant was taking over, even as he was soon to take command of the Republican National Committee.

About eight o'clock that night General and Mrs. Eisenhower and the Nixons arrived at the auditorium. Although the party was tumultuously cheered, the General did not strut down the aisle like a conqueror. He walked to the rostrum as part of a crowd. Unmistakably he was a happy man. He was smiling that smile which neither individuals nor multitudes can withstand.

When he stepped to the front of the platform, he radiated humility and sincerity. By his own admission he was a newcomer to political conventions, but he seemed fully at ease. Although modesty and confidence are seldom found together, no one could fail to sense that Eisenhower possessed both. Already he had evolved his own gesture to acknowledge the cheers of crowds. It was a great, expansive V-for-victory formed by flinging both his arms jubilantly into the air.

In his speech of acceptance Eisenhower said, "I know something of the solemn responsibility of leading a crusade. I have led one. . . . I accept your summons. I will lead this crusade."

2. The Donkey Moves In

Stevenson Opens Windows

He had not spoken three minutes before the thousands in the Amphitheatre and the listening millions realized that the low ceiling of convention thought and oratory had suddenly been lifted.

As governor of Illinois, Adlai Stevenson was facing a routine assignment. Like Chicago's Mayor Martin H. Kennelly, he was present at the Democrats' opening session as an official greeter. Under the circumstances, the usual, indeed the expected, chamber of commerce bromides would have been acceptable. In no time, however, it became clear that the balding, pleasant-mannered man on the rostrum was incapable of holding himself down to such banalities.

Plainly, Stevenson was no typical politician. He neither looked nor sounded the part. He had convictions without dogmatism, and eloquence without demagoguery. Instead of sinking to the thundering tirades which cauliflowered the ears throughout both conventions, he invited his hearers to exercise their reason.

No ordinary man would have dared to say to such partisans, "Where we have erred, let there be no denial, and where we have wronged the public trust, let there be no excuses." No ordinary man, speaking to men and women anxious to think the right all on their side, would have insisted that "self-criticism is the secret weapon of democracy." No ordinary man would have warned a party long in power that "we dare not just look back to great yesterdays. We must look forward to great tomorrows." Only a state governor who happened to be a statesman could have had such thoughts and used such words.

In a windowless auditorium Stevenson opened windows on the dilemmas of the outside world. That he was a possible candidate, in spite of his reluctance to be one, did not mislead him into any of those degrading intellectual concessions which might have eased his nomination. He treated the many as if they were the few.

Blessed with a fine mind, he shared the fruits of his thinking with the convention as if all its delegates were equally anxious to think and equally equipped to do so. This in itself was an act of courage. The Governor spoke as a man whose exceptional gift for phrasing was obviously the expression of a large spirit. Supposedly on hand to do no more than spread a welcome mat, he delivered a speech worthy of being a keynote address. On the first day at the first session he soared to an altitude which the Republicans had achieved only on the last night of their convention when General Eisenhower accepted their nomination.

Such a start raised hopes high for a few heartening and exciting moments. Only a dreamer, however, who carried his idealism to the point of lunacy, could have expected such a gathering to remain long at such heights. For there is a "me-tooism" about the outward inanities of conventions which crosses party lines.

The nonsense by which sense is reached; the intolerable squandering of time; the tedium that leads to excitement; the endless stream of poor speakers who have nothing to say and say it at cruel lengths; the tiresome practice which demands that each nominating speech be followed by spiels from four windjammers who say less well what has already been said; the parade of clergymen who in their overlong invocations are frequently tempted to reduce God to party, if not precinct, dimensions; the huddles of caucusers in crowded aisles;

the eagerness of adults, both on the floor and in the balconies, to behave like children; the trooping toward the rostrum by delegates carrying state placards as proofs of loyalty; the blare of bands; the screams of enthusiasts for their candidates; the mass demonstrations by those miserable hirelings who function as the Hessians of hoopla; and the general surrender of individual judgment to mob psychology —all these remain the same.

One of the most inescapable features of the 1952 Republican and Democratic conventions was the utter, incredible, and baffling ease with which the right changed sides, black turned into white, the hero became the villain, and the villain the hero. Truth in politics appears to be reversible. Its disregard for facts is as great as its consideration of party needs.

Doldrums and Diversion

No observer could fail to note that the Democratic Convention was lacking in that life-and-death struggle between two major contestants, and the drama that went with it, which had added to the excitement of the Republican battle. Although the ring was crowded with middleweights, welterweights, and several lightweights (who kept shadowboxing feebly near or outside the ropes), the two heavyweights were not even present. One was President Truman, at first far distant in the White House, and then, after he had given the nod, waiting next to the Amphitheatre in the Saddle and Sirloin Club. The other was Governor Stevenson, who continued to insist almost up to the time the balloting began that he was not a candidate, and who never visited the headquarters set up in his name until after the final returns were in.

Around the Conrad Hilton and the Blackstone the tension and the noise were certainly not as great as they had been when the Republicans met. No doubt this was due to the seeming friendliness of the avowed candidates. Harriman, Barkley, Kefauver, Kerr, and Russell were photographed together before the opening session, wreathed in smiles, shaking hands, and as friendly as the Five Little Peppers. On the Sunday before the convention they were rushing as a team from one television or radio program to another with the eagerness of authors seeking publicity for recently published books.

Although amiable when subjecting themselves to such group interviews, none of these Presidential quintuplets hesitated in the presence of the others to insist that HE was the man for the job and the only one certain to win. Such trumpeted self-belief and such unzippered ambition may create a certain queasiness in those trained to value modesty, even when such unblushing self-confidence is no more than a pose. But politics lives by its own realities, makes its own demands, and is bound to do strange things to men who have a lust for public office.

In their television interviews Barkley came across as the most genial of raconteurs; Kerr, the log-cabin millionaire, as a good-natured, breezy tycoon with a nice sense of humor; Russell as a voluble and capable Southerner, candid in his misgivings about the FEPC; Kefauver (without coonskin cap) as a frozen-faced and enduring collegian, always ready to summon a smile when a camera was near; and Harriman, impressive in his earnestness, as a handsome, gifted, and cultivated man, scrupulous in punctuating his sentences with no less cultivated "ain'ts."

The surface harmony of these aspirants, and at first seemingly present among the Democrats as a whole, was in marked contrast to the open bitterness between the Taft and Eisenhower camps and the political ideas the two men represented. But this concord soon proved an illusion. At least it did among the thousands of delegates and at the very core of the party.

Even before the first meeting there were disturbing rumors that a storm was raging in the committees. It soon reached the convention floor, striking with hurricane force. It was an ugly storm, furious and alarming, which at many moments threatened to do permanent damage. At its center was a conflict between North and South which laid bare ancient animosities. Joint service in two world wars and all the placating years since the Civil War would, you might think, have healed these wounds. Nonetheless a convention held in 1952 appeared at several angry sessions to be almost the same house divided against itself that the nation had been in 1860.

When the Republicans foregathered, they had their heated struggle over the seating of several contested Southern delegations. Although the problem posed by these delegations may have been used for political expediency, it raised a moral issue. The battle of the Langlie resolution was fought, and fought brilliantly, against the questionable means by which the delegates in certain Southern states had been chosen. The issue at stake was something which the general public found easy to understand. Corruption within the party had to be exposed and wiped out before any charges of corruption could be brought against the opposition.

Among the Democrats the sectional conflict, which started as a matter of party procedure, got out of control in a leaderless convention and stirred up many fundamental antagonisms. A fight undertaken in the interests of unity resulted in distressing signs of disunity. What precipitated this division was the amendment to the Moody resolution, which amounted to a "loyalty oath." The object of this amendment was to see to it that the only delegates seated would be those who promised to use "every honorable means" to assure that the names of the candidates chosen at the convention or of the electors pledged to them would be entered in November on the state ballots under the designation of the Democratic party.

This resolution was not presented until late Monday night after Governor Paul A. Dever, an anti-Marquand Bostonian, had sweated and croaked his way through a keynote address almost impossible to listen to, which rose (or descended) to such perplexing eloquence as "from our lips, let us storm the bastions of our destiny beyond the stars." No wonder, to achieve such a purpose, Governor Dever asked for "divine assistance."

Franklin D. Roosevelt, Jr., a personable and gifted, if over-camera-fond young man, fought for the resolution tirelessly and patiently, both in the convention hall and at the committee hearings. No doubt he hoped to convert the "loyalty oath" into a weapon which he could use as effectively in the interests of the Harriman-Kefauver forces as Lodge, Dewey, and Brownell had employed the Langlie resolution in Eisenhower's behalf.

In the case of the "loyalty oath," however, the big gun turned out to be no more than a troublesome firecracker. The tall talk about victory, and all the endless hours misspent trying to win it, ended in a compromise which amounted to defeat for the champions of the resolution. What they had offered as a pledge dwindled into a mild statement of good intentions, and all the Southern states remained in the convention more or less on their own terms.

If ever there was a case of "much ado about nothing," this was it. Nevertheless the repercussions of this debate were far-reaching, though anything but helpful to party unity. They made clear that the Democrats were suffering from the same "political schizophrenia" which, according to Governor Stevenson, afflicted the Republicans. In both parties the FEPC had its vigorous friends and no less vigorous enemies. In both the liberals were in open warfare against the diehards. In both young leaders were struggling with the old for domination. Ultimately, in the interests of harmony, extremists in each party accepted inoffensive platforms and moderate candidates.

Routine Foolishness

Apparently no convention reaches its serious goal without comic relief. Did the Republicans manage in the person of Governor Fine to make a little man big for a few dizzying days? The Democrats were still more ingenious. They found an even littler man to helium into importance. This was Thomas J. Gavin, the Kansas City brewer who, because he served as Truman's alternate and carried the President's sealed voting instructions, was briefly a favorite of photographers and the darling of reporters. Although Gavin's swiftly transient fame may have been ridiculous, Gavin himself proved to be a disarming fellow when he said, "I know how hot I am now and how cold I'll be after I cast that ballot."

If Gavin won universal gratitude as an exhibit on the midway, each long, short, dull, and thrilling day supplied everyone with the needed lighter interludes. Among the people I was grateful to for such moments were:

The steward in the dining car on the way to Chicago who hurried over to assure me, after two men had left their table carrying a "Draft Truman" sign, that "placards carried by guests do not necessarily reflect the New York Central's point of view."

The trapeze artists in the lobby of the Conrad Hilton, who, as a logical argument on behalf of their candidate, went through their act under a sign which urged, "Swing to Ewing."

The disciple of Philip Wylie who was so disgruntled by all the women on one morning's program, and particularly by the scolding and schoolmarmish ways of National Vice-Chairman India Edwards, that he threatened to picket the rostrum with a sign reading, "India for the Indians."

The man sitting next to me during a Russell demonstration, whose only comment, as he looked at aisles choked with signs proclaiming, "America is safe with Russell," "Industry is safe with Russell," "Your son is safe with Russell," was, "What about your wife and daughter?"

Senator Kerr who, when border states were mentioned on *Meet the Press*, smilingly replied, "I don't know what you mean by that. I would remind you that all states have borders. I can't imagine a more embarrassing situation for a state to be in than not to have one."

The delegate from Massachusetts who rose to say, when asked if he cared to address the chair, that he didn't "wish to waste his time addressing a disorderly house."

The incurable huckster who in a Kefauver parade, while other enthusiasts were carrying such slogans as "Estes is bestes'," raised a placard, "I am pledged but I like Schlitz."

Chairman Sam Rayburn, with his faint resemblance to Mussolini, for the bulldozer determination with which he plowed through confused happenings and for the sudden deafness he could develop for "No's" he did not wish to hear.

Where the Republican Convention sank to its low point in taste with Senator Dirksen's turning on Dewey, the Democratic Convention reached its nadir at the Wednesday session. It was then that Senator Kefauver, instead of sitting with the Tennessee delegation where he had a right to be, made a spectacular entrance in a box at the front of the hall and by so doing started a wild demonstration. His excuse for this incredible behavior on the part of a Presidential hopeful was that he was escorting his old Pappy to a seat. But the excuse, however filial, satisfied few. Among those it displeased was Vice-President Barkley. When he addressed the convention that evening as a contestant who had withdrawn from the ring, he delivered a reprimand by pointing out that, if he were a candidate, he would not have appeared because he recognized "the proprieties that ought to prevail among men who seek office."

Among the low points of the Democratic Convention I also counted the strange fact that the name of Dean Acheson was seldom, if ever, heard. Republicans had their own opinion of Acheson and were not reticent in stating it. But for a party which in its platform endorsed a foreign policy he had shaped, and boasted about the measures he had taken in unifying Europe against Communism, to leave Acheson unmentioned was the basest and most cowardly kind of ingratitude.

Eleanor Roosevelt and Barkley

If the convention had its ravines, it also had its peaks. Among these everyone who was there would include, I am certain, Eleanor Roosevelt's speech, the ovation given Barkley, the three slow-moving ballots which resulted in Stevenson's nomination, the climactic entrance of President Truman and the Governor as the nominee, and, of course, Stevenson's speech of acceptance no less than his welcoming address.

Television brought the highlights, sidelights, and lowlights of both conventions into millions of homes. By the skillful guidance of its coverage it enabled watchers to see many more things that happened than those sitting in the Amphitheatre could hope to see. Its close-ups of candidates, delegates, and strategists alike were more revealing than thousands of written words could ever be.

Already television has rendered enormous services to democracy by informing the electorate. In 1956 these services will increase. Unquestionably, due to TV, future conventions will be quite different from their predecessors. They will be streamlined and their programming will have to be adjusted to the needs of the new medium that records them. The long delays, the interminable speeches, the empty nonsense, the windy praise of those who nominate, and the duplications of those who second will doubtless be eliminated.

Even in Chicago in 1952 there was talk of holding offstage those polls which delegates are entitled to demand. Although I do not know about others, I do know that I should miss these polls. Not unnaturally, when requested they invite boos because they bring the whole machinery of a convention to a standstill. Yet there was something splendid, however silly, exasperating, or time-wasting, about them. What they proved was that one very average American citizen was able to keep the President of the United States, the thousands of persons in the auditorium, and the whole world waiting while he exercised his democratic right.

What TV can never supply a substitute for is the excitement of being a part of a convention crowd and sharing its mood. No stay-at-home, for instance, could have felt to the full the group emotion of those present when Mrs. Roosevelt, Barkley, Governor Stevenson, and President Truman appeared.

When Mrs. Roosevelt swept forward, swiftly and lightly, to the rostrum to the jubilant strains of "Happy Days Are Here Again," the past and the present merged. Time turned into an accordion. Nineteen hundred and thirty-two was in everyone's mind; 1932 and all those long, eventful years of Franklin Roosevelt's Presidency. Part of the cheering was for him, for what he had stood for, and for what he had done. Part of it, no less certainly, was for Mrs. Roosevelt, and for the same reasons. She did not face the convention only as a President's widow. She won its cheers as a person who has become an outstanding personage in her own right. It was as such a personage that she spoke, never stooping to partisanship, but speaking earnestly about world affairs and the UN, in both of which she had played a contributive part.

Barkley the next evening was greeted with an even more tumultuous, though quite different, ovation. The tribute he received was paid to a public figure who had served his party long and with distinction. It was in the nature of a farewell to a man who has shown a genius for friendship. Its affection was so genuine that it must have removed whatever bitterness he felt because of having been forced by labor's shabby treatment to withdraw as a candidate.

What Barkley said may have been forgotten, but no one who heard him will forget the way in which he said it. He spoke without notes for almost an hour. Although his speech was a very simple and sincere restatement of Democratic faith, his performance was an incredible feat. At its conclusion there was another demonstration, which Barkley permitted to run too long. Before it was over, however, an extraordinary thing occurred. So many people, prominent and otherwise, rushed up to shake Barkley's hand that the platform began to look as if he were holding a White House reception.

Stevenson Again Opens Windows

No orator is more eloquent than votes when they are being counted. The tension was almost unendurable on Friday as, little by little and then in great numbers, the votes swung to Stevenson. Out of deference to President Truman, who was waiting nearby to introduce Adlai Stevenson to the convention, the nomination of the candidate for Vice-President was postponed until the next morning. Then Senator John J. Sparkman of Alabama was chosen at a session strangely hurried and deserted, considering the historical importance of the office.

The President's long-delayed entrance with Governor Stevenson was impressive. So was the sceneshifting which had preceded it, with the clearing of the platform, the substitution of mahogany desks and chairs for the plainer furniture that had hitherto been used, and the mysterious actions of Secret Service men and aides, all of whom scurried around as if they were stagehands performing their duties with the curtain up.

For the second time within five days Governor Stevenson addressed the convention. Once more it was unmistakable that no ordinary man was speaking. His modesty, his fine command of the language, his deep awareness of the burdens of the Presidency, his humor, his stark sensing of the challenges of our times, the elevation of his thinking, and the largeness of his spirit were again made clear.

It was not only the Democrats who had reason to be proud and happy because of the man they had chosen. It was the nation as a whole. Americans, regardless of party, could feel the same pride, the same pleasure, the same grateful relief that they knew when the Republicans selected Eisenhower.

Learned and observant students of our institutions from De Tocqueville through Bryce have feared that one of the weaknesses of democracy is its fondness for mediocrity. Bryce even wrote in 1896 an ably argued chapter to explain "Why Great Men Are Not Chosen Presidents." He would have to rewrite that chapter. A worried nation could feel the more secure knowing that, no matter which of these two candidates won, an exceptionally able man would be in the White House. Both were selected by delegates of the people. Both choices were made out of the seeming madness and confusion of such political circuses as conventions. Both were of a caliber to refortify faith in the democratic process.

II

THE ROAD TO THE WHITE HOUSE

The General, the Governor, and the Grassroots

It was close to nine in the evening and we were nearing La Guardia when General Eisenhower emerged from his private compartment on the plane carrying him from St. Paul to New York. Seeming for the moment a man without worries, he moved up and down the aisle to chat with the reporters and members of his staff who had flown back with him for his A.F. of L. speech at the Commodore the next morning.

At one point the General asked for details about the flight the following afternoon which would enable him to rejoin his campaign train at Davenport, Iowa. Having come east on a chartered Capital airliner, he assumed he would take the same plane west. An aide, however, pointed out that, since a Presidential nominee must play no favorites, the return trip was booked on United. On hearing this, Eisenhower broke into his all-conquering smile. "If he didn't look out," he said, "this kind of thing could make a fellow take himself seriously." Still smiling, he added, "I suppose to take the same plane out and back would be too simple for politics."

Both Governor Stevenson and the General must have learned during grueling weeks of campaigning that there is nothing simple about running for the Presidency. Although they may have guessed the ordeal that lay ahead, they could not, even as men accustomed to the rigors of public life, have foreseen the unrelenting and terrible demands that would be made upon them.

Certainly, those who in the ease of their homes read the daily reports of the campaign, followed the texts of the two candidates' prepared speeches or whistle-stop talks, listened to them on the radio, or saw them in the newsreels or on television could not be expected to realize in full how merciless was the strain which Eisenhower and Stevenson faced. Even those of us who traveled with them could only surmise from our own weariness at the end of each long day the fatigue of the two men when at last they were permitted to sleep. If by that time their staffs were groggy and we who observed them as reporters were worn out, they must have been exhausted. But if they were (and here is the first inexorable law of the political jungle), they could not, they must not, show it.

Unless they wish to lose votes and start rumors racing, candidates must appear supercharged with energy, health, and good nature at all times and under all conditions. Regardless of when they have gone to bed, how they have slept, or how they feel, they must be up, prepared to greet the rising sun as if it could cast a ballot.

After bolting their breakfast, they must leave their hotel suite or step out on the back platform of their train looking well groomed and exuding affability. No matter how stiff their arms from all the waving to crowds they have had to do the day before, they must turn themselves once again into semaphores of graciousness. Although their fingers may be swollen from yesterday's handshaking, they must offer their hands without wincing to each and all of the state and local dignitaries who board their train, meet their plane, or encircle their automobile when it comes to a stop.

If they travel by motorcade, on approaching a crowd they must either stand up or perch on the top of the back seat, bareheaded and beaming in rain or heat, for block after block, or in big cities mile after mile, all the while going through the calisthenics of salutation. During parades their smiles must be permanent fixtures, as neon-bright as they can make them. They must seem as pleased with silent bystanders or small groups as they are with streets lined with enthusiasts, and grin with the same delight at hecklers as at rooters. If they are met by senators or governors for whom they have no personal liking, they must, while with them, in the interest of party unity hide their dislike under a peck, if not a bushel, basket.

This is by no means all. They must be prepared to accept gifts of every kind, ranging from brooms and pumpkins to rugs and pictures, and, what is more, act as if they know exactly what to do with them. The candidates must also remember the state and town in which they happen to be. This is not as easy as it sounds when so many places are visited during a crowded day. They must have done their homework so as to rattle off the name of the mayor or chairman, and be able to refer to the local product whether it is steel, clocks, Billy Sunday, football teams, or Ellen Glasgow.

They must survive such a schedule as confronted the General the first day I joined the party, when within thirteen hours he made thirteen speeches in twelve cities and traveled 139 miles by automobile and 232 miles by train through Indiana and Illinois. Or they must brave such an itinerary as Stevenson's when he arrived in Bridgeport at noon after flying from Springfield, Ill., and moved northward through Connecticut to deliver nine back-seat or public-square talks and a major address in the evening at Hartford. At the end of such punishing days, which run well into the nights, candidates must go to sleep knowing that what they have just done will in all probability have to be done all over again the next day.

Everything they say publicly is the nation's property within a few hours after their having said it. And anything they say privately to the persons sitting next to them at lunch or dinner or in their car, or to well-wishers lucky enough to push close to them, runs the risk of being quoted proudly by chance hearers who feel they have brushed shoulders with history. The press, notebook in hand, is always at their heels; the newsreel cameras are constantly turned on them. When they speak to a local audience, radio and television may be carrying them to the world. When this happens, they are judged unfairly but inevitably, not according to the gifts they might bring to the Presidency, but on the basis of such talents they may possess as radio and TV performers.

Between the endless parades of their public appearances they must somehow find time to keep up with what the opposition is saying, confer with their staffs, write or redraft their prepared addresses, and at least read the speeches which are written for them. They must be in touch with their National Committees and maintain what peace they can between those ever contrary-minded groups that travel with them as advisers—the close personal friends who, rightly or wrongly, are apt to be the champions of firmness or idealism; and the cynical professionals who, wrongly or rightly, are inclined to be the apostles of compromise and expediency.

In the midst of all their other harassments, they must be able to deal with such sudden and major crises as the revelation of the Nixon and Stevenson funds. All the while they must talk, talk, talk, using their vocal cords more unsparingly than if they were filibustering. Yet, as surely as their spirits must show no signs of drooping, their voices must betray no hints of hoarseness. If they repeat their jokes, illustrations, and themes, as they are bound to do; if each, for example, starts off whistle-stop talks in the morning by saying brightly, "Well, at least the school children must be glad to see me since I got them out of school," they must convince others and give the impression of having convinced themselves that they are forever saying something different. Their daily obligation is to make news. After all, the purpose of their tours is not only to be seen by as many people as possible but to steal headlines from their opponents.

As candidates for the Presidency, Eisenhower and Stevenson played these multiple roles. They were at once exhibits and personalities, public figures in their own right and rallying points for the hopes and convictions of millions of their fellow citizens. In spite of their areas of agreement, each was the symbol of a different approach to the problems of the United States at home and abroad. Each was the leader of his party and at the same time to some extent his party's captive.

The thousands who turned out to see and hear them may have seemed to be attracted by a bobbysox curiosity, but theirs was a vastly different interest. These crowds were drawn by reality, not make-believe. They knew that their lives and living would be affected by the men they waited hours to get a glimpse of and held their children up to see. They sensed that this fight-to-the-finish was *their* fight. They realized that power was the prize, power huge and awesome, and that history was in the ring. Inescapably, therefore, these men, one of whom was bound to be the implement of great events, were judged and followed as more than men. They were mortals who had been transfigured into the symbols of opposing political faiths. In addition to serving as spokesmen for the issues which divided the two parties, they were to most people the embodiments of those issues, and hence had become issues themselves.

Ike and Adlai, a Study in Contrasts

Few men could have been less alike in personality, train-ing, and endowment than the General and the Governor. They pre-sented a sharp and insistent study in contrasts. No reporter who traveled with them as I did, first with Eisenhower and then with Stevenson, could avoid noticing how deep-seated these dissimilarities were.

There were, to be sure, qualities the two men had in common that must be mentioned at the outset. Election years are not notable for dispassionate judgments. They are the open season for mud-slinging, for prejudice at its most violent, for abuse at its ugliest, invective passing for truth, and partisanship which though blind is ever vocal. During them many seem to feel that, in order to be for one candidate, they must vilify the other. It is hard to see, however, how anyone making a pretense to fair-mindedness could fail to admit, even as the campaign grew in heat, that the General and the Governor were both men whose goodness and modesty were be-yond question. They were equally determined to clear up "the mess in Washington." They were equally honest, equally concerned with efficient government, and equally convinced that, to be healthy at the top, it must be healthy at its lowest levels. Each was animated by the same genuine patriotism. Each had the same passion for peace. And both, in their very different abilities, were uncommon men.

The General enjoyed the advantage of touring not only as a can-didate but as a national hero who was internationally known. For ten years he had been a world figure. Those who had never seen him felt as if they had because they had seen so many pictures of him. They recognized him the moment he appeared and were thrilled to have him in their midst. They sensed at once that he was no pro-consul type of military man. He was "Ike" to young and old, "Ike" the liberator, not the conqueror. They may or may not have wanted "a General in the White House," but they did want to see the General whose crusade freed Europe.

Although Eisenhower looked older than at the war's end (who didn't?), he looked years younger close to than he did on television or in most of his photographs. Neither his balding forehead nor his thinning gray hair could detract from what was irresistibly boyish about him as he acknowledged cheers or relaxed in private. He seemed, at sixty-two, in the best of health and, when understandably tired, renewed his strength after a nap with remarkable swiftness. His skin, though crisscrossed with a fine mesh of hard-earned lines, was carnation pink, his eyes a shining blue. He was broad-shouldered and erect, and wore civilian clothes as trimly as if they were uniforms. Above all, as he rode through the streets or stepped forward on a platform, there was a bounce to his personality so buoyant that people felt it and responded to it. His smile was more than a release of high spirits; it was a radiation of light. And when, to greet crowds, he spread his long arms wide in a V-for-victory sign, his gesture was as winning an expression of confidence and affability as this world knows.

Stevenson, a newcomer to politics on the national scale, was not always spotted immediately. In spite of placards and buttons bearing his picture, his many television appearances, and countless photographs which had been printed daily for months, there were times when some of his admirers were said to have cheered his manager, Wilson Wyatt, under the impression they were cheering the Governor. It seems safe to say, however, that those who had once seen him, and certainly those who had watched him as he spoke, were not apt to forget him.

Although he appeared to enjoy campaigning, was always ready with a retort, and had an unfailingly gracious manner, Stevenson's approach to a crowd was very different from Eisenhower's. When he waved, it was not with his arms straight out. He tended to keep his elbows at his sides and to make tentative, half-finished gestures. His pleasant smile was less expansive than the General's and found its truest center, not in his mouth, but in his blue eyes, which had in them all the wit and humor that were in his speeches.

Though he was as bald as Eisenhower, if not balder (corrosion of the hairline, the Governor called it), the hair that he had was black. He was ten years younger than the General and looked it. Stevenson moved swiftly with the energy and ease of a man whose body was at the command of a nimble mind. In spite of seeming almost shy, there was something about him which demanded attention and respect. His was the face of an intellectual. It was as sensitive as it was alert, and quick to register the subtleties and depths of his thinking. In appearance the Governor might at first have been taken for a successful lawyer or businessman, or even a popular professor. If he refused to fit neatly into any of these categories, it was because of another quality or dimension. He might not have had about him the aura of a hero who had made history, but he created the impression of a man who was capable of making it.

As soon as he began to speak, his authority, more accurately his bigness, made itself felt. Then, especially in the case of his major addresses, it was as if a giant switch were thrown on and Stevenson's personality and strength suddenly blazed forth in their full light. Almost every time the General spoke, at least when I traveled with him, the reverse was true. Except in three or four of the twenty speeches I heard him deliver, the light, the extraordinary light, which was his when bowing, waving, or acknowledging applause, went out the moment he started speaking.

There were good reasons for this. When Eisenhower journeyed through Indiana, Illinois, and Minnesota, his troubles were many. He had given his reluctant endorsement to McCarthy, he had had his famous breakfast with Taft, and he had been persuaded to appear publicly with Jenner. Furthermore, the General must have been appalled, if not angered, by what his staff had done to him instead of for him in the Taft matter. The senator, when he flew into New York the night before their meeting, handed to Senator Carlson, the Eisenhower representative who met him, a copy of his statement so that the General could study it. Carlson, however, was reported to have pocketed the statement on the grounds that the General needed rest. The result of this misplaced consideration was that Eisenhower went unprepared into his all-important conference with Taft. The General's staff committed another blunder a few days later when it allowed eighteen hours to pass before telling him about the Nixon fund. Had either or both of these mistakes occurred at SHAEF, the roof would have blown off, and rightly, too.

The Two Men as Campaigners

The General had his other worries when he started out on his special train. Since this was his first whistle-stop tour, naturally he was concerned with how well he could put it over. During most of the first day and part of the second he seemed ill at ease. Before beginning one of his off-the-cuff speeches, he would beam upon the crowd to its obvious delight. Then, instead of allowing people to savor his personality (which is the real purpose of a whistle stop) while thawing them out with an anecdote or a GI story, he would, as a rule, snap off his smile abruptly and assume a grim frown to make it clear that he took solemn things solemnly.

His strategy, of course, was to imply that, because the Governor could at times be wonderfully witty, Stevenson was not to be taken seriously. Unfortunately, Eisenhower often forgot to mention Stevenson or to indicate that he had him in mind. Hence, when the General would declare that he found nothing funny in the Korean war, taxes, high prices, or corruption in government, many people clustered in front of him looked somewhat surprised, if not confused. They had never regarded any of these things as jokes either, and wondered why Eisenhower bothered to make the point.

Few who had a proper admiration for the General, and were traveling with him when I was, could have been happy during those first two days and nights as he spoke from his train or the steps of city halls. His sincerity was radiant, his goodness unmistakable. Yet at most of these smaller stops he seemed inwardly uncertain in spite of his outward assurance. Clearly he was a novice at the game, a man whose mind was made hesitant and harried by listening to too many different advisers who were telling him to do too many different things. He was a great leader who, for the moment, had mislaid his leadership and was being led.

Some of his talks were more telling than others, and he was better the second day than the first. He was at his best before a large crowd at Aurora, a huge crowd at St. Paul, and when delivering homilies to the students at Notre Dame and Carleton and St. Olaf. But something had happened to the Eisenhower who at London's Guildhall had delivered one of the memorable speeches of our time, and later in a smiling mood had said to Mayor La Guardia on receiving honorary citizenship, "New York simply cannot do this to a Kansas farmer boy and keep its reputation for sophistication." That other Eisenhower had gone into eclipse. The fire was temporarily extinguished. The delivery was no longer ignited by his personality. The short sentences, once so eloquent in their directness and military conciseness even when he was not using a script, had been replaced by long sentences apt to lose their way. The complication of their structure could in itself be interpreted as a betrayal of confusion.

It was upsetting to watch the ease with which the seasoned political reporters turned away from the General to scramble back on the train or bus as they guessed he was nearing his peroration. It was disquieting to hear them discuss the lack of interest of his speeches and make fun of his repeated point about the hundred hidden taxes on an egg by referring to it as "The Egg and Ike." Nonetheless, their joking in his early days as a campaigner was understandable from their point of view. The General had given them gray copy, had said little that was newsworthy, and indulged mainly in platitudes. He had made the familiar attacks without offering the needed solutions. He had spoken as the echo for wide-spread grievances but not yet as the voice for a new program.

It is true that reporters are overexposed and cynical judges. It is no less true that at most of these whistle stops Eisenhower received greater applause at the beginning of his speeches than at the end. Nevertheless the crowds poured out to see and hear him. What is more, they listened to him, often with rapt attention and always with manifest affection and respect. Although the General was green at politics, the proof of his political rightness no doubt lay in his having said these simple things to a people whose basic hopes are simple. Among the imponderables of the election was the appeal of Ike's earthbound oratory with the occasional eloquence of its plain phrases and the incontestable honesty and fervor of his beliefs.

The different attitude of the reporters following Stevenson was noticeable at once. They rushed out whenever he spoke, eager to hear what he was going to say. That staggering felicity and facility he has with words made them look up to him as if he were a top-flight member of their profession. Although they realized he would have to repeat himself from day to day, they did not mind. They knew they could rely on him to say new things and even make some of the old ones sound new.

Many of these hard-boiled pressmen listened to the Governor not as if they were doing a duty but as if they were pursuing an enthusiasm. They admired his courage in stating without equivocation beliefs bound to be contrary to the interests of the groups he was addressing. They were delighted by his wit and enchanted by his phrases. They were fascinated by the clarity of his thinking and impressed by the eloquence of his long serious passages. The freshness of his approach in speech after speech amazed them, and they wondered how long he could keep it up. Regardless of their political convictions, the reporters recognized how right *Time* had been when it pointed out that, whether or not Stevenson got in the White House, he was certain to get in the next edition of Bartlett.[1]

Not surprisingly, the Governor's qualities which won him the respect of the press attracted the intellectuals, too. But Stevenson's appeal, as I know from my own observation, was by no means limited to writers, teachers, highbrows, or the college-bred. I heard him talk to small groups from the back seat of a car. I heard him make extemporaneous speeches under the most trying conditions in public parks or in front of town halls. I heard him in overflowing auditoriums read carefully reasoned addresses to Northerners and Southerners of every trade and kind. I heard him speak to the A.F. of L. in New York. And in every case his audience followed him with interest, as pleased with what he said as by his manner of saying it.

Some Democrats, afraid of any deviation from politics as usual, expressed the fear that the Governor ran the risk of talking over the heads of his hearers. Republican leaders made the same complaint, that is, when, in a contradictory mood, they were not doing their best to persuade voters that, instead of being a man of thought, Stevenson was only a comedian, a professional entertainer whom they at one moment likened to Bob Hope and at the next to Bing Crosby.

Stevenson had perhaps the most silencing answer to those who condemned him for his gift of laughter. No one could be more

[1] P.S. He did—thirteen times.

anguishingly aware than he or more articulate about the pains and problems of the modern world. But he realized that, just as men cannot live by bread alone, so they cannot always dwell with sorrow. He knew that laughter is no sin and that we are a people who love to laugh. To explain the jokes he told and the lines he brightened with his wit, he was fond of quoting Lincoln, who in the midst of the terrible Civil War years said of humor, "If it were not for this occasional vent, I should die."

Insult, if picturesque or vitriolic enough, is by tradition accepted as wit during the primitive slugging of a campaign. But real humor, shown by a public man *in public,* is uncommon in this country. Wit has been considered dangerous and irony fatal. The fact that Stevenson dared to employ all three was only one proof of how new and refreshing a type he was in American politics.

The millions who heard or read his welcoming address at the Democratic convention and his speech of acceptance realized instantly, and with unforgotten excitement, that here was a man as exceptional in his spirit and endowments as he was in his attitude toward the electorate. What the Governor had done in Chicago, when he treated the many as the few, he continued to do throughout most of the campaign. He seldom condescended to his hearers. As a citizen of Illinois steeped in the Lincoln tradition, at his best he showed Lincoln-wise that behind his humor and eloquence lay a Lincolnian melancholy and mysticism. As a graduate of Princeton and a close student of Wilson, in his more important addresses he brought to politics an altitude of mind unknown since Wilson's day.

When at a Town Hall luncheon in Los Angeles Stevenson delivered a fine lesson on the responsibility of voters, he did not hesitate to refer in passing to Disraeli, Shaw, Plato, and the London *Times Literary Supplement.* When in Richmond he touched upon the problems of the South with great frankness and understanding, he was no less prepared to discuss Southern literature than the Constitution of the Confederacy. What is more, in his discussion of Southern writing he did not stop with *Gone With the Wind,* but included William Faulkner. When Stevenson addressed the A.F. of L. in New York, though he won many loud and often easy laughs and an ovation, he confessed his speech was intended for the heads, not the hands, of his audience. It was to the heads of the voters that he was again and again intrepid enough to address himself. To reach their thoughts, his whole concern as a candidate was, as he said at Quantico, to find the right words, the true, faithful, explicit words, which would make the issues plain and his position on those issues clear. Surely, Stevenson was not to be blamed for having the ability to find these words any more than he was to be condemned for having a style at once so sprightly and illuminating that he became the favorite columnist of many people, including some who would vote against him.

The Governor in his speeches was constantly saying, "This reminds me" or "I am reminded by"; the General in his, when making a serious point, was apt to say "I am told" or "Someone told me." These expressions, which both men used automatically, were no doubt revealing in themselves.

Many things happened, foreseeable and unpredictable, as the campaign continued. The Stevenson fund, like the Nixon fund, and the Eisenhower and Sparkman income-tax reports made their headlines. The triumph which the Young Republicans had achieved at Chicago became an almost forgotten victory. Stevenson's attempts to disentangle himself from the Truman administration proved unsuccessful. Other figures—Taft, Jenner, McCarthy, Byrnes, Shivers, and Truman himself—elbowed their way back into the ring as symbols of complicating issues. By their often embarrassing reappearances they altered the nature and tone of the contest that Eisenhower and Stevenson would have fought if they had been free to fight it alone and in their own way.

As was bound to happen, the campaign deteriorated in quality and grew in bitterness. Both candidates were put on the spot by the tactics and statements of those supposedly coming to their aid. Both were forced to talk too often for their own good. Both showed an increasing tendency to treat the facts of history as if they were rubber and in their party zeal to state half-truths as whole truths. Eisenhower gained in ease and his speeches bettered perceptibly. Stevenson, though toward the end he frequently reached the high tone of his earlier addresses, was for a short period tempted (or advised) to slug it out on a plane unrepresentative of his real self. Through it all, however, it became increasingly clear how fortunate we were to have such men to choose between.

III

THE TRUMANS LEAVE THE WHITE HOUSE

A Significant Traffic Light

"I am just Mr. Truman, private citizen, now."

In response to cries of "We want Harry," he had come out of Dean Acheson's Georgetown house to speak to the three hundred people, old and young, rich and poor, white and colored, but most of them misty-eyed, who had gathered there to say good-by to him.

Twenty minutes earlier a red light at Seventh and D Streets had abruptly reminded those of us following him that Truman was no longer President. For the first time in nearly eight years an automobile in which he was riding had had to stop for traffic. There were other such stops before he and his little motorcade reached the Acheson home, and on the way other reminders.

Secret Service men, though attending him, were not clustered around Truman's car. No police escort cleared his way. Few among the hundreds of thousands who a short hour and a half before had waved and called to him, as he rode to the Capitol with General Eisenhower in a black Lincoln convertible, recognized him in the limousine which carried him and his family to the Achesons' for lunch. Two or three motorists, also going about their private business, even tried to cut into the motorcade as it neared Georgetown, not realizing it was a motorcade and unaware of Truman's presence.

The listening and the seeing world had heard and watched the proceedings just completed in the Capitol Plaza. No ceremonies which elevate mortals to power are more impressive in their pageantry than these time-honored rites in their simplicity. Compared to the medieval color and pomp of a coronation, they are as plain as the clothes Ben Franklin wore at Louis XVI's court. The spectacle of an inauguration is not a show of wealth or might or temporal grandeur. It is a reaffirmation of principles in which simple dignity replaces ostentation and is in itself a display.

The man driving through Washington unnoticed had ridden up to the Capitol as President of the United States, possessed of all the rights and powers of that office. When he appeared on the temporary platform shortly after noon the color guard had raised its flags in his honor and he had been greeted by "Hail to the Chief." Just before he left, less than an hour later, he had heard those familiar strains again. This time, however, the scarlet-coated Marine Band was saluting another chief.

During that hour, against the background of the Capitol with its dome topped by the statue of Freedom, America had demonstrated its beliefs and aspirations in ways movingly American. "The Star-Spangled Banner" had been sung by a Negro woman. A Catholic archbishop, a rabbi, and a Protestant bishop had offered prayers for this land, its citizens, its new government, and especially its new President, beseeching God, in the rabbi's words, to "keep him with great kindness" and permit us as a people "to walk always in the dignity of free men."

The new Vice-President had been sworn in. So had the new President, who was as visibly moved as were his wife and the thousands on hand to watch him. Truman, sitting in front of Hoover, our other ex-President, had listened intently to President Eisenhower as he delivered his inaugural address. The actual transfer of power from Truman to Eisenhower had taken less than a minute and required a mere thirty-five words in an oath terrible and terrifying in the responsibility it imposes.

The clouds had lifted on a day that threatened to be gray, and grateful people described the sunshine as being "Truman weather" or "Eisenhower weather" depending on their politics. Solemn as the event was, the cheerfulness was not all in the sky. In the difficult moments of waiting, the Trumans, Mrs. Eisenhower, the Barkleys, and the Nixons were as conversational as neighbors on a front porch. When the ceremonies were over, there were handshakes and friendly partings, including a kiss from the new First Lady for Mrs. Truman. Then the Trumans slipped away to the cars assigned to take them to Georgetown. The change of administrations had been achieved, the continuity of government guaranteed. In spite of all the bitterness of a bitter election year, one party had supplanted the other with that public show of good nature we like to feel is in the American tradition.

The Homburg and Other Crises

Behind the scenes it had not always been so easy. There was the Homburg crisis. Its origins were doubtless innocent, its repercussions unforeseen. It was created by Eisenhower's announcing quite casually in New York that he was going to wear a Homburg. Because Truman had not been consulted as to his preference, to those in and about the White House this seemed a discourtesy, trivial but upsetting. Immediately toppers went out of fashion and official Washington, old and new, spent hundreds of dollars to acquire the new uniform of the day which the man who was still Commander in Chief had not designated.

Until Truman emerged from the White House on January 20, there was much speculation among newspapermen about what he would wear. When asked this question at his last staff meeting on the day before the inauguration, he took again the stand he had taken at his final press conference three days before. His sole interest was to turn over the Presidency to his successor expeditiously and smoothly, and to show the world that government in a free country changes hands without rancor. As he is reported to have said at his final Cabinet meeting the week before, "I refuse to have my last quarrel over a hat." He wore a Homburg. Since both men were for the most part bareheaded when they rode up Pennsylvania Avenue, the Battle of the Hats must take its place as one of history's less decisive and most unnecessary skirmishes.

Then there was the question of whether the Eisenhowers would call on the Trumans. Twenty years had passed since a Republican had occupied the White House, an interval long enough for precedents to have been misplaced by both parties. Such courtesy calls had often been paid in the past. Even a dinner on the night before the inauguration used to be given by the outgoing President and his wife for their successors. These dinners, endured in the name of courtesy, must have been terrible ordeals when political opponents, who had not been calling each other pretty names in public, tried to break the ice—and bread—together in private.

This time no such social interchanges took place, although until the very morning of the inauguration Truman's hopes remained touchingly, almost boyishly high that a courtesy call would be paid. The Eisenhowers may have felt that they had paid their calls—she when on December first Mrs. Truman had shown her over her future home; he when, after his post-election vacation in Augusta, he had flown on November 18 to Washington to be briefed.

In any case, the word had spread that the General did not wish to enter the White House again until he was President. That the rumor had some basis in fact was indicated when the official party set out for the Capitol. Then the Eisenhowers, instead of following tradition and going inside to meet the Trumans in the Blue Room, remained in their car at the North Portico until the President, Mrs. Truman, and Margaret came out.

There was an awkward second when it looked as if the General, at a loss for the moment and plainly embarrassed by the broadside of flash bulbs, were going to stay in the car. But at the prompt appearance of the Trumans, he and Mrs. Eisenhower no less promptly stepped out to greet them. From then on these minor yet disquieting threats of friction disappeared. The greetings were cordial among the women, hesitant between the men. Almost at once, however, the President was grinning and Eisenhower was smiling as only he can.

A tape recording of what the two men said to each other while bowing to the crowds on the way to the Capitol would be a collector's item. Few conversations could be more difficult than attempts at small talk under such circumstances. When Truman, after his arrival in Kansas City, revealed the subjects touched upon, it was not surprising to learn the weather was among them. Apparently it served its usual purpose by leading to somewhat livelier topics. The crowds, for instance. And the orderly transition from one administration to another.

Finally there came a question, which was followed by an answer that must have removed the sting from many a harsh word spoken before and after the campaign. As the procession approached the Capitol, the General is said to have asked, "Who ordered my boy John home from Korea? He has been giving me hell about it." "I did," Truman replied. "Just tell him that contrary old man in the White House did it."

Truman's Mood

That "contrary" man in the White House, who at sixty-eight looked anything but old, had been in the most benevolent of valedictory moods throughout his last weeks as President. Certainly, during the scattered six days when I was permitted to try to absorb at first hand the atmosphere of the Executive Mansion at a moment of impending change, President Truman was the least "contrary" man imaginable.

The world was aware that he enjoyed the central heating of temper. Some of those close to him at the White House insisted he showed his temper rarely. Others described his moments of irritation by saying that, very humanly if not Presidentially, his temper sometimes "got out of hand." At least one high official, a devoted admirer, conceded that, when the President exploded, he "blew like a whale."

Quick-tempered or not, the Truman I saw just before the inauguration was as mild-mannered, long-suffering, and gentle an individual as could be encountered. In personality, conversation, and manner he bore no resemblance, even coincidental, to the quick-to-anger figure of popular legend or the "pour-it-on Harry" of the whistle-stop tours, famous for slugging it out with verbal brass knuckles.

When I asked him how it felt to have his breakfast coffee curdled day after day by newspaper attacks, he said, "I've been in politics too long to be hurt by that kind of thing. I don't care what they say about me. I only get mad when they say anything against Mrs. Truman or Margaret." There was a pause. Then he added jokingly, "Come to think of it, I'm still mad at that s.o.b. music critic." Even this anger soon cooled. At least the AP reported from Kansas City that, after reading the article written by the one-time offender, Paul Hume, praising him for all he had done for music in Washington, Truman said, "Of course I'll write him and thank him for it. He can put it with his other letter."

Truman's mellowness during his final weeks as President did not mean that he believed less militantly in the services performed by his and Roosevelt's administrations. He reviewed these services with undiminished pride in his State of the Union message. When asked several times if he would change anything if he had it to do all over again, his answer was invariably "No." In other public papers he had repeated his pleas for racial and religious tolerance in the fulfillment of government contracts and defended federal civil servants from "reckless attacks." By executive order four days before he left office he had transferred offshore oil lands to the Navy. President Truman had done this not to embarrass the incoming administration, which was pledged to give them to the states, but because he felt duty bound to write himself and his party into the record as having done so.

In spite of these restatements of policy, there had for some weeks been a marked absence of name-calling. I mean such name-calling as had rekindled the fury of Republicans when, at a press conference in December, the President referred to Eisenhower's journey to Korea as "political demagoguery." That phrase had shocked many Democrats as well as Republicans, although Truman had gone on to say he would be "the happiest man in the world" if some good did come from the trip and he hoped some would.

Whenever I saw him, Truman was unfailingly equable and considerate of everyone on every level who worked with him or came to see him. The dreadful responsibilities he still bore, the appalling daily schedule which continued to be his, the abuse that had been heaped upon him, the annoyances of moving, the pangs of farewell, the drastically changed life that would soon face him, the uncertainties of his own future, and the verdict of history—none of these disturbed him. With the possible exception of Mrs. Truman, he was the most lighthearted person at 1600 Pennsylvania Avenue.

He was spruce, kindly, and above fatigue. He held himself erect, moved briskly, and was in top-notch physical form. The long hours and merciless labors of the Presidency had left him unwearied and unworried. He had the true professional's mastery of his job and relaxation in it. Although occasionally his lips were drawn thin, as a rule he was ready to smile or laugh. Whoever talked to him had his full attention. He dominated a staff meeting or delegation not by raising his voice or bullying, but by the quiet eagerness with which he sought information or stated a decision.

Although he was no longer taking so many morning walks as he once did, he was still getting up at five-thirty or six. He was still signing a pile of documents and carefully reading four newspapers— *The New York Times* and *Herald Tribune,* the *Baltimore Sun,* and the *Washington Post*—each morning before going to his office. Thereafter he faced a daily routine until ten-thirty or later at night which would have worn out almost anyone else. Once in a while, even during those overcrowded last days, he found some relaxation in the late afternoon in paddling around in the White House pool, the water of which was kept at a higher temperature than he liked at the order of his physician, General Graham. When he could, he napped briefly after luncheon. In spite of such a man-killing routine, his physical and mental resilience was incredible. Only his eyes, as they peered through his thick glasses, looked tired at moments. They were worn out by the endless pages of small type he had to read daily.

I was amazed, when I arrived at the, as yet, empty Executive Offices at nine on the morning of the inauguration and wandered into the waiting-room outside the President's office, to find Truman there. "Mr. President," I asked, "isn't this awfully early?" "Not for me," he replied, "I've been up for four hours clearing my desk."

Since December carpenters had been building a reviewing stand for the Eisenhower parade just across the lawn from the North Portico. Their daily hammering might have suggested the construction of a scaffold to some occupants of the White House. Not to Harry S. Truman. From the moment he had made up his mind not to run again he had adjusted himself to the change that lay ahead.

As a politician long accustomed to the hard blows exchanged in elections, he had forgotten most of the wounds he had given and received during the campaign. As a Democrat, he was sorry to have had his party lose. As a President, he was anxious to have the policies for which he had battled continued here and abroad. As a man, however, he looked forward to the freedom Americans have but which is denied their Presidents.

"I come from hardy Kentucky stock that prized their independence," he told me. "I'll be glad to be home. When I get there, I'll be able to go to the post office whenever I want to, take a walk down Main Street, and even go to the bank."

On the day before the inauguration, Truman paid a visit to the Hamilton National Bank. Although only a few blocks from the White House, he had to be taken to it in a limousine accompanied by a carful of Secret Service men. His last visit as President to his Washington bank was quite different from his first.

One morning when he was new at the job, he wanted to cash a check. In his innocence he put on his hat and walked out the front door on what seemed a simple errand. To his horror he held up traffic for half an hour, and such a crowd gathered around the bank that no one could get in—or out. He finally had to be rescued by the Secret Service. After this experience he let someone else do his banking for him. He discovered he could not shop or buy even a valentine for Mrs. Truman or Margaret. As he put it in *Mr. President,* "It is something to be Chief of State."

"But what about all the power a President has?" I asked. "How does it feel to have it and to be giving it up?"

"The Presidency," he answered, "is the greatest job in the world. The President has more power than anyone in history—Caesar, Genghis Khan, Napoleon, or Victoria at the height of her empire. He must always remember, however, that he is a private citizen of a democracy, who will become one soon again. His one job is to consider the best interests of all other private citizens. He must also remember that a decision of his can affect hundreds of millions of people."

"It must be terrible to know that a sneeze of yours can be heard around the world."

Truman's reply was, "The President must be careful not to sneeze just so as to have that sneeze heard around the world."

Such power means facing labors that would have appalled Hercules. During the weeks before the change these labors were even more arduous for the President and all around him than they would ordinarily have been. Moving at any time is an ordeal. Moving on a Presidential scale is an occupation admitting no union hours and permitting no rest. More accurately, it is a private torture which must be so conducted that the public business can be carried on as if nothing were happening.

Presidential Moving Day

Because there is no avoiding it, on an Inauguration Day the most spectacular moment in this slow scene changing occurs between eleven-thirty, when the outgoing President leaves the White House, and two-thirty, when it must be ready for its next occupants. Only the permanent White House staff and the personal servants of the departing and arriving Presidents are present at this Cox and Box shift. One family's suitcases vanish in some mysterious fashion and those of their successors arrive no less mysteriously. Meanwhile the bedrooms, hotelwise, have to be prepared for the incoming guests so as to create the illusion that they have never been occupied before. Meanwhile, too, the kitchen staff, which has served one family the breakfast of its choice, must be ready to serve dinner to another family whose tastes are as yet unknown.

The Trumans had begun their moving when the President decided not to run again. What had started at the leisurely pace all people hope will continue, when they have warning that they are going to change homes, had become more and more frenzied in its tempo. Such large items as Margaret's piano must have been troublesome enough. But then there were all the gifts, welcome or goofy, with which a Presidential family is burdened. There was also the sizable library (300 crates) the President had himself collected.

Worst of all, there were the backbreaking, hernia-causing steel files (some seventy-five for Mrs. Truman's correspondence, some four hundred for the President's papers) which, until the completion of the Truman Library at Grandview, Mo., were to be housed in the Jackson County Court House or the Federal Reserve Building in Kansas City. No wonder, when someone asked the President about his plans, he said he was uncertain about everything except that it would take him at least three months to find his socks and neckties in all the stuff shipped to Independence.

During the Trumans' final weeks the transformation had reached its climax. While painters in the Executive Offices moved from room to room, in some miraculous fashion in the White House and in both wings not only was the illusion of serenity maintained but each day's business was accomplished as if nothing unusual were happening. The whole permanence and impermanence, the change and yet the continuity of free government, find a symbol in this moving out and moving in.

In the Cabinet room the old leather chairs disappeared one by one, and new leather chairs, smelling new and with no name plates on their backs, replaced them around the coffin-shaped table presented by Jesse Jones to Roosevelt in 1941. The corridor leading to the President's office was suddenly denuded of the President's cartoons of himself, his honorary degrees, and his photographs of Civil War generals.

As for the President's office itself, each day took its toll. The four liberators of the Western Hemisphere, Washington, Bolívar, San Martín, and Hidalgo, were among the first to go. The Du Plessis portrait of Franklin presented by De Gaulle soon followed. Another day a silhouette of FDR, a framed photograph of the "Mighty Mo," and some lithographs of the Wright brothers' plane had been removed. Then the desk was cleared of its keepsakes—the gold four-leaf clover, the tiny ivory statue of Gandhi, the four handsome desk pens, and the small reproduction of the *Chicago Tribune's* front page announcing "DEWEY DEFEATS TRUMAN."

Next the table behind the President's chair was emptied of its family photographs. It was as if an autumn wind had stripped a tree, leaf by leaf. Finally, even the American and Presidential flags were no longer standing at either side of Truman's chair. The apple-green walls had been washed. The chairs, the bare desk, and the oval light-green rug with the seal of the President of the United States woven in its center were ready for the next President.

There remained only the globe, used by General Eisenhower in Europe from 1942 to 1945 and presented to President Truman in July, 1946. Truman had given it back to the General in December, 1952, as a historic memento. "Look at that globe," the President said to me one morning. "It looks large, doesn't it? Its diameter is thirty inches. But don't forget that it has shrunk to the size of an orange."

One might think the nation's and the world's problems would

have been enough to overtax Truman's strength during those hectic days and nights. A President, however, enjoys no vacation from every kind of demand on his time and energy. While the State of the Union and budget messages were being prepared in draft after draft, while his final Annual Economic Report to Congress was being readied, and he himself was writing his farewell address to the nation, a flood of documents and letters was deluging the President's desk and hundreds of people were clamoring to see him.

Meantime the never-stopping avalanche of Presidential mail poured into the White House. During certain crises, as when Mac-Arthur was dismissed, as many as 100,000 letters were received in a week. Although the figure once sank as low as 5,000, the number averaged 12,000 to 15,000. All of this mail had to be answered. Whenever possible, the government department concerned did the answering. Even so, the White House secretariat faced an overwhelming task.

There were letters from all parts of the country and the world. Some came from very literate people who confessed they were writing for the first time to a public figure, others from those whose respect for the President was as great as their knowledge of spelling and grammar was small. There were incessant requests that birthday greetings, messages of condolence, or salutations to business, professional, and veteran groups be sent. There was crank mail and fan mail. There were letters of praise from distinguished historians or unknown citizens in remote villages. There were threatening letters, which were at once turned over to the FBI.

The President at his own request was given a daily digest. Among the unfavorable comments he read such lines as these: from a man in Pittsburgh, "With all your ego I suppose you think you are about tops. We never had a President who has done our nation so much harm"; from Wisconsin, "I would suggest that history record your dynasty in red ink"; or from Connecticut, "You evidently intend to leave office with the reputation of having slipped a stiletto between the ribs of the American people which in the last election gave you and your kind the thoroughest reprimand ever dealt through electoral processes to any bunch of politicians in the history of the world."

The letters of praise almost always outnumbered those of abuse and by a large percentage. This was particularly true during the final weeks. A farm woman in Maryland wrote, "Maybe we worshiped FDR like a god apart, but it has been you we've loved because we felt you one of us." From New York came, "As a Negro, I am most grateful to you for your tireless efforts to secure for my people those rights and those privileges guaranteed us by the Constitution." From Tennessee there was a note saying, "Your good wife and fine daughter have both set splendid examples for those who will follow." A Georgian's comment was, "You, the fightingest President of them all, have a special corner in my heart and in the hearts of millions of us little men."

The mail was not the only chore. Day after day in his office the President was expected to function like a cuckoo in a clock. Every fifteen minutes (unless the caller was very important and hence merited a longer interview) Truman would rise on the minute to greet a new visitor. The visitors were a varied lot. They included Winston Churchill, girls in the graduating class of Holy Cross Academy of Brookline, Mass., industrialists, politicians, members of the American Biblical Encyclopedia Society who gave the President the first volume in English of the *Torah Shelemah*, a group of Presbyterian ministers, the March of Dimes poster children, the Commission on Immigration and Naturalization, foreign diplomats, and, of course, Cabinet members for their regular appointments.

In addition to everything else, the Trumans faced in their final weeks a long series of leavetakings. There was the last press conference, the 324th. There were the last Cabinet meeting and the last staff meeting. There were a round of farewell dinners and an endless stream of high officials who called to say good-by. There was Mrs. Truman's reception for everyone who worked in the White House and their families. The White House takes its tone from the top. The Trumans had made it a happy place to work in and be in. They had the affection of the whole staff. Regardless of the person I talked to or his job, I heard only words of admiration for Mrs. Truman, Margaret, and the President, and expressions of gratitude for the way they did things, for their courtesy and their imaginative thoughtfulness.

Happy as the Trumans were to escape from the imprisonment of the White House, they must have had their regrets, too. They had left their mark upon it. It was under them that it had been remodeled. No one who saw the television tour Truman himself conducted can have failed to realize not only how much he cared for the place but how intimately he knew its history.

Truman's Sense of History

Few Presidents have been more interested in history. He told me that he was brought up on Carlyle, Macaulay, Guizot, Plutarch, and Gibbon. As every reader of *Mr. President* knows and as everyone was aware who listened to his conversation, historical parallels were constantly on his lips. History, as he talked about it, was a key to Truman's character. He did not see it, as Toynbee or Trevelyan would, in terms of long cycles and complicated social and economic forces. His was an old-fashioned approach. He saw it in terms of its great men and believed, as he once said to William Hillman, "There is nothing new in the world except the history you do not know." Darius, Alexander, Julius Caesar, Rienzi, Napoleon, Hitler were figures he often mentioned. To him their lives were object lessons in the abuse of power.

If Truman oversimplified history, it was because, in spite of his years in high office, he remained an essentially simple person. He was simple in tastes, simple in the unswerving loyalty he gave his friends, and simple in his conviction that the major struggle in the present world is a fight between the godless and the God-fearing, the moral and the unmoral.

His untarnished simplicity did not mean that the Harry S. Truman who quit the White House on January 20, 1953, was the same person who said to reporters the day after he had become President nearly eight years before, "I don't know whether you fellows ever had a load of hay or a bull fall on you. But last night the moon, the stars, and all the planets fell on me. If you fellows ever pray, pray for me."

The humility with which he assumed office had disappeared long before Truman left the White House. Although it had been replaced by the unmistakable cockiness of a man who knew his job, the basic modesty persisted. So did the basic simplicity. Both were apparent when in his farewell address to the nation he said, "When Franklin Roosevelt died, I felt there must be a million men better qualified than I to take up the Presidential task. But the work was mine to do and I had to do it. I have tried to give it everything that was in me."

He could, and did, point with pride to many things. The country's prosperity. His resolute stand on the FEPC. His support of the UN. His veto of the McCarran Act. His dislike of McCarthy. His decision to use the A-bomb, to establish the Berlin airlift, and to take a strong position in Greece and Turkey. His championship of the Marshall Plan and NATO. And the supreme test of Korea.

Farewell to the Chief

Certainly, his actions will loom large in the history of our times. Was he a little man forced by circumstances to do big things, or a big man prepared to face the challenge of the problems he had to solve? Who can tell the shadow a person will cast tomorrow until tomorrow's sun has risen?

One thing is certain. Many people everywhere felt that he was one of them. They may not have been authorities on politics and international affairs, but they liked him and they liked his family. If they admired his virtues, they forgave him his frailties. These only made him more human.

This is why, when he was no longer President, three hundred people cheered him with such neighborly warmth in front of the Acheson home. This is why that same night thousands gathered at the station in Washington to see him, to wave to him, to call for "Harry," "Bess," and "Margaret," and to sing "Auld Lang Syne" and "For He's a Jolly Good Fellow." Due to President Eisenhower's thoughtfulness, "Mr. Truman, private citizen" traveled on the Presidential private car which had carried him to many whistle stops and on many journeys. Having fought hard and long for freedom for others, he was at last heading for his own Independence.

IV

THE GENERAL WHO BECAME PRESIDENT

Inauguration Day

He took the oath on two Bibles, George Washington's and the one he had himself used as a cadet at West Point. If he had had his way forty-two years before, he would have used this second Bible at Annapolis, not the Point, because at twenty the Navy had been his preference. If Truman had had his way, the General who might have been Admiral Eisenhower would have been the third Democrat to have been sworn in as President in twenty years rather than the first Republican.

The two men, between whom friendly conversation was difficult as they drove to the Capitol for the Inauguration, had found talk easy on another ride some seven and a half years before. Truman was then attending the Potsdam Conference and while discussing other things, including the General's ambition "to retire to a quiet home," had overwhelmed Eisenhower by suddenly turning to him and saying, "General, there is nothing that you may want that I won't try to help you get. That definitely and specifically includes the Presidency in 1948." [1] Eisenhower's reply had been a hearty laugh, and he had tried to treat the offer as the "very splendid joke" which he sincerely hoped it was.

Whether this offer was mentioned by Truman or Eisenhower as they rode toward the Capitol on January 20, 1953, has not been revealed. Neither could have forgotten it nor been unaware of the ironic twist in events which had made Truman's choice the incoming Republican President. This twist was all that was left of the joke. No man worthy of the office can ever have undertaken the Presidency with a light heart, and no man could have made plainer

[1] *Crusade in Europe* by Dwight D. Eisenhower, Garden City, Doubleday & Co., Inc., 1948.

51

by look, manner, and voice his consciousness of the gravity of the task ahead than Eisenhower when he took the oath.

In spite of the cheering crowds, in spite of the excitement of the day, and the pride and pleasure he had the right to feel, he must have wondered as noon drew near, even as he must have wondered time after time during the irritations and fatigue of the campaign, why he had ever said "Yes." Over the years he had said "No" publicly and privately in various decisive ways. He had thought of himself as a soldier and, as such, shown so little interest in national politics that the Democrats did not learn he was a Republican until late in 1951, soon after he had made the same discovery himself.

He had no desire to be President when Truman first made his offer, or when he repeated it before and after 1948. He had no desire to be President when liberal Republicans tried to draft him in 1947–8, or when in increasing numbers, as 1952 approached, they knocked on his door at Columbia and later flew to Paris, hoping to persuade him to be their candidate. At a press conference in Abilene, on his triumphant return from Europe a month before his talk with Truman in Potsdam, when asked about his political ambitions, he had declared that he would like to go further than Sherman in making his position clear. After Dewey came out for him in 1950, he had issued a formal refusal at Columbia, adding, "I don't know why people are always nagging me to run for President. I think I have gotten too old."

Eisenhower recognized that by flatly rejecting the offers of both parties he appeared "to violate that concept of duty which calls upon every good citizen to place no limitation upon his readiness to serve in any designated capacity." He had his reasons, however, "cogent" ones, which he never expressed more specifically than when, in his letter to Leonard V. Finder, he declined to have his name entered as a Republican candidate in the New Hampshire primaries of 1948. There he stated his conviction that "the necessary and wise subordination of the military to civil power will be best sustained, and our people will have greater confidence that it is so sustained, when lifelong professional soldiers, in the absence of some obvious and overriding reasons, abstain from seeking higher political office."

Politics, he pointed out, is a profession, serious, complicated, and in its true sense noble. He saw no dearth of men fitted by training, talent, and integrity for national leadership. "Nothing," he insisted, "in the international or domestic situation especially qualifies for the most important office in the world a man whose adult years have been spent in the country's military forces. At least, this is true in my case. . . . My decision to remove myself completely from the political scene is definite and positive." But the anti-Taftite Republicans, eager to have him run, had worn him down and won him over by convincing him that there were "obvious and overriding reasons" which made it his duty to accept.

His decision to do so, reached in anguish, had been the more difficult for other and personal reasons. He had bought at Gettysburg the "quiet home" to which he dreamed of retiring. At Columbia he held a distinguished position which, by rounding out his career as a college president, had allowed him to follow the Lee pattern that had long been his ideal. For nearly forty-two years he had been in the Army, serving his country with such distinction that no one could say he had not done more than his share.

He had his understandable misgivings about the damage he might do to his reputation as a soldier by entering politics. According to Merriman Smith,[2] he had stated these to a group of reporters at the White House after a call on Truman upon completing his term as Chief of Staff. Asked if he had any Presidential ambitions, Eisenhower had plopped down on a red leather couch in the lobby and said earnestly, "Look, you guys, I don't want to get myself spread all over the papers with this, but I want you to get something straight. I don't believe a man should ever try to pass his historical peak. I think I pretty well hit my peak in history when I accepted the German surrender in 1945. Now, why should I want to get into a completely foreign field and try to top that? Why should I go out and deliberately risk that historical peak by trying to push a bit higher?"

He was doing precisely this when at sixty-two he raised his right hand to take the oath. The General on whose Bible his left hand

[2] *Meet Mister Eisenhower,* by Merriman Smith, New York, Harper & Brothers, 1955.

rested had felt the same apprehensions as, at fifty-seven with a great reputation already made, he prepared to leave his "quiet home" at Mount Vernon to assume the same office for the first time. Washington had written a friend, ". . . in confidence I tell you (with the *world* it would have little credit), that my movements to the chair of government will be accompanied by feelings not unlike those of a culprit, who is going to the place of his execution; so unwilling am I, in the evening of a life nearly consumed in public cares, to quit a peaceful abode for an ocean of difficulties, without that competency of political skill, abilities, and inclination, which are necessary to manage the helm."

Once Chief Justice Vinson had administered the brief oath, Eisenhower shook hands with him, next with Truman, and, surrendering to impulse, crossed the platform with outstretched arms and kissed Mamie. It was a family moment between a happy husband and a proud wife, a gesture from the heart, youthful in its exuberance and executed without self-consciousness to the delight of all. Then Eisenhower returned to the microphones, no longer the smiling private citizen, his boyishness erased, solemn and already solitary in the cares of office.

No house lights could be dimmed, no spotlights brought up full to obscure the background and give him sole possession of the stage. They did not have to be. In the spread of chilly sunshine the famous and illustrious, the incoming and the outgoing, who were clustered behind him, blurred as individuals for a few minutes, and he faced the huge crowd and the listening-watching world alone. He was not alone in the sense that everyone is ultimately fated to be. His was the loneliness of the leader. He had known it before and many times in Europe, especially in the predawn conferences near Portsmouth when history's course depended upon the decision which he, and only he, had to make about D-Day. In what Jefferson called the "splendid misery" of the Presidency he would know this loneliness often, and no one even among those closest to him could spare him its pains.

He put on his horn-rimmed spectacles, and the crowd settled down to hear the new President read his Inaugural Address. Instead, he asked permission to "utter a little private prayer of my own. And

I ask you to bow your heads." As thousands obeyed, he read the prayer he had worked hard on during the night. "Almighty God," said he, ". . . give us, we pray, the power to discern clearly right from wrong. . . . Especially, we pray that our concern shall be for all the people, regardless of station, race, or calling. May cooperation be permitted and be the mutual aims of those who, under the concepts of our constitution, hold to differing political faiths; so that all may work for the good of our beloved country, and Thy Glory. Amen."

The sophisticated, to whom nothing is more embarrassing than simplicity, were embarrassed by Eisenhower's prayer. Some Democrats and hard-boiled Republicans had read politics into his becoming a Presbyterian just before the Inauguration. Forgetting that he had postponed joining Mamie's church until after the election so as not to make political capital of his religion, they were pleased to recall he had been brought up in the River Brethren sect and had not been a regular churchgoer for years. The disillusioned were startled by his early mention of the Almighty, since they would have agreed with the cynical view that " 'God,' in the unwritten glossary of American politics, is a word in the last paragraph of a political speech." [3]

The surprised did not include those who had traveled with Eisenhower on his campaign train, followed his postwar talks, or remembered the faith in the brotherhood of man that rang out in every line of his Guildhall speech, with its eloquent plea that "we should turn to those inner things—call them what you will—I mean those intangibles that are the real treasures free men possess." They had come to realize the strength of his religious feeling and to accept it as being as much a part of him as his passion for peace, his smile, his charm, his fondness for fishing, golf, and bridge, or, for that matter, his temper.

He paused after the "Amen" of his prayer, raised his head, then lowered it again and began reading his Inaugural Address with the same dedication. Although it had its good single lines, such as "we know that we are not helpless prisoners of history; we are free men," it was not an easy speech to listen to even close to the platform in

[3] *Life,* March 22, 1954.

the press section. It said what it was bound to say. Therefore, in spite of its tonic confidence, it offered no surprise. It praised peace, condemned appeasement, stressed the need of a sound economy, supported the UN with vigor, and sagely pointed out that "whatever America hopes to bring to pass in the world must first come to pass in the heart of America." Without mentioning Communist Russia, it emphasized the continuing struggle between the armed forces of good and evil in the world, and recognized that "destiny has laid upon [the U.S.] the responsibility of the free world's leadership."

It was scarcely new; indeed, it was unexcitingly familiar. At least it was until we realized that what was novel about it was that we could dismiss as commonplace its picture of the new and terrible world in which we found ourselves and our new position in it. Twenty years before, on this same spot, when Franklin Roosevelt in his First Inaugural had lightened the darkness of the depression by saying, "The only thing we have to fear is fear itself," he had mentioned the outside world once, and only once, and then to dedicate the "nation to the policy of the good neighbor."

This was the measure of the change. It was also the measure of the task Eisenhower faced when, at the end of a long day, including luncheon at the Capitol, reviewing a ten-mile parade, and attending two inaugural balls, he finally returned with Mrs. Eisenhower at one-thirty in the morning to the unquiet home which is the White House.

Soldier Presidents

The Eisenhower who entered into the captivity of the White House had been a reluctant candidate and was at first to be a reluctant President. The difference between being Supreme Commander in Europe and Commander in Chief at home, with all the nonmilitary powers, responsibilities, and annoyances of that office, was enormous, and he took up his new duties with much of the same understandable uncertainty that he had shown as a newcomer among educators when president of Columbia.

Legend has it that, after he had been at Columbia for six months, Eisenhower chanced to run into an old and important professor who had been avoiding him. The professor's hat was pulled down, his eyes were on the ground, and he was walking fast, plainly doing his best to slip by unnoticed. But Eisenhower recognized him, went up to him, shook his hand warmly, and said, "Delighted to see you, Professor. There's a question I've been wanting to ask you. Frankly, what do you think of me as president of Columbia?" The professor is supposed to have raised his head, looked Eisenhower straight in the eye, and replied, "General, what would you think of me as Chief of Staff?"

Naturally people everywhere, including his warmest supporters, wondered how a man who had made history as a general would serve it as President. History is what is always being made and then refusing to stay made, and nothing alters with its changes more than the reputations of those who have made it.

Few incoming Presidents have enjoyed Eisenhower's personal popularity. This popularity did not stop with him. It included Mamie. Not since Douglas Fairbanks and Mary Pickford had America found a couple it so took to its heart. The two of them together during the campaign had conquered people everywhere with their wide-screen smiles, their bubbling good spirits, their charm, and the miraculous manner in which they managed to combine neighborliness with dignity. When it comes to the gracious art of taking curtain calls, no actors ever excelled these two who were taking theirs at the beginning of the show.

Ike entered the White House as a hero, and "Hail to the Chief" acquired a new meaning when played for him. He was well aware that the luster of the hero can soon wear off or easily tarnish. In the back of his mind, as his term began, must have been the recollection of another general, also a great one and a popular hero. That one had lost his greatness in the White House and not regained it until, discredited, overwhelmed by debts, and tortured with cancer, he relived the great days of his past as he raced with death to finish his *Memoirs*.

The superficial parallels between Grant and Eisenhower when they assumed office were many and striking, though, fortunately for the country, their administrations proved to be very different. Certainly, it could be said of Eisenhower that he was the embodiment of victory. His devotion and integrity were beyond question, and it was clear that he wanted nothing for himself except a chance to serve the nation. He had a distaste for shabby deals and believed the tools of government had got soiled. He wanted to balance the budget and unleash the country's productive system in private enterprise. He was no politician, and as President he would have liked to continue to be above party politics. He was for peace, and people were tired of being plagued by hatreds and the terrible tensions under which they had been living for more than a decade. The polls showed that the majority was relieved to have a famous soldier to guard what had been won, to have things cleaned up and the old ways resumed.

These same things could be said of Grant. In fact they were said, and almost word for word, though deliberately printed here without quotation marks, by Bruce Catton in his *U. S. Grant and the American Military Tradition*. There was even the possibility of another similarity, and this one was disturbing.

An old gag insists the hardest thing on earth is to get an idea into a soldier's head, and the next hardest is to get it out. Grant had got an idea into his head which contributed to his calamitous failure as a President. The fault, at least in part, was not in himself but in his stars—four of them—and the thinking habits which had become second nature to him during his military career. Underlying all of his beliefs was the regular army officer's view that Congress, the dispenser of appropriations, was the boss. This is why, as Catton goes on to say, when Grant became President, he provided "an enduring illustration of the fact that it can be risky to put a professional soldier in the White House, not because the man will try to use too much authority in that position, but because he will try to use too little."

Catton wisely avoided the dangers of generalizing about a profession by saying that it *can be*, rather than that it *is*, risky to have a soldier President. Even so, the inevitable question was whether Eisenhower, having had the same training as Grant, would be misled into the same lamentable error. During his campaign he had, as a novice, on several disheartening occasions seemed bossed instead of the boss. Until he assumed office there was no way of knowing whether the qualities of leadership which had made him a hero would fully reassert themselves. One could only guess, looking for hints as to what he might be in what he had been, and remembering that far more important than his training was the kind of man he was. After all, Patton, Bradley, and MacArthur had this training, too, and emerged from it as scarcely interchangeable personalities. Eisenhower was as different from them as they were from one another or, for that matter, as he was from Grant.

The Man Who Had Been General

But what was he really like, this particular man, the tenth general to become President? Few public characters have been more public, few more Boswellized, than he even before he entered the White House. Americans who had never met him not only liked and trusted him but felt they knew him as an intimate. There were many reasons for this, not least among which was that they found it easy to identify themselves with him. He was an individual who could serve as a type; the male animal, species *Americanus*, if ever there was one.

That he had a smile which for spread and radiance was beyond the invention of commercial artists and an effulgent personality did not harm him. There was, however, much more to Eisenhower's appeal than his smile and his personality. Still more winning was the fact that he was the exceptional man who appeared to be average. Unspoiled by fame, he had not lost the common touch. No doubt he was far more complicated than he seemed. But his face was as open as a sunflower, his manner direct, and his goodness as hearty as his laughter.

He had once described himself as the most optimistic man in the world, and Americans liked him for that optimism. In a land where youth is a fetish, they were also pleased to see that, like many another graying American, he had never quite misplaced the boy in him. He could ponder, scowl, or pinken with controlled anger, but suddenly in his grimmest moments he would roar with laughter and the Penrod or Tom Sawyer in him would break through his frowns.

Above everything, he communicated the sense of being dependable. Not only GI's who had served under him but people everywhere, as the campaign progressed, saw in him "the father image" and would have understood what Ernie Pyle, no polisher of the Brass, meant when he said, "If I could pick two men in the world for my father, except my own Dad, I would pick General Omar Bradley or General Ike Eisenhower. If I had a son, I would like him to go to Bradley or Ike for advice."

The dictionary insists that "sophisticated" means "being deprived of simplicity" or "made artificial." Most definitely, Eisenhower was not sophisticated. This is not to say he was "small town" or ingenuous. He had uncommon poise and the dignity which comes from being natural. He did not forget Abilene when he became a leading citizen of the world. He remained as American in spirit as in accent. He had shown a genius for continuing to be himself and being at ease in any company or country. In spite of having had, as Elmer Davis pointed out, "more experience in dealing with coalitions than any man since Metternich," he had grown wise in the ways of the world without becoming worldly.

No one could deny that Ike was a man's man and a regular guy. He was the outdoor type that found it hard to stay indoors too long. In the tradition of most successful American businessmen he liked to play golf, to fish, hunt, and cook in the cool air of mountains, and to relax of a free evening with the "boys" at poker or bridge.

To the dismay of introverts he was an extrovert and happy, and to the distress of the intelligentsia he was not an intellectual. An ardent amateur painter, he made "no claim to the artistic temperament" and modern art baffled him. He was indifferent rather than antagonistic to the arts, and his tastes were conservative. He found comfort in the traditional and was at home with the obvious. He seldom went to the theatre or a concert, and rarely read a book. When he did, in moments of tension it was apt to be a western. He had a way of referring to writers as "word men" which not only put them in their place but him in his place, too, as a man of action.

The intellectuals, who had accepted these simplicities when he was a general, smiled at them as soon as he became a candidate, and laughed at them after he had become President. If dedicated Democrats, they made fun of his antipathy to reading. Among the stories which went the rounds was one (doubtless apocryphal) that had to do with a call made at the White House by Arthur Hays Sulzberger. As he rose to leave, the publisher of *The New York Times* is supposed to have seen behind the President's desk a copy of the *New York Herald Tribune*, and Ike, realizing Sulzberger had seen it, to have smiled and said, "But, Arthur, I don't read that either." Another joke, and a cruel one widely spread, was based on the rumor that Eisenhower insisted on a one-page digest of documents submitted to him. The loaded question was, "Why? Do his lips get tired?"

They tried their best, the intellectually rarefied, to reduce Eisenhower to a Babbitt. If he had to be placed in terms of a Sinclair Lewis character, Dodsworth was the one. There was something in him of Sam Dodsworth, who was strong and decent, who had "the energy and reliability of a dynamo," who was plainly "a man of importance," and had spent his life "in not letting himself do anything so destructive as abstract thinking." But Babbitt, no.

The error of the intellectuals was the old and familiar one of denying intelligence to a person who is not an intellectual. It was as silly in its way as the form it took in reverse when anti-intellectuals questioned Stevenson's practical intelligence on the ground that he was an egghead or tried to paint him as a comedian, incapable of serious thought, merely because he could be celestially witty.

Most certainly Eisenhower was not an intellectual in the sense that Stevenson was. He neither shared his free-wheeling intellectual interests nor had his originality with phrases and ideas. His cultural range was infinitely more limited, his mind much less agile. It was specific not conceptual, strong rather than subtle, and ungiven to meditation. Its being a very different kind of mind, however, accustomed to dealing with very different problems, in no way meant that it was not an exceptional one.

Precise, vigorous, and incisive, it spoke for a firm will, a humble heart, and a temperament which, in spite of its fire, knew the value of patience. When dealing with subjects with which it was at home by experience or conviction, it could express itself with color no less than force and clarity.

Eisenhower and the Language

The campaign had, for the most part, obscured the true qualities of Eisenhower's mind. During it Ike had been at a mean disadvantage. As he doubtless would have been the first to admit, he was then a babe in the jungle of American politics and the intricacies of domestic problems. Yet day after day he had to talk about things of which he knew little or on which he had been briefed too recently to master his homework. If in his extemporaneous speeches his sentences often got lost, it was because he was often lost himself.

He was no less uncomfortable in his formal addresses when he had to read what had been written for him. He had no liking for ghost writers, and as Supreme Commander had had no need for them. He had resented it in 1945 when some reporters assumed he did rely on them. Butcher [4] points out that Eisenhower was his own ghost writer at that time, adding, "only he seldom writes a speech, just thinks his thoughts in advance, gets his ideas in order, then has the ability to deliver them."

It was out of his unghosted best that the Guildhall speech had come with its richness of spirit, its world-linking vision, and such stirring sentences as "Humility must always be the portion of any man who receives acclaim earned in the blood of his followers or the sacrifices of his friends," or "To preserve his freedom of worship, his equality before the law, his liberty to speak and act as he sees fit, subject only to provisions that he trespass not upon similar rights of others—a Londoner will fight. So will a citizen of Abilene."

Those who had come to think of the General as being a dullish because inarticulate candidate had joined Eisenhower himself in misplacing for the time being the man who had been Supreme Commander. It was surprising during the campaign to discover in John Gunther's [5] penetrating study of him that for years Eisenhower had had two bibles, Fowler's *Modern English Usage* and a book

[4] *My Three Years with Eisenhower,* by Captain Harry C. Butcher, U.S.N.R., New York, Simon and Schuster, 1946.

[5] *Eisenhower, The Man and the Symbol,* by John Gunther, New York, Harper & Brothers, 1952.

called *Technical English*. It was no less surprising to read that on a Sunday afternoon after the Sicilian expedition, when his aides were off and he was dictating to Gunther a memorandum to the people of Malta, he kept changing words here and there as he paced up and down the room, and he exclaimed at one point, "Let's make it epigrammatic; let's make it exquisite!" Then he added with a chuckle, "I suppose you think 'exquisite' is a hell of a word for a soldier to be using."

As a political campaigner, Eisenhower may have made it difficult at times to remember that he cared about the language. But, during the war and the years immediately following, he had demonstrated again and again his ability to command it as well as men. Among those who recognized and admired this ability were Roosevelt and Robert E. Sherwood. Unable to get permission from the security authorities to reprint a long cable sent by Eisenhower to FDR explaining the Darlan affair, Sherwood apologized for running a paraphrase of it in his *Roosevelt and Hopkins* [6] by saying, "No paraphrase can do justice to Eisenhower's actual choice of words." He recalls hearing Roosevelt, who was "deeply impressed" by the General's "remarkable statement," read it aloud to Hopkins "with the same superb distribution of emphasis that he used in his public speeches . . . as if he were making an eloquent plea for Eisenhower before the bar of history."

The lucidity and lean strength with which the General could write or speak were not merely the expected traits of a military style when it is good. His prose, though soldierly, was at its best also personal. The stamp of his character was on it; his mind, heart, and spirit came through it. It could be eloquent in its use of words, but just as often its eloquence was the result of feeling rather than of phrasing.

Nothing could be more revealing, as an expression of a big man's bigness, than the widely forgotten alternate communiqué Eisenhower wrote the day before the Normandy invasion and fortunately never had to issue.[7] More than a communiqué, it was a self-portrait.

---

[6] *Roosevelt and Hopkins,* by Robert E. Sherwood, New York, Harper & Brothers, 1948.
[7] John Gunther, *op. cit.*

"Our landings," it said, "in the Cherbourg-Havre area have failed to gain a satisfactory foothold and I have withdrawn the troops. My decision to attack at this time and place was based upon the best information available. The troops, the air, and the Navy did all that bravery and devotion to duty could do. If any blame or fault attaches to the attempt it is mine alone."

Although I have heard Eisenhower speak many times and under all sorts of circumstances, one of the best speeches I ever heard him or, for that matter, anyone else make was at a small dinner in New York when he was president of Columbia. The hostess at the end of dinner toasted him. She expressed her thanks to him for the confidence he had inspired during the war and went on to praise his *Crusade in Europe* in some detail. He blushed as he rose to reply, and said, "Thank you very much. No one has said kinder things about my book. But such is my abiding faith in mankind that I look forward with hope to the day when such books as mine will never have to be written again." Then he sat down. Three sentences, no phrases in themselves memorable, but everything said, and admirably said because admirably felt.

Those who worked closely with Eisenhower during and after the war admitted he was too restless to read long reports and preferred to learn by ear rather than by eye. They were quick to point out, however, that he learned with incredible speed and had a durable memory. Making no claims that he was an intellectual, they described his intelligence as being "fantastically big-sized" and "definitely in the big league."

They were genuinely impressed by the order of his thinking and his uncommon powers of concentration. As proof, they cited the way in which he had produced *Crusade in Europe*, one of the least ghost-written of books. He talked it, walking up and down in a small upstairs room in the Chief of Staff's quarters at Fort Myers. He talked it, his thoughts already drawn up in formation, never needing a note to work from to remember a campaign, and sometimes dictating four thousand words at a session, words that scarcely had to be changed.

Grant's *Memoirs* came as the résumé of a career that was over, Eisenhower's *Crusade in Europe* as the unconscious foreshadowing of a career destined to enter a new and larger phase. It was, therefore, at once a record and in some respects a prophecy.

A Lesson in Coalitions

As Supreme Commander of the greatest combination of land, sea, and air forces in history, Eisenhower had faced a problem in united command that was unparalleled. He was well aware of how inept coalitions can be in waging war because of their "divided counsels and diverse political, economic, and military interests." As he dryly noted, "Even Napoleon's reputation as a brilliant military leader suffered when students in staff colleges came to realize that he always fought against coalitions." Yet out of the diversities that Eisenhower faced he had managed to create phenomenal unity.

Churchill [8] saluted him for setting "the unity of Allied Armies above all nationalistic thoughts." He praised Eisenhower's "firm, far-sighted, and illuminating character and qualities," asserting that "at no time has the principle of alliance between noble races been carried and maintained at so high a pitch."

Eisenhower had laid the foundation for this unity in North Africa. Sherwood remembers that Harry Hopkins, on his return from Casablanca, told him Eisenhower had said to Patton, "I don't mind if one officer refers to another as that son of a bitch. He's entitled to his own opinion. But the instant I hear of any American officer referring to a brother officer as that *British* son of a bitch, out he goes." As Sherwood says, Eisenhower maintained this basic policy all the way into Berlin, where he added the adjective "Russian" to "British."

The skills shown by the General as a coordinator, diplomat, and executive had their significance for the future. So did the fact that the word "team" was already and constantly on his lips. No less significant were certain of his personal qualities and thinking habits, the overtones of which at first eluded some observers. A case in point is a correspondent mentioned by Kenneth Davis.[9] In the autumn of 1944 this correspondent, who had spent several weeks

[8] *Triumph and Tragedy,* by Winston S. Churchill, Boston, Houghton Mifflin Company, 1953.
[9] *Soldier of Democracy,* by Kenneth S. Davis, Garden City, Doubleday & Company, 1945.

with Eisenhower, was asked to give an informal talk about him to some OWI employees in London. Davis recalls that the correspondent found the preparation of his speech difficult. He was disturbed because he could find no internal life in the General, no awareness of meanings, and "none of that moody grandeur, depth, etc., which inspire men to be better than themselves."

One of his notes read, "Ike mirrors events, colors them with his personality, but never (in the deep sense) *causes* them." Then the correspondent changed his mind and wrote, "But that's absurd. To color such mighty events as these is in itself a creative act. Moreover, SHAEF is perhaps the greatest fact of this war, and SHAEF is certainly Ike's creature. It didn't exist before him and it couldn't have existed without him. History may yet write Eisenhower's special qualities down as determining forces in the world stream. Must avoid the intellectual fallacy—belief that if a thing is simple it is without significance, or if obvious without truth."

The correspondent's final notes about Eisenhower were all affirmative. One said, "Do not his vital attitudes constitute a psychological base for world-wide cooperation? Tolerance, gradualism, etc. Are not these attitudes possible to all mankind?"

No reader of *Crusade in Europe* can fail to be impressed by Eisenhower's genius for conciliating without surrendering, and being adaptable but resolute. He may have known no more about European politics when he assumed command in North Africa than he did about American politics when he became a candidate. The Darlan mess was his disillusioning initiation. Although severely criticized at the time for his share in it, he had manfully accepted the blame and come out of it with his reputation unrusted. After that, he had learned so much so rapidly that in Sherwood's opinion, "His phenomenal and painful education of himself in the complex politics of Europe was perhaps the most brilliant of his great achievements."

On the grand planning level Eisenhower had to listen to Churchill, Roosevelt, and Marshall. Once the plan was agreed upon, however, the final military decisions were his. As Supreme Commander, he had what he would not have as President when surrounded by civilians—the power to give orders which had to be obeyed. He was working with men whose minds he understood on a task they were all trained to do. There was no obligation to persuade or placate. He had only to command. He protected his position and himself from involvements that might have been disruptive by his wise decision to deal only with the highest echelons. Army trained, he knew how to delegate authority; tough when need be, he exercised his own authority with such discretion that it did not seem autocratic.

Some of the men he had to work with in Europe, though in uniform, were by temperament prima donnas. They were rugged individualists, rugged to get along with. But they taught him as much as they tried him. Indeed, when he became President and had to cope with such Republicans as McCarthy, Jenner, and Knowland, he may even have been grateful to De Gaulle, Patton, and Montgomery for the basic training they had given him in handling difficult men.

After all, he had done the seemingly impossible. He had managed to keep peace with De Gaulle, in itself a sizable operation. Although Churchill once remarked that this "Cross of Lorraine" was the heaviest cross he had to bear, Churchill did not carry it alone. Ike shared the burden. Then there was "Blood and Guts" Patton, he of the pearl-handled revolvers, the show-off who in action showed up superbly. Realizing that he had in Patton a Peck's Bad Boy as well as a military giant, Eisenhower from the time of the unhappy slapping incident in Sicily used the rod and spared the child until the moment came in Normandy to release the giant and employ his brilliant gifts. Montgomery, also very able, was a headache of another kind. He, as Eisenhower notes, like Patton "conformed to no type" and "deliberately pursued certain eccentricities of behavior." Yet, when the war was over, he wrote Ike, admitting he was "not an easy subordinate," and acknowledging, "You have kept me on the rails in difficult and stormy times and taught me much."

The same Eisenhower who, when President, was to live by the almost impossible rule of refusing to indulge publicly in personalities showed on page after page of *Crusade in Europe* his remarkable insight into the men with whom he worked. They could infuriate him by disappointing him, and he is reported to have ventilated this disappointment in blistering, non-Biblical terms. His anger, however, was momentary: a release, not a judgment. His considered appraisals in *Crusade* reveal his scrupulous fairness. Frank as they are, they are large in their tolerance, and always eager to offset faults with virtues and follow the minus sign with the plus. They prove that Ike was carried away neither by his enthusiasms nor his irritations, and that, though he gave much in friendship, he was beyond being taken in. As summaries, they are unexpectedly subtle in their perceptions and in the gradations which color them as verdicts.

Characteristically shrewd yet warm was his tribute to Churchill, that roaring and magnificent old lion who won Eisenhower's admiration but left him uncowed. As Ike saw him, "He was difficult indeed to combat when conviction compelled disagreement with his views. . . . He could become intensely oratorical, even in discussion with a single person, but at the same time his intensity of purpose made his delivery seem natural and appropriate. He used humor and pathos with equal facility, and drew on everything from the Greek classics to Donald Duck for quotation, cliché, and forceful slang to support his position. I admired and liked him. He knew this perfectly well and never hesitated to use that knowledge in his effort to swing me to his own line of thought in any argument. . . . In countless ways he could have made my task a harder one had he been anything less than big, and I shall always owe him an immeasurable debt of gratitude for his unfailing courtesy and zealous support, regardless of his dislike of some important decisions."

Ike, Religion, and Democracy

Eisenhower in Europe had himself changed in the process of changing history. He had gained a knowledge of European leaders and affairs such as few, if any, incoming Presidents have possessed. More than that, he had found a mission, which was peace; rediscovered religion; and convinced himself that democracy was the political instrument of his quickened faith.

He had not used words idly when in his D-Day message to all soldiers, sailors, and airmen of the Allied Expeditionary Force he said, "You are about to embark on the great crusade"; when he called his book *Crusade in Europe*; or when, in his acceptance speech in Chicago, he identified his coming campaign as a crusade. Nor was he indulging in rhetoric when after V-E Day, at a reception at Frankfurt-am-Main in reply to a toast proposed by Marshal Zhukov, he described the war as "a holy war," adding, "More than any other war in history this has been an array of the forces of evil against those of righteousness."

Eisenhower had come to hate war with a soldier's fury. The one he had helped to win had been terrible enough, but by the time he became President the A-bomb and the H-bomb had so increased war's annihilating scope that he could maintain unanswerably, "There is no alternative to peace."

The barbarism of war had forced him to look for those "inner things," the intangibles of faith. His religion was an expression of his goodness at its simplest. Although its sincerity was beyond question, its form was without definition. Untroubled by theological niceties, it was concerned only with the nondenominational verities. To the consternation of some churchmen it appeared to make a religion of democracy. If it linked the two, it did so on the basis of a rudimentary association of ideas. Since all men are equal in the sight of God, it found democracy worthy of belief because it preaches that all men are created equal.

Peace was part of Eisenhower's religion. As the leader of a coalition that had triumphed in war, he emerged from the war a strong believer in a coalition to preserve peace. He saw clearly that democracies must learn that "none of them today can stand alone." With equal clarity he recognized that peace could not last and that the world would be divided into hostile camps if Soviet Russia and the United States, in spite of their fundamental ideological cleavages, found no way of bridging their differences with mutual trust.

In the Berlin of the late summer and early autumn months of 1945 he had, therefore, one paramount objective. As he wrote in *Crusade*, "overshadowing all goals for us Americans was the contribution we locally might make towards establishing a working partnership between the United States and Russia." His persistence in this matter and his faith also in the ultimate success of the United Nations were both rooted, as he stated, in his experience as Supreme Commander.

Even then the dissensions, misunderstandings, and animosities, which were to become rigid, were beginning to creep out of the rubble of Berlin. At that time, however, and when he paid his official visit to Russia at Stalin's invitation, relations remained friendly on the surface. The Soviet smile, more enigmatic than the *Mona Lisa's,* was still visible. The cordiality which backed it was soon to vanish and the smile too, though like the disembodied grin of the Cheshire cat it persisted for a while among the military. Before the grin vanished, Eisenhower had established a friendship with Marshal Zhukov warm enough to allow them to discuss their differences with candor. The Marshal would reappear ten years later at Geneva. So would the smile, no matter how briefly.

The possibility of cooperation, so bright in the first victorious months of 1945, soon faded and disillusionment seeped in like a fog. Yet Eisenhower forgot neither the reality nor the dream. He knew that, faced with the Soviet threat, it would be "criminally stupid" for us not to be strong. In his Inaugural he could have said, as he had some five years earlier in *Crusade,* "Seriously and soberly, aware of our strengths and our weaknesses, sure of our moral rectitude, we must address ourselves to the new tensions that beset the world."

Though disheartened, he was not discouraged by the tragic changes which had taken place since his first days in Berlin. Until the year of Geneva the Soviets may have refused to smile, but the General who became President had not lost his hope that in the interest of peace they could be persuaded to smile again.

V

"CRUSADE" IN WASHINGTON

The Two-Headed Elephant

One version of the story has it that, at a stop Stevenson's motorcade made in New England during the campaign, an Italian mother held up a screaming and fragrant baby for the Governor to kiss. A gentleman as well as a candidate, Stevenson stooped down to oblige. Having done so, and quickly, he grinned as he raised his head and said, "Good heavens, don't tell me he wants a change too!"

Change was very much in the air in 1952. Change was the siren song, number one on the political hit parade. Twenty years was a dangerously long time for a party to be in power and a dangerously long time for a party to be out of power. To many, change was a guarantee of our democratic health. It proved that the two-party system was still functioning.

In effecting this change Eisenhower's personal triumph was overwhelming. No President had ever received so many votes, or because of the increase in population had had a chance to, and no plurality since Roosevelt's in 1936 had equaled the General's six and a half millions. He carried all but nine states and captured 442 of the 531 electoral votes. Many independents turned to him, convinced there was sense behind the slogan "It's Time for a Change." They may have been uncertain as to what the change would be, but they were confident they would like it because he brought it about. Even some habitual Democrats, who in the manner of Sir Joseph Porter, K.C.B., had always voted at their party's call and never thought of thinking for themselves at all, could not resist the call of Ike.

Yet, in spite of Eisenhower's notable victory and the widespread talk of change, it would be to misread the facts to say that the desire for change amounted all the way down the line to a clear-cut repudiation of what had gone before. Where Ike was swept into the White House, his party barely squeezed into control of Congress. In the House were 221 Republicans, 210 Democrats, one independent, and three vacancies. The balance in the Senate was still more precarious. There 48 Republicans faced 47 Democrats, with Wayne Morse basking in the notoriety of having become an independent.

Obviously, the General, who had faced the grimmest hazards of war, began his term confronted with the grimmest hazards of politics. No less obviously, to win support on controversial bills he would have to rely at home on those talents for leading a coalition which he had shown abroad. His Republican majority in both the Senate and the House was too slim to be counted on, and his administration could be effective only if it gained Democratic support.

To complicate matters more for Eisenhower, the Republican party bore one name and was two parties. It was in Stevenson's phrase a "two-headed elephant trying to swim in both directions in very rough water," a party divided between the younger men and the powerful Old Guard who in 1952 were "still fighting valiantly to keep us out of World War II." As the Chicago conventions had dramatically demonstrated, the Democrats were no less sharply split between diehards and progressives than the Republicans. The difference now, however, was that the Republicans, no matter how small their majority in Congress, were in power and the Democrats out, and the Old Guard, which had not been able to block Eisenhower's nomination, was in a position to challenge his leadership, embarrass him as President, and obstruct his program.

He cannot have been happy to have important committees headed, because of seniority, by such persons as McCarthy, Jenner, and Langer, who were Republicans though not of his kind. Nor can he at first have faced without dismay the fact that the Senate majority leader was Taft, his bitter rival in Chicago, and a man as strongly nationalist (to use the polite word for isolationist) as Ike was internationalist. To the world Eisenhower was "Mr. President"; to the Senate Taft was still "Mr. Republican." This was a menacing distinction. Taft's defeat in Chicago had been vinegar which in time he had been big enough to swallow. Doing so had not been easy for him with his dynastic feeling about the Presidency. At Ike's inauguration, when complimented for forcing a smile, he had said, "I'm a three-time loser now. I ought to be getting pretty good at it!" [1]

[1] *Eight Weeks to Live,* by Jhan and June Robbins, Garden City, Doubleday & Company, 1954:

Taft's opinions may often have invited disagreement, but his integrity always commanded respect, and in his last months his gallantry achieved splendor. Although this tall, open-faced Ohioan with his broad grin and twang went his own fearless and contrary way to the end, urging in his last speech (which his son had to read for him) that we should "go it alone" in Korea and forget about the UN, he had been loyal to his party and to Eisenhower in seeking to make the administration a success.

The swift and mysterious cancer that killed Taft six months after the January day on which he had dreamed of being inaugurated could not destroy his willingness to help the man who had defeated him. In the hospital three weeks before he died, he said to a visitor, "I've got to snap out of this in a hurry now! Eisenhower needs me."

Eisenhower did need help. He was an amateur in American politics, and so were the "eight millionaires and a plumber" (the cruel phrase of the moment) who were in his Cabinet. He and they had to learn their jobs just as his administrative assistants had to be White House-broken. Although his official family did include, in Nixon and especially in Lodge, professionals in their knowledge of the men and intricacies of the Hill, it stood in desperate need of more of them.

When Eisenhower became President, even Republicans who were old in the Senate and the House were new to being in control under a Republican President. No Republican Senators in 1953 had held office when a Democrat was not in the White House. Having long enjoyed the irresponsibility of being free to attack a Democratic program, they now faced the responsibility of supporting the Republican program if they wished their own party's administration to succeed. With some of them opposition had become a habit which they seemed unable to break. Due to their disunity, they made strange use of the power they had been struggling twenty years to get.

Although Taft had forgiven Eisenhower for being elected, the Taftites had not, and the McCarthyites were still more grudging. They used their gifts not to aid but to make things difficult for him. Some from the very first may have worked against him behind the scenes, not daring to say publicly what they said privately. Others may have made known the disagreements in policy, to which they were entitled. Nonetheless it was odd to have Knowland, who had followed Taft as majority leader, remain in that position after he had spoken out violently against Eisenhower's stand on Red China and been one of the twenty-two senators to vote against the condemnation of McCarthy.

McCarthy's break with the President in December, 1954, was open, violent, and scandalous. Six months earlier, during the Army-McCarthy hearings, he had dared to speak of "twenty-one years of treason," an appalling remark in itself without the added insult of the twenty-first year. In his rage after Eisenhower congratulated Senator Watkins on the "very splendid job" he had done as chairman of the committee that recommended McCarthy's condemnation, the junior senator from Wisconsin went even further. He then issued an incredible statement in which he apologized to the American people for "an unintentional deception" when he had stumped the country urging them to vote for Eisenhower. He said he had been mistaken when he had promised that, if the Eisenhower administration was elected, the nation "could be assured of a vigorous, forceful fight against Communists in government." Moreover, he attacked the President's unwillingness to take drastic action about the American fliers held in Red China as a "shrinking show of weakness."

McCarthy was by far the most incorrigible and abusive of the anti-Eisenhower Republicans. There were others who, though their manners were better and their attitudes less truculent, were scarcely more helpful. Fortunately, this Republican administration did not have to depend entirely upon Republicans. Such Democrats as Georgia's veteran Senator George of the Foreign Relations Committee and Lyndon Johnson, the indefatigable Texan who as Senate floor leader was a master at marshaling votes, were of immense aid. Where they and many other Democrats were big enough time and again to put the country above their party, Republicans in disconcerting numbers were unwilling to put even their party above their party differences.

The obstructionists within the Republican ranks were not the only reason for the administration's slow start any more than the Democrats, though they did assist, were responsible for Eisenhower's successes. Nonetheless the situation was such that Walter Lippmann could observe that the Eisenhower administration did not really begin to succeed until 1954 after the Republicans had lost even their slim control of Congress.

The General as President

With Eisenhower's inauguration "the change" made itself felt at once, and nowhere more markedly than in the White House. There it expressed itself not only, as was inevitable, in the personality of a different President but also in terms of this new President's totally different concept of his function.

Both Franklin Roosevelt and Truman, in spite of their dissimilarities, saw leadership, positive, unflinching, and aggressive, as an obligation of the Presidency. In the manner of Jackson and Theodore Roosevelt, they made the office explosive with the dynamite of their wills no less than their personalities. Many may have feared or deplored the powers these Chief Executives never hesitated to use, but they did not.

FDR reveled in the Presidency. He rejoiced in it as an athlete relishes a sport at which he excels. With him the political manipulation it entailed was at once an art and a game. When he said "my friends" in his Groton-Harvard accent, he did so knowing to his delight that many who heard him were his enemies. As surely as he was never troubled by the fear of fear, he was never afraid of being hated. He was the squire of all he surveyed. But he was more than a squire. He was a knight too, sometimes errant, sometimes misled by his anger, often devious in his methods, and on occasion downright cruel. No one, however, could doubt his audacity, including those to whom he seemed a Red Knight. He jousted with history, his cigarette holder uptilted like a lance, while the majority cheered him on as their champion.

Truman was no less willing to influence people by making enemies. The truth, which already had been worn down into a widely admitted bromide, is that he, who could be so little about the little things, could be superbly large about the big ones. Some of the toughest decisions any American President has ever had to make were made by him. His courage was immense, his patience short, and his vocabulary husky. No character in a western ever

shot from the hip more readily than he. Humble at first, he grew
in his assurance until his confidence reached the point of cockiness.
But he never shrank from action, seldom pulled his punches, and
when he took a stand the world knew where he stood.

Though when whistle-stopping Truman could "give 'em hell" in
the most undignified terms, he had the highest veneration for the
dignity of the Presidency. His loyalty, which was undiscriminating
and on occasion got him into hot water, was unshakable. Nonetheless it was an eloquent expression of his jauntily shadowless but
strongly positive character. His *Memoirs* [2] are as studded with the
phrase "without hesitation" as a watermelon is with seeds, and he
comes through the pages as a man capable of swift and brave action,
uninhibited by introspection or reflection, whose firm belief is that "If
[the President] exercises his authority wisely, that is good for the
country. If he does not exercise it wisely, that is too bad, but it is
better than not exercising it at all."

Debatable as this may be, Eisenhower at first did seem overly
averse to using the power that was his. His weakness was that he
underestimated his strength. He did not appear to realize that the
Republican victory had been his individual triumph. The resulting
ironies at the start were many. One of the most colorful of personalities, he gave the impression of being a colorless President.

He who had won battles seemed determined to avoid fights. Once
again he was running a coalition, but this time it was often hard to
know who was in command, since some of those in his own party
who should have been his allies acted as if they were his foes and he
did everything he could not to antagonize them further. Although
his goodness was never in question, his decisiveness was frequently in
doubt. Sometimes, as in the case of his statement at Dartmouth
against book burning, he would take an admirable stand on his
own and then retreat from it a few days later, apparently on the
advice of those close to him.

This did not mean that Eisenhower lacked strong convictions or
that his private feelings were not vigorous in spite of the restraint
he forced himself to show in public. He had his own notions about
the office he held and his behavior in it. From the beginning the

---

[2] *Memoirs,* by Harry S. Truman, Vol. 1, *Year of Decisions,* Garden City,
Doubleday & Company, 1955.

difference between him and his two immediate predecessors was more fundamental than their being pros at politics and his not being, in his own words, "too smart politically."

His record was ultimately to prove that he was far smarter than he admitted. Yet even in the uncertain first months it was clear that the very qualities in him to which those overfed on turmoil and excitement turned with relief were of a kind that avoided drama rather than delighted in it. Where Roosevelt and Truman had gloried as administrators in bold primary colors, Eisenhower from the outset confined himself to the pastels of moderation.

He has been a stabilizer not a catalyst, a gradualist, a middle-of-the-roader, a decentralizer, and by inclination a states'-righter. Wherever possible, he has wanted to get the government out of business and private enterprise back in. "Getting back on the rails" is a phrase constantly on his lips. He has been resolute in his unwillingness to intrude upon the prerogatives of Congress and careful not to exceed his own.

In struggling to establish harmony within his own party and with the opposition he has carried tolerance to superhuman lengths, admitting so graciously the right of his most ruthless opponents to have their opinions that it has sometimes been difficult to determine his. Nowhere has his sustained moderation been a more muscular feat of will than at his press conferences, as I know from having attended several over the years and from studying and restudying the printed transcripts.

In spite of his smile, his kindliness, and his immense dignity, Eisenhower is by all accounts a quick-tempered man with a vocabulary supported by plenty of heavy artillery. Moreover, his face is so swift to mirror his changing moods and thoughts that the wonder is he ever excelled at poker. The questions asked at a press conference are not all meant to please. Many are as deliberate in their needling as they are tricky in their phrasing. When he answers them, the anger felt at moments by the General has shown itself in the steely tones of his voice, in the narrowing of his eyes, the pinkening of his face, the tightening of his lips, the stiffening of his back, or the sudden swelling of a vein in his forehead. Yet by some Herculean effort this irritation has seldom found its way into his words. Though at times the conflict has been plainly a fierce one between the reactions to which he is entitled as a man and the responses he thinks proper for a President, his manners have won out over his emotions, and his sense of office downed his sense of outrage.

In the seventy-five press conferences held before his illness Eisenhower has revealed himself to the public more fully than anywhere else, and in them his growth in office can be most clearly measured. In these conferences he has spoken for himself in his own extemporaneous words on any number of unforeseeable subjects. He has done this instead of being spoken for by those speech writers who, since Hamilton did some ghosting for George Washington, have made it hard in many cases to know how much that a President says in his messages, major addresses, and state papers has been said for him by others and how much he has said for himself.

A few years ago Yale's president, A. Whitney Griswold, read somewhere that in Washington a university was about to start a course for ghost writers, who "will be taught to write in such a way that orators will at all times understand what they are saying." A good idea, too, both for the orators and their hearers, once one is persuaded to believe in ghosts. In official Washington such a belief comes more readily than elsewhere for, so far as writing is concerned, it is the world's greatest ghost town.

At no place even in that ghost-ridden city are more ghosts to be found than at the White House. There, though Lincoln's may remain largely unseen, of recent decades others have been most tangibly present, slaving individually or in groups to draft and redraft Presidential speeches, with the aid of department heads and also of the President, until their communal effort is at last assembled in acceptable form. Then it is presented to the world as a President's and accepted as such, though most people, including the President, really know better.

The Authors League and the law courts have an ugly word for a writer who, without acknowledging he is doing so or giving proper credit in public, appropriates the words of others. His being able to put some personal touches on the final draft ("possess it" is the phrase) would not endear him to them the more. Writers are not supposed to be too busy to write, because writing is their business. Presidents (and other government officials) are luckier. To be read, they do not have to write; they have only to be able to read. Necessity is the mother of this lack of invention. Common sense demands it, and convention has long accepted it. Bowing to a "must," no one questions Chief Executives if they seldom write all the words which they do not hesitate to read as if they had and which find their way, first into print and then into history, associated with their names.

Unavoidable as this practice of committee authorship is, it speaks more for a President's views than for the man who is President. Since it is authorship by adoption not creation, it is bound to be impersonal. But a Presidential press conference, free as it is of all such ventriloquism, is different.

The President Meets the Press

A Presidential press conference is an institution, madly, magnificently, and almost pugnaciously American. Nothing like it exists in any other country, and there must be many moments when a President wishes it did not exist here. It can be compared to many things—a verbal steeplechase, a regular rendezvous with a grand jury, a major drama in which the star is asked to ad-lib his way through the central part, or a hazardous gauntlet run voluntarily in the interests of democracy. Toward the end of his first year in office Eisenhower used another image when at such a conference he said he would mount the usual weekly cross and let the reporters drive the nails.

The war that knows no armistice in Washington is the fight for headlines. It is fought the year around by opposing parties, department heads, senators who would like to be in the White House, and congressmen who hope to remain in the House. A President has to fight it too, fight it long and hard, and one of the most effective ways for him to dominate the news, defend his administration, and explain his policies is to submit to the ordeal by interrogation which is a Presidential press conference.

There were rumors before he took office that Eisenhower would discontinue such conferences. No doubt what lay behind these rumors was the fact that, though he had got along with reporters in the war years, the General had been ill at ease with them during the campaign and created the impression of shunning them. He was still ill at ease with them in his earlier conferences. Even so, he went manfully through what he must have thought of as a painful duty, and no President has been more cooperative than he in attempting to answer all the questions put to him, in avoiding "no comment" as a way out, or in permitting the full transcripts to be published.

Since the conferences have been filmed, Eisenhower has accepted the new realities brought about by television, on which he is bound to speak for himself in the first person. Accordingly, he has often allowed the conference rule to be suspended which required all of the President's remarks to be printed in indirect discourse, except those, of course, which he authorized to be quoted directly. Meant to be a protection, this was a rule which, even before the cameras intruded, could not be defended against its own absurdity because all readers knew that the "he" in the published transcripts was the President speaking, and that when he had spoken he had said "I."

The President has not often discussed important matters in such informal terms. Now and then he may have given extemporaneous talks on topics of his own choosing. In these he has been free to avoid controversy by burnishing the homilies and spilling good will. He has lost such freedom in the choice of subjects at his press conferences. There he has been on the spot, and a hot spot it can be. Naturally, it has taken time to master the hazards of these inquisitions. Within twelve months, where Eisenhower had been awkward, he had grown skillful in thrusting no less than parrying. Relaxation had replaced his former tenseness, and his answers, at the outset hesitant because of insufficient knowledge, had become assured, backed as they were with much detailed information.

When asked at the twenty-sixth conference at the end of his first year if he liked these meetings, he was able to reply that, though he sometimes begrudged the time they took, "all in all he thought he liked them would be his answer." A half year later Roscoe Drummond noted the change in Eisenhower's attitude by saying that he was no longer on the defensive and, though at first he had acted as if he were the guest of the correspondents, the President had by then made it clear that the correspondents were his guests.

Quite properly, before facing the press, Eisenhower has been briefed by experts on the subjects about which questions seemed likely. At the conferences he has had James C. Hagerty, his able press secretary, and Murray Snyder, Hagerty's assistant, sitting behind him to one side, ready to correct him if he makes mistakes or to supply facts when asked. Once he has crossed the street, however, from the Executive Offices of the White House and taken his stand behind the desk in that tawdry chamber of horrors, the Indian Treaty Room on the fourth floor of the old State Department Building, Eisenhower has been on his own and speaking for himself in his own words without the protection or the static of ghost writers.

The dangers of such confrontations are as great as the opportunities. Only two hundred people may be on hand, but because of who they are the world is present. One minor slip in a President's phrasing can result in a major official embarrassment which may cause agitation in chancelleries the globe over. Eisenhower has been deeply conscious of these challenges and in his manner of answering the questions of others he has inescapably said much about both his private self and his public self and the struggle that sometimes goes on between them.

Self-Portrait by Eisenhower

All of us talk in order to make ourselves heard, forgetting that while doing so we may make our innermost selves seen. A thousand instances come to mind of people who, without meaning to, have in the course of casual remarks on other subjects written thumbnail sketches of themselves. In this respect senators enjoy no immunity, nor does his high office exempt a President. An unforgettable illustration of this can be found in the record [3] of a conference held in the East Room of the White House on August 19, 1919, when the Senate Foreign Relations Committee met there on the invitation of Woodrow Wilson. Among the senators present were the elder Henry Cabot Lodge, Borah, and Hiram Johnson.

The conversation was admirably high-pitched, courteous and statesmanlike until Wilson explained that the obligations imposed by Articles X and XI of the League were moral, not legal. At this point another senator, Warren Harding, asked a question which, considering the tempest that lay ahead in the Teapot Dome, was to prove uncomfortably prophetic.

"Right here, Mr. President," he inquired, "if there is nothing more than a moral obligation on the part of any member of the

[3] *The Senate and the League of Nations,* by Henry Cabot Lodge, New York, Charles Scribner's Sons, 1925.

League, what avails Articles X and XI?" Wilson's answer was, "Why, Senator, it is surprising that that question should be asked. . . . A moral obligation is, of course, superior to a legal obligation, and, if I may say so, has a greater binding force."

This question and this answer are more than an interchange of words. They are miniatures which Harding and Wilson unwittingly did of themselves. In the same unintentional fashion Eisenhower has in his press conferences little by little painted a detailed portrait of himself both as man and President.

At one he said "he thought it was a free country, and one could use words as one saw fit." Like everyone else he uses words in his own manner. Sometimes in his answers he has used them clumsily, often with more fluency than felicity, on the whole with studious restraint, occasionally with fervor and admirable precision, but seldom with sparkle.

Although his single phrases, such as "the anvil of reason," have been pungent and his statements at their finest when he was taking a moral position, he has rarely recaptured in his conferences the conciseness and color which distinguished his spoken style as a General. When he has been confused, Eisenhower's replies have inevitably shown it. But, though his sentences have often lost their way, his qualities have not been lost in them. His honesty has been his most unfailing eloquence. That, and the sense he creates of being a Gibraltar of a man, unshakable in his basic decency, simple in his virtues, and unafraid for America even when a hurricane of fear lashed around him in the worst years of the recent hysteria.

Truman has said that no one can really fill the Presidency. Doubtless on this point Eisenhower would agree with him. Certainly, it is impossible for any man "normally accouched," in Shaw's phrase, to know all that a President is expected to know and to have informed answers on all the questions thrown at him.

At the start it was embarrassing to learn from following the transcript of conference after conference how uninformed Eisenhower was on some major questions, how little he read even the newspapers, how insufficiently at that time he had been briefed, and how often he would say he had not heard or thought about matters very much in the news. His lack of information was human and understandable and he commendably honest in acknowledging it.

But, when it continued to show itself again and again, it prompted one of Washington's foremost journalists to describe Eisenhower privately as the "only lazy President" he had observed in his many years in Washington. As the months went on, however, and the proofs of Eisenhower's increased knowledge of his job became unmistakable, even this correspondent changed his mind.

Certain habits of Eisenhower's colloquial speech have not altered. Few public men could ever in a half hour have used "well" and "now" so frequently as traffic islands on which to pause before advancing an idea. Few could ever have said so often, after indicating that they were unprepared or reluctant to answer, "But I will say," "But I must say," or "I can say," or "I do say," and then plunged, out of courtesy or a feeling of obligation, into an answer. "Well," as he has used it, has been generally a filler-in while he collected his thoughts and a signal that he intended to reply. With him "now" has marked the conclusion of one point in an argument and his transition to the next step in its development. Although both words in his use of them have Webster's blessing, his overreliance on them has created, especially for readers of the transcripts, the impression that Eisenhower was inarticulate when he was not.

He still has the respect for the language that John Gunther noted and, when asked for permission to be quoted directly, has said he would not mind, providing Hagerty could look the passage over and see to it that "he hadn't tied up syntax and construction and ended his sentences with prepositions." The most adroit of talkers, when pursuing an idea under relaxed conditions, can be guilty of misplaced predicates, lost subjects, false starts, and awkward constructions, as the transcripts of their conversations show. If Ike has frequently been guilty of these errors, it must be remembered that he has usually answered the most difficult questions under the most trying circumstances.

Faultless English is an ornament in effective government, not a necessity. When Eisenhower has faced reporters, he has had other things on his mind than satisfying grammarians or delighting stylists. To consider his habits of speech at all would be an irrelevance if it were not for the unconscious disclosures they have made about his habits of mind.

His smile, though all-conquering, is by no means all of him. It is the irresistible spokesman for his geniality, his gregariousness, his exuberance, and his optimism. But Eisenhower is a fighter as well as a beamer.

He has been frank in pointing out to reporters that, while he has tried to cultivate patience, he does not believe he is primarily a patient man. He has said, "I never give up a battle until I am licked, completely, utterly, and destroyed, and I don't believe in giving up any battle as long as I have got a chance to win." He has described himself as "a rather stubborn individual when he thought he was being taken in any way or for any reason." And indicated it was not without significance that he was the son of a Pennsylvania Dutch father "who had all the temper of the Pennsylvania Dutch."

Yet this potentially choleric man, who can apparently raise hell when provoked in spite of his calm façade, was beyond contradiction when he told reporters, "I have never in my life spoken badly of another individual in public, that I know of. I have never attacked any man's motives; I have talked about policy, about beliefs, about convictions, or about the practices of an administration." In *public* he has been scrupulous in following such an austere course; the opinions he has released in *private* are another, and doubtless livelier, matter.

From the time he took office he has insisted that in public discussion restraint is the wisest policy. He has opposed conversational "shooting from the hip," "shotgun answers," and "mudslinging." Instead of charging head down when attacked or betrayed by members of his own party, he has preferred, almost in the manner of Ferdinand the Bull, to sit by quietly and smell the flowers. He has refused to "muddy the waters" by needlessly controversial answers and not allowed McCarthy, even at his most abusive, to goad him into "name-calling."

In spite of the displeasure his face has often registered, his answers have been models of forbearance which, though they may have eased or avoided public tensions, cannot have relieved Eisenhower's own. There have been exceptions, human, harmless, mild, welcome. When questioned, for example, about Democratic National Committee Chairman Paul Butler's charge that he had shown a lack of capacity to govern and unite the American people, Eisenhower's reply was a curt, "I think too often politicians look into a looking glass instead of through a window."

Then there was the "Nonsense" which was his sole comment on, though not an answer to, Stevenson's contention that the Republican party was half Eisenhower, half McCarthy. There was, too, his statement (as sharp as any Eisenhower was to make) on the Army-McCarthy hearings in which he said, "Our only hope now was that America might derive from this incident advantages comparable to what we had suffered in the loss of international prestige, and, he ventured to say from his correspondence, national respect, self-respect."

Such rejoinders have been rare, because Ike has struggled valiantly, and with nearly saintly success, to speak at his press conferences for his concept of the Presidency rather than in terms of his personal feelings. Nonetheless, often in the most casual asides, Eisenhower the individual has inescapably broken through. Although his speech has often been as commonplace as Marquand's Melville Goodwin, U.S.A., he has emerged as a man humble and good and very much the kindly father, billboard size, presiding with patient dignity over the bickerings and misbehavior of his often unruly children.

Naturally, the General has spoken many times in a soldier's images, falling back on his old profession to find equivalents for the new problems he has faced. Yet he has been known to refer with amused tolerance to "the military mind," distinguishing between his own as it has been forced to function in the White House and the minds of his former colleagues as they have continued to think along exclusively military lines. As President, his has had to become the over-all view. Hence, while granting that General Ridgway had as Chief of Staff the right to oppose an arms cut, Eisenhower has not hesitated, having once been Chief of Staff himself, to point out to reporters that Ridgway's responsibility was "a special one or, in a sense, parochial."

"Never," by his own admission, is a word he does not often use; "purely academic," a phrase that he often does. He has made it clear that he is not, and has not been, "particularly interested in turning back and trying to unearth every mistake of the past." He attempts "to avoid calling on history in terms of comparison," in spite of having an expert's knowledge of military history. The present and the future are Eisenhower's concern.

At his first meeting with the press he neatly ducked a question about Truman and the Korean war by saying he would not take that one on because he had enough troubles of his own. His aim has been to keep moving ahead, not insisting that everything be done at once or by any means approving all that was done, but hoping for tangible proofs of progress. In seeking to promote this progress he has refused to think "there was anything sacrosanct about his decisions," and trusted that he has not "yet gotten stupid enough to believe that he knew all the answers in advance."

Eisenhower, Marshall, and McCarthy

A question asked Eisenhower on August 4, 1954, pierced his public armor and moved him to say, "Ladies and gentlemen, there are some things which cause me to be almost emotional." The question was about George Marshall, and he answered it with an emotion which belied his "almost," no doubt because the subject was a thorn in his conscience.

Three times General Marshall has played master builder in Eisenhower's career—by recommending him for Allied Commander in Europe, for Army Chief of Staff, and NATO Commander. No one, including Truman, has greater love or a more abiding respect for Marshall than Eisenhower, as he reaffirmed in the tribute he paid him that August morning.

Unquestionably, Eisenhower was happy to have another chance to speak out for his old friend and boss. Ike had suffered, and so had his reputation, because of a much-publicized incident which had occurred two years before when, to his obvious discomfort, he was being initiated into politics. Then, during his early campaign days, he had been persuaded, in the hope of securing needed Republican seats in the Senate, to do two things which must have pained Eisenhower since they involved seeming disloyalty to Marshall.

Although in August, 1952, he had praised General Marshall in Denver as "the perfect example of patriotism," in September he had ridden across Indiana and been photographed on his train with Jenner, who had dared to call Marshall "a living lie" and "a front man for traitors." Worse still, it subsequently became known that Ike had dropped from his Milwaukee speech a paragraph praising the General in order to keep peace with McCarthy, who had accused Marshall of making "common cause" with the Soviets.

Many were shocked by this and many alienated. Among them was Truman, who is said to have told his aides, "I can't have any use for a man who treats Marshall that way. . . . You don't kick the man who made you. . . . This Eisenhower must have a weak character."

The Wisconsin incident is reported to have been the end of the friendship between Eisenhower and Truman and the beginning of their "feud." Two Republicans close to Eisenhower, and with him at the time, have confirmed the factual rightness of Fletcher Knebel's telling [4] of the backstage story of the Milwaukee speech.

What Truman (and the country) did not know, according to Knebel, was that Eisenhower was very angry when Governor Walter Kohler and other Wisconsin Republican leaders requested him to delete the Marshall paragraph; that the request precipitated an argument which raged on the campaign train from Peoria, Ill., to Milwaukee; and that Ike, still very angry, consented to drop the reference to Marshall only when he was told it might start a riot if interpreted as an insult to McCarthy.

Apparently, as late as when Eisenhower was dining in a hotel before the speech, the dispute ("perhaps the most acrimonious of the whole Eisenhower campaign") continued in a corridor for forty-five minutes between Governor Sherman Adams, now assistant to the President, and Republican Chairman Arthur Summerfield, now Postmaster General. "Adams," says Knebel, "argued that Ike's anger rode high, that he felt he must defend his old friend, whatever the political cost. Summerfield argued that he had given his word to Kohler and other Republican leaders. If he went back on his word now, nobody would trust him again. It was the kind of argument for which there is no rebuttal in practical politics."

Maybe so, maybe not. From the point of view of staff work, it was an error for reporters ever to have known there was a paragraph to be dropped. From the point of view of Eisenhower, the other and the bold stand is the one that today it seems certain he

[4] "The Inside Story of the Ike-Truman Feud," by Fletcher Knebel, *Look,* September 6, 1955.

wishes he had taken, as Sherman Adams and some of his advisers wanted him to do and most of his admirers regret that he did not.

Eisenhower's Feeling about the Job

No wonder, with such surrenders to expediency held lightly in politics and dismissed as inevitable, that Eisenhower found the Presidency irksome at first or that once, when asked about a second term, he answered, "Sufficient unto the day is the evil thereof." Even after he had been nearly two years in the White House and the novice had become adept and the led once again the leader, he could admit that "sometimes a man gets tired of all this political clicketty-clack."

He had not undertaken the job "with any idea it was going to be a picnic." Nor had he found it one. He was abruptly submerged in the "frustrations, disappointments, and inhibitions" that are the penalty of the office, and neither the state of the nation and the world nor the division within Republican ranks eased his burden. Asked if there might some day be a woman President, as Truman had suggested, his reply was that he thought women "had too much sense to want to take the job."

From the very outset reporters and politicians have plagued Eisenhower with questions about his running again, and for the soundest of political reasons he has dodged definite answers. The game of "keep 'em guessing" is one that he has appeared to enjoy, and his deliberately tantalizing evasions have been inventive, whether serious, joking, or whimsical.

At a press conference as late as the spring of '55 he referred to the squirrels scampering on the White House lawn "with a freedom he would dearly love." In Maine in June of that year he accepted a deer for the Washington Zoo, saying he hoped it would be happy in its new home, and then adding, "But it may be like a lot of other folks that go to Washington; they find out they have left a lot behind." Once, and only once that I know of, has Ike been as definite as a man can be on the second-term question. This was in mid-April, 1954, when, according to Speaker Joe Martin, he offered to bet Martin that he would not run again, declaring, "I don't want a second term. Four years in the White House is enough for one man."

He has hated the restrictions it forced on him as plainly as at first he disliked much of what he had to do, and seemed to avoid doing some of the things which many either hoped he would or felt he should do. Whenever he could, he has escaped to Burning Tree, Camp David, Atlanta, Gettysburg, Denver, the high Rockies, or Secretary Humphrey's plantation in Georgia, disregarding the careful, even gleeful, count which Democrats kept of his absences from Washington.

With Dewey, who in Ike's phrase "had earned the right to make his own decisions . . . after plugging away in public service for a good many years," he once enviously discussed "the joys of private life." Beyond question, the liberator has dreamed of Gettysburg and his own liberation. The dream has been a constant one, in spite of the fact that during the first two years Eisenhower changed perceptibly in his attitude toward his job and in his manner of doing it.

Observing this change required no special discernment. It was as marked as the difference between the amateurishness of the Abilene speech announcing his candidacy, delivered in a storm in which King Lear would have felt at home, with the rain pelting Ike's head and pulping his manuscript while he read on and on poorly but gallantly to a thinning crowd, and the commanding poise and assured professionalism of his White House television talks, as he has given them seated behind a desk or leaning, arms folded, against it, his performance assisted, if not directed, by Robert Montgomery.

Among the reasons for the change was that during those first two years Eisenhower had learned in his own way and on his own terms the hard, the terrible, the impossible job of being at once chief of state, head of government, and head of party. Moreover, four months before his heart attack on September 24, 1955, he had made two discoveries which might have surprised him in 1952. One was that he had come to find the Presidency "a wonderful experience . . . intriguing, even if at times . . . very fatiguing"; the other that, without having to remind himself or be reminded, he was an enthusiastic Republican.

Ike Discovers He Is a Republican

"Bein' de Lawd ain't no bed of roses," says the Lord in *The Green Pastures*. Neither is being the President of the United States any bunch of carnations, especially in the mid-twentieth century. His every important decision or statement is scrutinized by all other governments, his every act or phrase apt to be pounced upon at home as a political issue. The world is always with him, and many worlds at that, both huge and small.

Almost anywhere one's finger lights on a globe—India, Morocco, a divided Germany, Korea, Egypt, Vietnam, Japan, France, Israel, Indo-China, Austria, Burma, Yugoslavia, Iran, Formosa, or Red China—there is a source of recent trouble, an actual battleground, or a point of future tensions. Above all other dangers (and usually provoking them) is Communist Russia, which, except for the years of the Second World War, has remained unchanging as our foe in spite of changing Soviet regimes or expressions.

A President lives with these crises and this menace the clock around, having to make almost daily decisions any one of which may affect the future freedom of many nations, including our own. Like Roosevelt and Truman before him, Eisenhower has had no vacation from such anxieties.

Meanwhile, day after day he has been assaulted, as a President is bound to be, with domestic problems of every kind and scale. In his case these have ranged from "wetbacks," food surpluses, the boosting of tariffs on Swiss watches, or attempting to live up to his promise of balancing the budget, to civilian defense, the need of visiting in person and rushing relief to disaster areas, public versus private power, inflation, the economic plight of farmers, highways, education, desegregation, or the Defense Department's "new look."

Few Presidents have been treated more shabbily than Eisenhower by those in his own party to whom he might have expected to turn for support. His Presidential honeymoon was over almost before it started. His troubles have not been lightened by such obstructionists as Knowland, Dirksen, Jenner, Millikin, Bridges, or Bricker. Nor has life been made the easier for him by the Communist scare and the attendant fear which gripped the country like a seizure during the first two years of his administration; by the appalling wrongs done to many Americans in trying to get a muddled security system to work; by the nightmarish years of McCarthyism; or by Brownell's wild charge in Chicago that, in Harry Dexter White, Truman had knowingly promoted a Red spy.

Neither were Eisenhower's difficulties reduced for him by Nixon's branding the Democrats as the party of treason during the off-year election campaign in '54; the sorry confusions in handling the Salk vaccine; the poor advice upon which Ike took the position from which he ultimately retreated in the Dixon-Yates controversy, and the strange legal course subsequently followed by the AEC; or the strange reasoning which enabled Harold E. Talbott to think he was guilty of no impropriety when as Secretary of Air he did private business on Air Force stationery.

If, in spite of these and other daily tensions and tribulations, Eisenhower was able to find kind words to say about the Presidency on May 31, 1955, he had better reasons than that the job enabled him, as he in effect said, to meet "such interesting people." Where he had at first proved Henry Adams was right in his contention that Grant showed "a great general might be a baby politician," Ike by this time had learned much about American politics. His initial insecurity had vanished, the stammer of his uncertainty been conquered. He was running things, not being run, and his party was by then as Eisenhower-dominated as the Republican convention had been Taft-rigged.

From the beginning he had taken certain definite positions. He had opposed the Bricker Amendment's dangerous weakening of the President's and the federal government's power to conduct foreign affairs. He had preached and practiced decentralization. He had been against Red China's admission to the UN under existing conditions. He had pleaded for maintaining our military strength because "weakness cannot cooperate with anything." He had been an ardent champion of the UN and persuasively explained why "we cannot go it alone." He had also refused to criticize the Congress in public or meddle in the work of its committees.

Yet, strong as his position had been in these respects, at the outset he appeared to be weak in his conduct of domestic affairs. He had seemed to govern by evasion and by carrying tolerance to a point where he created the impression of having lost control by his hesitancy to assert it. As time went by, however, it slowly became apparent that Eisenhower did have a policy. It was the old, old one of giving his enemies enough rope to hang themselves. Furthermore, it eventually worked. The general he could have pointed to as a model was Quintus Fabius Maximus, known as Cunctator, "the delayer," who scored against Hannibal by his "masterly inactivity."

Once Eisenhower had told reporters he hoped he could have "the courage to be patient." He had demonstrated that he had this courage in countless ways. He had shown it by keeping cool when the hotheads got overheated. He had shown it by abstaining from fights into which his own temper might easily have involved him. He had shown it by maintaining in public that Knowland was his friend and by talking as if he were unaware of McCarthy. He had shown it most fortunately by overriding, according to rumor, the Joint Chiefs of Staff three times when they had recommended an all-out war against Red China.

If, after all he had endured, Eisenhower could bring himself in May, 1955, to refer to the Presidency as a "fascinating business," it was not merely because of his domestic triumphs over his Republican enemies. He admitted even then he had never developed "any liking" for politics "in the derogatory sense." But, beyond what he had once called "the alleys of government," he saw an opportunity which to him was an obligation or, more truly, a cause. This was the influence he could exert because of his position in minimizing the chances of war and working toward a peaceful world. Peace was the General's old goal in his new job, and "with his whole being" (another of his favorite phrases) he believed fighting for it was "the kind of thing that would engage the interest of any man."

By peace he did not mean merely that our guns were silent and our forces not in battle. He meant peace the world over, because for him a divided world was one world when it came to the calamity of war. John Donne was not more convinced that "No man is an *Iland,* intire of it selfe" than Eisenhower was that every free nation, including the United States, is "a part of the *maine.*" As he once put it, "when the freedom of a man in Vietnam or China was taken away from him, he thought our freedom had lost a little."

Again and again Eisenhower had said as President that he would go anywhere to meet anybody if it would do any good. Some have contended that he had run the race which led to the hardships of the White House not to save the Republican party but to save the Republic from the "go-it-alone" policy he feared Taft might pursue if elected.

That Truman should have thought of Eisenhower as a Democratic candidate for President is not surprising. At the time of the Potsdam Conference Ike thought of himself, and was thought of, as a man very definitely with a country but without a party. Gunther insists that in the 1947–48 boom, when Democrats and Republicans alike were pestering him to be their candidate, Eisenhower "loved the chimerical idea of being nominated by both parties." No doubt any Presidential aspirant could be persuaded to see the advantages of such an idea. Eisenhower's toying with it did not betray vanity. It spoke only for his distaste for politics and his political naïveté.

Even when elected, his hope was to be above politics and beyond party. When he had been in the White House a little more than two years, he could still say that he had "never believed all wisdom was in one party" and that "without being stuffed-shirt about it" he had tried "to draw up a program for all Americans," who, he graciously added, "included Democrats." After all, he owed much to Democrats and thought as they did internationally.

Paradoxically, the Republican losses in the 1954 Congressional election were a victory for Eisenhower, since thereafter he was recognized as the indispensable leader of his party. He was quick to perceive the implications of the change and his Republicanism grew with his confidence. No one could have mistaken him for a Democrat when, in February, 1955, he spoke in Washington to the Republican National Committee, or when in the summer of that year, two weeks before his illness, he gave in Denver a fight talk to the forty-eight Republican state chairmen. "Mr. President" had become "Mr. Republican."

When he had finished speaking in February, one committeeman is reported to have said, "Why, that's the first real, honest-to-goodness Republican political speech I've ever heard him make." In Denver he had gone even further. There he was proud to talk in vigorous, doorbell-ringing, precinct terms, because the Republican party had plainly for him ceased to be a party and become "a great cause."

At the Denver meeting he was touched by the telegram he received from Republican workers which said, "We like Ike better than ever." He acknowledged it in his speech by saying, "May I return the compliment and say that when I see these faces before me

I like the Republican party more than ever." In his reply there was something of the surprise M. Jourdain felt when he learned he had been speaking prose all of his life without knowing it. There should not have been. For on domestic matters by temperament and conviction Eisenhower had as President been speaking Republicanism from the very start.

Definitely he was not Old Guard. Just as definitely he was not a New or a Fair Dealer. But, middle-of-the-roader though he was, the accent of his spirit was unmistakably Republican. It made itself heard in many ways—when he condemned the extension of certain features of the TVA principle as "creeping socialism"; when he said that wherever possible he wanted to get the government out of business and private enterprise back in; when he fought hard to balance the budget, stated his administration was "liberal as to people, conservative in economics," and defined his own position as representing "dynamic conservatism."

Domestically, his was a program, protective not adventurous and practical rather than imaginative, in which the chief originality was a return to what the administration held to be the sanity of old and tested ideas and methods. It was dedicated to prosperity, and to achieve this Eisenhower did not hesitate to surround himself with the prosperous. As President, he followed the same practice of dealing with the highest echelons that he had when Supreme Commander in Europe. It was natural for him, as a champion of free enterprise, to feel that those who had risen to head large corporations proved the reality of the American dream. Since they had succeeded in their businesses, it was to them that he turned for the expert knowledge which might help him in his new business of being President.

He was at home among the successful and in no way more conservative than in his taste in friends. His stag dinners were indications of this. No one expected him to recruit his companions entirely from Skid Row or, for that matter, from the Actors' Equity, the faculty of Bennington, or the American Academy of Arts and Letters. But his guest lists did so resemble a *Burke's Peerage* of American business that they provoked much mocking comment, and the White House finally stopped releasing the names. Typical of this criticism, and not unmerited, were the verses which appeared in *The Reporter*:

Do you think, dear Ike, for a change
You could invite somebody strange?
Somebody who's not head of a corporation
Or chairman of any board in the nation?
Somebody, say, who's written an ode,
Or has no fixed abode?
Don't you think maybe you ought to see
Somebody outside the business community?
A failure, say, or a juggler or even a mystic,
Or someone wholly humane but atheistic?
Maybe you think, dear President,
That the people you ask to your dinners represent
A cross section of our opinion, but truly, Ike,
They are only the people who like
The way things are; and most of them
Belong to the N.A.M.
They won't be able to tell you what will come
Any better than poet or bum,
Who, having nothing to lose,
Can at least amuse.[5]

"The Team" and Ike

In his choices for the Cabinet and those working close enough to him to be included in "The Team," Eisenhower also showed that, far from being reluctant for political reasons to associate with the successful, he gravitated to them as a matter of policy. Some of the people he selected were comfortably off, some rich, and some very rich. Because of those who were extremely wealthy the accusation was instantly and inevitably made that the administration was being run by millionaires and had been so taken over by Big Business that in Stevenson's phrase it might become the "Big Deal."

At his first press conference Eisenhower answered these charges. He explained that, inasmuch as the Defense Department spends two-thirds of all appropriations, he had "deliberately gone out to find the men who had made the biggest record in business" to introduce businesslike practices and effect savings in that department. Elsewhere, he said, he had not paid the slightest attention to whether

[5] "Stag Dinners at the White House," *The Reporter*, February 24, 1955, p. 2.

the men he chose had been in business or not. He had tried only to find the people he thought fitting because of their character.

Obviously, Eisenhower would have been criticized even more harshly, and with complete correctness, had he been guilty of the folly of turning to failures. Yet by enlisting successes he invited attacks of another kind because of one of the most persistent of American paradoxes. The United States is the land of the success story where money is the measure of success. But, when it comes to having them serve in their government, Americans have long eyed with suspicion their fellow countrymen who have succeeded as capitalists in the greatest of capitalistic countries. Although they may have accepted those who have inherited money, they tend to penalize politically those who have made their own fortunes.

Eisenhower's administration ran head on into some of the non-demagogic reasons for this distrust. The political ineptitudes for which a few of its higher officials were at first responsible proved to many that experts in one field can be amateurs in another, and that running a big government is quite different from running a big business.

Then there was the question immediately raised by the so-called "conflict of interests" law in the confirmation of Charles E. Wilson, president of General Motors, as Secretary of Defense. Since the Defense Department bought heavily from General Motors, the Senate in demanding that Wilson sell his stock took an ethical position which only Wilson seemed not to understand. After several days and at appalling sacrifice to himself, Wilson did do what the Senate asked of him. No question of honesty was ever involved, and few even among the slim-pursed could view his dilemma without sympathy, or his decision without admiration. Nonetheless, as Arthur Krock noted in *The New York Times*, the failure of G.M. and administration lawyers, especially Brownell, to inform Wilson about the law, his "bull-headedness" in dealing with the Senate Armed Services Committee, and his seeming "listlessness" in understanding the morals of the problem combined to create a bad first impression and got the "Crusade" off to a limping start.

In time it became more sure-footed, and the blunders of inexperience were replaced by actions wise or unwise according to the individual's prejudice or judgment. Eisenhower's faith in his Cabinet and the other members of "The Team" was complete. "The men in charge," he said proudly in 1953, with the Christmas cheer of Bob Cratchit though this was in the spring, "are the finest in the world," and he was firm in supporting them when they were under attack.

Even when he was embarrassed by the Talbott case on his return from Geneva, Eisenhower expressed no bitterness, referred to Talbott as a "personal friend," praised his work as "almost brilliant," and refused to reach a conclusion until the evidence was all in. He did, however, make his own stand clear by saying to the press, "I do not believe that any man can hold, properly hold, public office merely because he is *not* guilty of any illegal act." A public servant, he insisted, repeating what he had said during the campaign, "owed to the government, to the people, that his actions had to be impeccable, both from the standpoint of law and from the standpoint of ethics."

Boys will be boys, and so will men, no matter how the calendar may contradict them. In no country do graying adults return more happily to a vocabulary remembered from their youth than in the United States. "The Team" is a school or college term as dear to aging American males as "The Girls" is to American dowagers in search of their vanished sorority days. In Europe before and after the invasion, "The Team" had been a term that Eisenhower used as freely as other officers. He fell back on it as President with obvious relish.

They were quite a group, these members of his White House "Team." On Inauguration Day the ages of those in the Cabinet stretched from John Foster Dulles' inexhaustible sixty-four to Herbert Brownell's precocious forty-eight. Oveta Culp Hobby, who was younger, was not to acquire official status until April when she became the first Secretary of the new Department of Health, Education, and Welfare.

Coming as they did from three Eastern, two Central, and two Western states, the original nine had the proper geographical spread. Their colleges (except for the two who had got along nicely without them) ranged from Princeton, the Sorbonne, and George Washington University (Dulles, *State*), Carnegie Tech (Wilson, *Defense*), Harvard (Sinclair Weeks, *Commerce*), and Oregon State (Douglas McKay, *Interior*), to Nebraska and Yale Law (Brownell, *Attorney*

General), Brigham Young University (Ezra Taft Benson, *Agriculture*), and the University of Michigan (George M. Humphrey, *Treasury*).

Santayana once heard a president of Yale exhorting the student body to "Be Christians and you will be successful." The members of the Eisenhower Cabinet had all been successful to solacing or spectacular degrees, and all were Christians, including two uncommitted Protestants, one Roman Catholic, one Episcopalian, one Methodist, one Unitarian, one Mormon, and two Presbyterians.

If "Hindsight" was not among them, in spite of General Marshall's having pointed out that Hindsight would be an invaluable member of any Cabinet, this omission was not surprising. Hindsight has always refused to accept public office, elective or appointive, preferring to write history rather than to make it.

Unlike some Presidents who have by-passed their Cabinets, Eisenhower has relied on his to assume full responsibility for the tasks their titles proclaim. He has not stopped there. In his eagerness to keep "The Team" informed, he has included some of its top members in his Cabinet meetings. Among these have been Sherman Adams, Assistant to the President, often described as Ike's alter ego or "President Number Two"; Henry Cabot Lodge, Jr., our Ambassador to the UN; Harold E. Stassen, first as Director for Mutual Security, later Special Assistant for Disarmament; and the Vice-President, Richard M. Nixon.

As is the way with Cabinet members, Eisenhower's have had varying fates. Some, no matter how efficient, have not made any impression outside their departments. Neither official press agentry nor countless photographs and articles have been able to bring them into focus. Public life has not kept them from remaining private. Others have taken more definite form.

Even now to the average citizen Attorney General Herbert Brownell, Jr., is hazy as a personality though familiar as a name. Apparently, like many another important political strategist, this highly respected lawyer with a pronounced flair for politics prefers to work behind the scenes, playing a telephone as if it were a Stradivarius, as he did when he was twice Dewey's manager and a key factor in the Eisenhower campaign. He is pictured by intimates as attractive, wise, and quiet. They report that, though his comings and goings are noiseless, he always manages to be present at a meeting when a decision is to be reached and has the kind of mind that quickly clarifies confused issues.

In Washington, however, he has sometimes added to the confusions. He has done this most notably in the crucial area of security. An effective security system is a need no one can deny. Equally needed is a fair one in accord with American principles and practices. From the Democrats the Republicans inherited a security system well meant but ill-conceived and full of pitfalls. Instead of correcting its abuses, Brownell "continued, defended, and expanded," according to Dean Acheson's charge,[6] "the most harmful aspects of the loyalty program long after their destructive and corrosive consequences were plainly apparent."

As Attorney General, he seemed at first torn between his legal instinct for caution and his politician's skill at manipulation, with the latter winning out. Certainly, he did not do himself or anyone else any good by his indefensible Chicago speech in which he linked Truman with Harry Dexter White. Since then, the lawyer in him has reasserted itself and he has regained prestige by zealous work, by being less hasty in bringing charges, and by learning when to keep silent, that most difficult achievement for people in private as well as public life.

Benson, as a Secretary of Agriculture faced with steadily falling farm prices, has been forced into a prominence which might not otherwise have been his. If in the popular mind he has ceased to be a person and become an issue, it is because even those who know little about him do know where he has stood on the farm problem.

He did his best to turn down the Secretaryship. On being offered it by Eisenhower, he said, "General, no salary in the world could persuade me to take the job." [7] Then he began to tell Ike why. He explained that he had favored his distant cousin, Bob Taft, for the nomination, but Eisenhower pointed out that so had a lot of other patriotic Americans. Benson next confessed that he had often stated his doubts about having a soldier in the White House. Eisenhower's swift response to this was to say that was all the more reason to get

[6] *A Democrat Looks at His Party*, by Dean Acheson, New York, Harper & Brothers, 1955.
[7] *Time*, April 13, 1953.

good civilians in the Cabinet. Finally, Benson advanced what he believed was his strongest argument—that he was one of the Twelve Apostles governing the Mormon Church and did not think a clergyman should take a political job that might compromise his principles. Eisenhower skillfully brushed this one aside with, "Mr. Benson, we have a mandate from the American people to restore their faith in the United States government. Surely you agree that is a spiritual job."

As Secretary, Benson has fought for the principle that the farmer should depend, as far as possible, on his own initiative rather than federal aid. Government by handout is bound to win friends, just as holding price supports down to a minimum is certain to win enemies. The latter has been the thorny course of Benson's choice, which Eisenhower and his administration have backed. In spite of howling demands for Benson's resignation, attacks of every kind, and the ever-present political temptation to outpromise the other side, this big, plain clergyman-farmer has faced his assailants with the courage his forebears showed when confronted by their persecutors. Fortified by his religion and his belief in the essential self-reliance of the American character, he has managed to remain so steadfast in the midst of troubles that even those who have sincerely opposed his views have found it hard not to admire his valor.

Type-casting would assign to George M. Humphrey the role of Secretary of the Treasury which is his. This former head of Cleveland's Hanna empire is a smiling, driving turbine of a man, as all-executive as a stack of back issues of *Fortune*, who in his non-governmental days thought nothing of traveling 100,000 miles a year on the theory that "there is no fertilizer like the footsteps of the boss."

Regarded as one of the strongest members of Ike's Cabinet, he has been the embodiment of an economic approach which is a major cleavage between the Republicans and Democrats. Both parties, in spite of their follies, are wise enough to recognize the need of having money—sweet money—flow. They divide on which is the healthier direction of the flow. Where Minnesota's Democratic Senator Humphrey [8] says, "I'm Percolate-Up Hubert," he describes the

[8] "George M. Humphrey—The Star of Ike's Team," by Fletcher Knebel, *Look*, December 13, 1955.

Secretary of the Treasury as "Trickle-Down George," meaning that the Republican Humphrey believes, as Ike does, that the nation's economic well-being is best achieved, not by governmental initiative, but by having prosperous industries disseminate the wealth in terms of wide employment.

Spectacularly successful in his own career, Humphrey has had only one rival in the Cabinet when it comes to being the American businessman's dream walking. This is Charles E. Wilson, who was also born in a small Midwestern town and rose, because of his phenomenal managerial skill, to head a huge corporation in a Midwestern city. Of the two, Wilson found it more difficult to adjust himself to the ways and methods of government. For some time this white-haired, blue-eyed, incredibly industrious executive, fresh from being "Mr. Big" in the biggest of private businesses, was a misfit in official Washington. He spoke as a tycoon, understood as a tycoon, thought as a tycoon, and when he became Secretary of Defense had a hard time putting away tycoonish things.

Noted for his efficiency at producing automobiles of high quality in great numbers, he got into trouble at first because he could not seem to find a reliable assembly line for the English language. In politics a man's enemies can hang him with a phrase or a sentence. When Wilson said, "What's good for the country is good for General Motors, and vice versa," he made undeniable sense about the interdependence of government and business. Yet his was a statement so easy to twist politically that Democrats could not resist trying to turn it into a noose. With equal glee they seized upon Wilson's canine remarks in Detroit when he made the mistake, as he later admitted, of talking about people in terms of bird dogs that go out and hunt for food and kennel-fed dogs that sit on their haunches and yelp for it.

Nixon, Checkers, and the Vice-Presidency

In mentioning dogs Wilson, as a high government official, wandered onto dangerous ground. To go back only as far as Fala and work down through Blaze to Checkers, the dog has figured in American politics, not of course so prominently as the underdog, but prominently enough.

Checkers was a family pet converted into a heartthrob for the nation. The silky black-and-white cocker spaniel was the climaxing emotional appeal made by Richard Nixon when, "as a candidate for the Vice-Presidency and as a man whose honesty and integrity had been questioned," he took to TV and radio to explain midway in the 1952 campaign a private fund he had accepted to pay his political expenses as a senator.

The broadcast from Los Angeles, in which Nixon insisted he had not spent one penny of the $18,000 on himself and had accepted it only because he thought it improper to charge taxpayers for his political activities, was sensational in ways unprecedented. Nixon knew Republicans were urging and Democrats demanding that Ike drop him, and that within the half-hour he would make or break himself. Without a script, with only a sheaf of statistics on the desk before him, he faced the nation, his manner showing no sign of strain, his voice no tension, and his wife Patricia, seated a few feet away, having no notion what he was going to say.

Within the first fifteen minutes of his allotted half-hour Nixon had told all, fighting with every weapon including tear gas. He had itemized his childhood and college hardships, his Navy record in the Pacific, and his early struggles as a lawyer as carefully as he had accounted for his yearly earnings, his campaign expenses, and the amounts he had borrowed in addition to the mortgages on his two simple homes in Washington and California. Checkers' turn came next. Though not a part of the private fund, Checkers had been a gift and became a political asset. Said Nixon, speaking of his two little daughters, "You know the kids love the dog and, regardless of what they say about it, we're going to keep it."

Was this broadcast, which was greeted with sneers, sniffles, sobs, or cheers, the soapiest of soap operas, a sort of *Poor Richard's Almanac* mixed with *East Lynne* and *Bob, Son of Battle,* as some complained? Or was it, as others insisted, a contest in which a brave young David faced without fear a cruel Goliath? The vast majority doted on the "show." Within a week the Republican National Committee had received two million telephone calls, letters, and telegrams supporting Nixon. At thirty-nine, with his collegian's looks and Boy Scout ingenuousness, he had routed his detractors. No matter how shrewdly calculated his points or close to high-school oratory his devices, his frankness came through as disarming, his honesty beyond question.

In the process of clearing himself Nixon had emerged not only as an office-seeking candidate but as an Everyman budgetarily. With his family, his mortgages, and his dog he was the typical young husband struggling to get ahead. He had done more than save himself. By denuding his finances Nixon had dramatized the ugly fact that an American without private means cannot afford to run for high public office unless he has outside help.

The most important conquest made by Nixon's broadcast was Eisenhower, who, with Mamie, had followed it on television in the office of the manager of Cleveland's Public Auditorium. Ike was deeply moved. When he later appeared before an overflow audience downstairs, he said, "Tonight I saw an example of courage. I have seen many brave men in tough situations. I have never seen any come through in better fashion than Senator Nixon did tonight." The next evening, when Nixon flew to Wheeling, West Virginia, as requested, he was met at the plane by Ike, who threw his arms around him, saying, "Dick, you're my boy."

Others have found Nixon harder to adopt. He has his warm adherents and his opponents no less warm, including those whose opposition is hot enough to have earned them the name of Nixon-haters. These have not been confined to Democrats, who had no reason to embrace him after what he said about their party in 1954. Personally agreeable, this spruce, intense figure, with his raven hair and black paintbrush eyebrows, his glowing black eyes, his roundish jaws with a "five-o'clock shadow" eternally on them, and his lean, sleuthing nose, is hard to place.

Few deny his capabilities yet many, though certain about these, remain doubtful about him. They admit (if not cheerfully, then because they have to) that he is unusually able; that the sharpness of his mind showed itself when he was on the House Committee on Un-American Activities in his questioning of Alger Hiss and Whittaker Chambers; that he can make an excellent speech; that he was successful as an ambassador of good will in the Far East; that he has performed an invaluable service as a liaison between the White House and the Hill; that he has grown greatly and gained the respect of those high in government who were at first inclined to dismiss him as "Junior"; and that, during the trying early days of Eisenhower's illness, when false steps would have been easy, he conducted himself with perfect loyalty, taste, and dignity.

Yet there is a strange lack of liking for him among many Republicans who do not dislike him. They concede his qualities without mustering their enthusiasm, and are hesitant in committing themselves where it might be expected they would be headlong. This resistance is not limited to Nestors in and out of his party who resent his youthfulness, thinking he has come too far too fast. It runs deeper than that. If by position he is among the envied and as a public personality widely unloved, it is because of stubborn doubts not about his smartness but his wisdom, and suspicions, hard to dispel, that he is more devoted to expediency than to principle.

Eisenhower clearly does not share these misgivings about his "boy." In addition to giving Nixon his friendship, he has given the position he holds an importance it has never had before. Is Benjamin Franklin supposed to have stated his opposition to our having a Vice-President by saying, "If they insist upon having one, I shall address him as 'Your Superfluous Excellency' "? [9] And did John Adams, the first Vice-President, write his wife, "My country has in its wisdom contrived for me the most insignificant office that ever the invention of man contrived or his imagination conceived"? [10]

By tradition, from Adams through Throttlebottom to Truman, the Vice-Presidency has been a political outpost or oubliette. In it a star's understudy has had prominent billing without being given a proper chance to learn the part that might be his. The office itself, however high-sounding, has been such a sure way of kicking a man downstairs by kicking him up that New York's Boss Platt, who thought he had neatly rid himself of the unbossable T.R. when he was elected Vice-President, described attending McKinley's Inauguration as "going to see Theodore Roosevelt take the veil." [11]

There are men, even big men with the radium of greatness in

[9] "The Vice Presidency," *See It Now*, produced by Edward R. Murrow and Fred W. Friendly, CBS-TV, 1955.

[10] *Ibid.*

[11] *Our Times*, Vol. 1, *The Turn of the Century*, by Mark Sullivan, New York, Charles Scribner's Sons, 1926.

them, who when in a ruling position have not been big enough to abide having near them such a reminder of their mortality as a Crown Prince. Franklin Roosevelt was one of these. Although he renewed the practice of having the Vice-President attend Cabinet meetings (where Truman during his eighty-two days discovered "little of real importance was discussed"), FDR's unwillingness to share the secret of the A-bomb with Truman and his slowness in informing him in wartime about the supersecret Map Room in the White House are impossible to defend.

Truman explains the reluctance of a President to become too close to his possible successor by pointing out that, no matter how friendly they may be, the two men "are, or should be, astute politicians, and neither can take the other completely into his confidence." Eisenhower, perhaps because of having a different brand of astuteness, has expressed his strong conviction that the Vice-President "should never be a nonentity," that he "should be used," and that he "should have a very definite use." Ike, who has referred to Nixon as "the most valuable member" of his "Team," has turned his beliefs into deeds by having Nixon represent him at home and abroad, speak for the administration on several important occasions, and in his absence take the chair at meetings of the Cabinet and the National Security Council.

Dulles, Sisyphus of State

Although technically the Vice-President is the Number Two man in our government because of being potentially the Number One, the second in importance is the Secretary of State. Always a post of dignity, the Secretaryship in the grave (not brave) new world of the present has become a position of crucial importance, carrying with it burdens almost as crushing as the President bears and almost as intolerable, if not impossible, to sustain.

Few may want to be President, fewer have the chance, and still fewer are equipped to be. Yet every American newspaper has columnists and nearly every American dinner table guests who appear to nourish the conviction that they are better qualified to head the State Department than whoever happens to be heading it. From reading or hearing these self-appointed Secretaries one would gather that foreign affairs are foreign only to those who deal with them and are therefore possessed of information which outsiders have no way of obtaining.

Freedom's future and ours, the world's peace, our international commitments, the number of our allies and our relations with them, the apportionment of our resources abroad, our persuasiveness as a spokesman for democracy, and the outcome of the Cold War which Soviet Russia has forced on us depend to an uncomfortable degree on the overburdened man a President asks to preside over that new building, huge and austere, which stands in Washington on lands reclaimed from a swamp once known as Foggy Bottom.

His administrative ability in running a department employing more than ten thousand people at home and twice that number overseas, his foresight in planning, his gift for appraisal, the adaptability of his mind, his skill as a negotiator, his wisdom in determining a policy or taking advantage of a situation, his powers of exposition and persuasion, and the strength of his personality and character all combine to matter greatly. For today an American Secretary of State is bound to be not merely a major force in any administration but a key figure the globe over.

Any contemporary holder of the office doubtless envies the easier task which faced his predecessors in simpler days. But the change in scope of the Secretary's job is permanent, and has been brought about by many factors. Among these count the ocean-shrinking contraption of the Wright brothers; the routing of "colonialism," that outmoded bulwark of European wealth, authority, and world stability; the resulting vacuums in power controls; Britain's economic inability, after the draining of the Second World War, to hold her own in the Mediterranean and the Far East; the splinters in party politics on which France, since its liberation, has walked the plank internally and internationally as a major power; the weapons developed by such of our scientists as Oppenheimer and Teller in the new race for obliterative armaments; the great, sullen awakenings from long slumbers of ancient civilizations in far-spread continents; the fierce struggle between two irreconcilable economic and governmental concepts which has reduced in scale, intensity, and possible horror the bloody religious cleavages of the past to so many boxing matches between pygmies; and the new pre-eminence of the United States that has forced her into a position from which she cannot retreat.

The ultimate authority of the man heading the State Department rests with the President under whom he serves. In periods of emergency certain Presidents have preferred to act as their own Secretaries of State, as Wilson did when (with Colonel House behind the arras) he relegated Lansing to the sidelines, or as Franklin Roosevelt did (with Harry Hopkins as his stand-in) when he undercut the authority of Cordell Hull by dealing with his Under Secretary, Sumner Welles.

John Foster Dulles has had Eisenhower's full trust and backing even as Acheson had Truman's. Ike's public praise of him has been frequent and unstinting. He has pointed out that he meets with him more often than with anyone else in the Cabinet, said that he knows of "no man who could have done better in representing the best interests of the United States in the most confusing and trying circumstances," and described Dulles as handling himself "like a master." He has gone further. At the first televised meeting of the Cabinet he even played stooge to him. (It is impossible to say "straight man," because no one in appearance, manner, and speech could be more monumentally a "straight man" than Dulles himself.) This was late in 1954 when Dulles, just back from Paris, reported that Britain, France, and the United States had agreed to rearm Western Germany under a Western European Union and NATO.

To be Secretary of State is said to have been Dulles's lifelong ambition, one he came by naturally. His maternal grandfather, John Foster, held the office under Benjamin Harrison, his uncle, Robert Lansing, under Woodrow Wilson. It was the former who took Dulles to the Second Hague Conference in 1907 and arranged for him, at nineteen and already in a cutaway, to serve the Chinese delegation as its secretary. Since then, world affairs have been as consuming an interest of his as law and religion.

One of the most successful of America's international lawyers, he has also been one of the most active of our Protestant churchmen. A strong religious feeling, which in a sense Eisenhower rediscovered during the war and came to link with democracy, has been a propelling force throughout Dulles's life and is, no doubt, one more bond uniting the two men. If the Bible and Blackstone have figured equally in Dulles's thinking, it is because the influence on him of his father, a Presbyterian minister in upstate New York, has been abiding.

Dulles did not have to become a clergyman to be a preacher. There has always been something about him of a John Pastor Dulles. When he speaks, a podium almost becomes a pulpit. His evangelical quality has been so pervasive that Eden is rumored to have described him as "a card-carrying Christian." No one who has followed his crusading career, heard him deliver an address, or read his fervent plea for strength through faith in *War or Peace* can question the intensity of his religious convictions.

"Massive retaliation," as a statement of our policy in case of an enemy air attack, is a phrase that has plagued him. Yet "massive" is an adjective which, in no retaliatory sense, is almost inescapable in a description of Dulles. Everything about him is massive—his head and shoulders, his mind, his energy, his capacity for work, his learning, his gravity, his righteousness, his literary style, his imperturbability, his droning monotony when he reads a speech, and his blunders or accomplishments (depending upon who is judging him).

Distinguished looking rather than handsome, Dulles is a formidable Gladstone of a man. He has the head of an elderly eagle, a nose and mouth like the beak of the Gryphon in *Alice in Wonderland*, wide, staring, light eyes that soften when he remembers to smile, an upper lip which droops as unevenly as a theatre curtain stuck at one side, and a strong body just wooden enough to suggest it has been carved.

Although in public he appears earnest to the point of grimness, Dulles's character is not so single in its emphasis as it seems, nor his nature so simple. As Beverly Smith has noted,[12] "He is a woodsman and a cosmopolite, a Spartan with a dash of the epicurean, a fervent rough-water sailor and a scholar, a gregarious world traveler and an (occasional) recluse." He usually has within reach "the Bible, the Federalist papers, a batch of whodunits, and Stalin's *Problems of Leninism*. In matters of duty he has an old-fashioned austerity; in personal relationships he is warmhearted to the point of fondness toward those who once come within the circle of his affection."

[12] "The Rugged Mr. Dulles," by Beverly Smith, *The Saturday Evening Post,* May 28, 1955.

In *Bird in Hand,* a nearly forgotten comedy by John Drinkwater, an English traveling salesman, when asked the kind of goods he sells, replies that he "travels in sardines." Dulles "travels in peace"; peace and the building of protective alliances for the free world. Few salesmen have ever traveled so far, so constantly, in a like number of years, and certainly no other Secretary of State. Compared to him, Eleanor Roosevelt at her most itinerant was a stay-at-home. The log of his journeys reads like the index to an atlas. Vienna, Formosa, Bermuda, London, Rio de Janeiro, Rome, Bangkok, Bonn, Venezuela, Madrid, New Delhi, Yugoslavia, Paris—there is scarcely a place where he has not been, and the range of his travels is a measure of the spread of today's troubles. Toward the end of his third year in office it was estimated he had flown 262,566 miles, or more than ten times around the globe.

His critics insist his long absences from the State Department mean that it too is often up in the air. He is bound, while off trying to mend our fences internationally, to leave the administrative structure of the Department untended. He is also bound to be out of touch (on occasion dangerously so) with intelligence reports, and to run the risk of having subordinates reach spot decisions in the Department's name which may embarrass him.

Dulles, however, is a firm believer in personal meetings and seeing things for himself. Hence his arduous schedule of flying, flying, flying; of writing speeches endlessly on the yellow pads he carries with him; of facing the rigors of protocol, reception committees, and state dinners, of sitting through conference after conference, whittling or doodling while he listens. Somehow he has managed to survive, unwearied at sixty-eight, the strains and stresses of such a routine.

Either major party on coming into power nourishes the illusion that its doing so means a clean break with the policies of the party it has replaced or a marked improvement on them. Yet, as surely as the grounds of Hoover's camp on the Rapidan remain very much the same whether renamed Shangri-la by FDR or Camp David by Ike, there are areas in our government in which fundamental policies do not, and cannot, vary greatly in spite of a change in administration.

Regardless of big talk at election time, or even after, this is particularly true of the State Department. There, because of our new role in the world, the scale of our international commitments, and the unresting threat of Russia, a definite continuity exists, demanded by circumstances and aided by bipartisanship.

Dulles is himself a product of this bipartisanship and from it has gained invaluable experience. Under Woodrow Wilson, for example, he took part in the reparations negotiations after World War I. Under Roosevelt he was named a member of the United States delegation to the San Francisco Conference on World Organization. And under Truman he was several times a delegate to the General Assembly of the UN and scored a distinguished success for his part in negotiating the Japanese Peace Treaty.

The policies he has traveled far and tirelessly to sell are on the whole extensions or adaptations of the ones he inherited. The great brave decisions—to move in where Britain had had to move out, to strengthen Turkey and Greece, to build NATO, to put the Marshall and Truman plans into effect, to maintain the Berlin airlift, and to save the UN and our prestige by fighting in Korea—had all been taken before he came into office and were largely the result of the courage and brilliance of Dean Acheson, his incredibly misrepresented, persecuted, and vilified predecessor.

Speaking before the Council of Foreign Relations in January, 1954, Dulles praised these measures as "the acts of a nation which saw the danger of Soviet Communism, which realized that its own safety was tied up with that of others, and which was capable of responding boldly and promptly to emergencies." No doubt he was right when, during the same speech, he described these as emergency actions imposed on us by our enemies. But when, after offering this as a reason for criticism, he created the impression that the Eisenhower administration within its first eleven months had changed conditions so that such actions were no longer necessary, he was being optimistic beyond the support of facts and indulging in partisan fantasy. In spite of alterations or even improvements in our foreign policies, the next years would prove that our continuing need for a peacetime draft, for huge military appropriations, for keeping forces overseas, for additional foreign aid programs, further pact-signing, and more regional alliances was also imposed on us by our enemies in an emergency which has lasted so long that it has almost begun to seem normal.

Plainly we live in a world of suspended war rather than true peace, and some insist that, in spite of all his efforts, Dulles, instead of cleaning up the situation in Korea, Formosa, Egypt, and other tension areas, has merely swept war under the carpet. His has not been an enviable labor. He has been damned if he does and damned if he doesn't. He has been criticized for being too conciliatory or too saber-rattling; for pursuing policies either too rigid or too flexible; by one group for visiting Franco, by another for seeing Tito; for threatening to withhold aid or for giving too much; for aiding Pakistan when we have sought the friendship of India; and for siding with Portugal about Goa when our hope has been to prove that we are against colonialism. He has been attacked by some Democrats because of being a Republican; by some Republicans because of being too much of a Democrat in his foreign policy; by isolationists because of being an internationalist; and, above all, because he occupies the great but ghastly position of Secretary of State.

He was never more vehemently assailed than when he invited protest by giving an exclusive interview to *Life*. However reasonable Dulles's statement may have been about knowing when to approach and withdraw from "the brink" of war, its manner of being made was massive in its tactlessness, its artlessness, and, above all, in its needlessness. As James Reston noted,[13] by making it Dulles "added something new to the art of diplomatic blundering . . . the planned mistake." Dulles, said Reston, "doesn't stumble into booby traps: he digs them to size, studies them carefully, and then jumps. . . . This is unfortunate for two reasons: It blurs Mr. Dulles's real achievements, and it diverts attention from the remarkably solid front that has been built up in both parties for the policy of collective security."

Dulles best explained the difficulties of his job, and the reason for its being difficult, on a February day in 1954. He was sitting then in a cold conference room in West Berlin, whittling on a pencil, as Molotov talked on and on, refusing once again in the name of Soviet Russia to sign the Austrian peace treaty after nine years of nego-

[13] *New York Times,* January 15, 1956.

tiations. When at last Molotov had finished, Dulles blew the dust
from his pocketknife, snapped it shut, slipped it in his pocket, leaned
forward, and said, "For about two thousand years now there has
been a figure in mythology which symbolizes tragic futility. That
was Sisyphus, who, according to the Greek story, was given the task
of rolling a great stone up to the top of a hill. Each time when, after
great struggle and sweating, the stone was just at the brow of the
hill, some evil force manifested itself, and pushed the stone down
again. So poor Sisyphus had to start his task over again." [14]

Looking straight at Molotov, that arctic negative, as the spokesman for the evil forces, Dulles added, "I think that the Soviet Foreign Minister will understand that it is at least excusable if we think,
and if much of the world will think, that what is actually under way
here is another illustration of the unwillingness of the Soviet Union
actually to restore genuine freedom and independence in any area
where it has once gotten its grip." He might also have cited this
treaty, since ratified, as only one more of the countless obstacles the
men in the Kremlin have been careful to place in the path of real
peace.

The Russians have seen to it that as Secretary of State Dulles's
has been the task of Sisyphus. As a man of conscience, he has suffered from the disadvantage of having to deal with the conscienceless, and as an honest man from having to give his word to those
whose words cannot be trusted. Yet he has remained undiscouraged,
laboring with all his massiveness to push men's hopes for peace and
freedom to the top of that hill down which they are always slipping.
At Geneva, owing to Eisenhower, he did have the satisfaction, and
the world the relief, of seeing these hopes rest at the summit for an
interval that was heart-lifting, however shortlived.

At the Summit

It was Churchill, that Renaissance man of today, that
last of the great Elizabethans, that most teemingly endowed of contemporaries who, speaking the language of his spirit, first used the
phrase "at the summit" to describe a meeting of the Big Four. Before it was held he had resigned as Prime Minister, but his disappointment because of not attending it, though real, cannot have

[14] *Time*, January 3, 1955.

been complete since the summit for many years had been wherever he happened to be.

In spite of Eisenhower's having said often that at any time he would go anywhere (including much-maligned Timbuktu) if his doing so would help the cause of peace, he had agreed with Churchill late in October, 1954, that a conference at the summit should not be held until after the negotiations about Germany, currently in progress in Paris, had been concluded. Even then he had raised the question of Russian sincerity.

As the spring of the next year came around Eisenhower, still dubious, stressed the need for caution. When the plans began to take form, he warned it would be foolish to imagine that miracles would occur because of a few days' talk, emphasized that the four heads of government would not attempt to solve specific problems, and characterized the meeting (with great accuracy, as it turned out) as "a testing of temperaments." A few days before flying to Geneva he expressed the belief that the chances of lowering the world's tensions were slightly better than he would have thought possible two years before, though he was still "trying not to expect too much." In such a mood, realistic but not without some hopes, he flew to Geneva.

Were those six days of talk from July 18 to 24 in 1955 wasted days during which the marble walls of the League of Nations palace looked down on yet another failure to bring peace and international sanity nearer? Were they, as some were quick to say, deceptive in the manner of a masquerade, and did they offer no more light to live by than a rainbow? They produced no real agreements, no tangible results, and those who had prophesied they would not could remain satisfied at least with themselves.

Within three months the Russian smile had faded; the Soviet enmity was again naked; Khrushchev and Bulganin, their recent protestations of friendliness forgotten, were off fellow traveling, once more attacking the United States and Britain; and the foreign ministers of the same four governments that had met in July gathered for another conference, though this time in a Geneva in which scant traces of "the Geneva spirit" could be found.

All this is darkly true. Yet in the brightness of the storm's momentary clearing it seems equally incontestable that a change beyond changing had taken place and one which Eisenhower alone could have brought about. This was the creation of a memory of what international relations could be because of what they had been, if only for a while. Eisenhower, the cosmopolite from Abilene, a soldier working for peace, was the best of ambassadors, because he was the simplest, the most sincere, and in many respects the least traditional. Where plans and counterplans had long failed, character succeeded for a reassuring interval. That he spoke of the spirit of friendship in a world which had apparently forgotten both friendship and the force of the spirit, and created this spirit himself, was a victory for lost hopes and ignored values. Friendship with him was no act, his desire for peace no matter of fancy words. Once again he triumphed by being himself.

Twice during the week-long declarations of policy about atomic sharing, the unification of Germany, demilitarized areas, NATO's future, and lifting the Iron Curtain, he interrupted the formal diplomatic interchanges.[15] On the second day, when Germany and NATO were being discussed and tempers were rising, he turned to the Russian delegation and singled out Zhukov.

"Marshal Zhukov," he is reported to have said, "is an old friend of mine. He knows that when we have spoken as soldier to soldier I have never said a word that is not true." Then he continued, "I have had enough of war," and forcefully explained that he had come out of retirement to command NATO only because he believed it was an organization for peace, that the United States would never indulge in an aggressive war or approve of one, and that Russia had nothing to fear from having a united Germany in NATO. At this point Bulganin broke in with, "That's all very well —we believe you." Though after this Bulganin stated his reservations, the world knew that the Russian Premier had said he believed in Eisenhower's peaceful intentions, and by acknowledging this had denied the stalest and noisiest of Communist charges against the United States.

On Thursday, the fourth day, Eisenhower surprised even some members of his own Cabinet at home by making a proposal which had been such a well-kept secret that neither Eden nor Faure knew anything about it, and the Russians were taken completely off guard. Halfway through the reading of a formal document, he took off his glasses, faced the Soviets again, and speaking extemporaneously said,

[15] *Time,* August 1, 1955.

"Gentlemen, I have been searching my heart and mind for something I could say here that would convince everyone of the great sincerity of the United States in approaching the problem of disarmament." He made two proposals—first, that the two countries should give each other complete blueprints of their military establishments; and, second, that each country should provide the other with facilities for aerial inspection of its military installations. Both offers were perhaps too simple to be possible and too sensible to be accepted. Yet they served their purpose because, by their sincerity and audacious simplicity, they captured the imagination of people everywhere.

On his return to Washington Eisenhower did not claim that the week in Geneva guaranteed the starting of a new era. He did, however, say that a beginning was made from which it was "just possible that something to the great benefit of mankind" might come. With satisfaction he pointed to one indisputable achievement. Not once during the six days of often "intense" debate and argument had there been "a return to the old methods of merely talking to constituencies in terms of invectives and personal and nationalistic abuse."

The truce in such invectives was short. The frowns soon reappeared, the cold war blew hot again, and within six months in his State of the Union message Eisenhower was forced to note that the Communists were relying on "division, enticement, and duplicity in their tactics against the free nations." "The Geneva spirit" faded, but it *had* existed. The world had had, in T. S. Eliot's phrase, "a wink of heaven." The door, seemingly sealed, had been pried open if only for a moment historically. Through it men and women on both sides of the Iron Curtain had had a glimpse of the very different universe they would be free to walk in if only nations (as the President once put it) "would recognize the folly of not getting along." More than anyone, Eisenhower had generated the "spirit" identified with Geneva. As a figure and force in the world, on this his second crusade in Europe he had reached a higher peak than when he accepted the German surrender ten years before. His career was at the summit.

Two months after Geneva, shortly before two o'clock of the morning of Saturday, the twenty-fourth of September, in the second floor bedroom he occupies when staying in the Denver home of his mother-in-law, Mrs. Elivera Doud, his heart attack struck. According to everyone with him, he seemed in the best of spirits and health during the first four days of that week when, at the Byers Peak ranch of a friend, he had fished, painted, cooked, and relaxed. On Friday everyone who saw him again commented on how well he looked, how ruddy, and on the springiness of his athlete's walk.

It had been a long day. He got up at five, cooked a hearty breakfast, drove the seventy miles to Denver, worked for several hours at the "summer White House" at Lowry Air Force Base, and played twenty-seven holes of golf, according to one observer "with the breeziness of a man twenty years his junior." To be sure, in the late afternoon at the twenty-sixth hole he had a slight touch of heartburn, but that quickly disappeared. He seemed in fine condition when, soon after dining at nine, he went to bed. Then in the early morning hours of Saturday came his coronary, first called "mild," later "moderate." By striking him it struck the country and the world.

In spite of his good health, Eisenhower for some time had been thinking of his age, the pressures of the Presidency, and the problems raised by a second term. At a press conference on the first of June he had spoken of what might happen if a President "is suddenly disabled or killed or dies." On August second he was quoted as discouraging an Ohio Republican delegation, which had come to the White House to urge him to run again, by saying he liked to see younger men given top jobs, by mentioning the physical erosion of a man in the Presidency, and by pointing out that no President had reached his seventieth year in office. Two days later, at the last press conference before his illness, he had indicated that he was not a prophet about his own health.

In Denver, two weeks before his attack, he had again stressed the need of younger Republicans, denied his own indispensability by insisting the Republican party was not so lacking in inspiration, personnel, and leadership that it depended on one man, stressed that "humans are frail—a man mortal," and dismayed the forty-eight state chairmen by urging them never to "pin your flag so tightly to one mast that, if the ship sinks, you cannot rip it off and nail it to another." Plainly, intimations of his mortality were very much on his mind.

The hundreds of thousands of messages which poured into Denver from everywhere were expressions of the tremendous affection in which Eisenhower was held; the reaction of stock markets abroad and here was a reflection of the hope for stability that the world had invested in him. Before Wall Street could open on Monday, stocks had dropped in London, Paris, and Amsterdam. In New York stocks declined an estimated fourteen billion, the heaviest dollar loss in history, the break was the sharpest since the 1929 crash, and the volume of shares traded was the largest since 1933.

Blessedly, his health returned, as millions prayed and followed his recovery. During the first weeks, when the regency had had to take over, the "Team" justified his faith in it by keeping the government "on the rails," running it efficiently, and for the most part smoothly. Meanwhile, as Eisenhower recovered, more and more pressures were brought on him to run again, with little concern for his health but with great concern for keeping his party in power by relying on its most certain guarantee of staying there.

The long-awaited decision, not announced until February 29, five soul-searching months after his heart attack, was in the final sense his and his doctors', but mainly his. Had he declined, no one, including those who hoped to hold onto office by riding on his coattails, could have accused Eisenhower of not having done more than enough for the nation. A second term, undertaken under the limitations and hazards he was scrupulous in making clear, would present its problems to him and to the country. The critics who had hesitated to attack him, finding it far safer to attack those around him, can no longer be expected to hold their fire. His Ike-into-icon exemption from such onslaughts, increased by his illness, is bound to vanish. His having been ill will not, and cannot in fairness, be held up as a shield to protect him, since he considers himself well enough to take on the Presidency again.

Eisenhower had brushed with death in the service of his country, and his heart attack had added to his career that touch of martyrdom which is part of the heroic legend. History, to which he has given much, had provided him in his illness with an "out" beyond question honorable. By not accepting it he has chosen to tempt fate.

VI

STEVENSON SPEAKING

A New Approach to Politics

It was all over, including the shouting—at least for that time—when a tired Stevenson appeared at 12:40 A.M. on November 5, 1952, at his headquarters in Springfield's Leland Hotel to concede Eisenhower's victory. His last words of the hundreds of thousands he had spoken during the campaign were very much in character since they recounted an anecdote and the anecdote had to do with Lincoln.

"Someone asked me, as I came in, down on the street," said Stevenson, "how I felt, and I was reminded of a story that a fellow-townsman of ours used to tell—Abraham Lincoln. They asked him how he felt once after an unsuccessful election. He said he felt like a little boy who had stubbed his toe in the dark. He said he was too old to cry, but it hurt too much to laugh."

Previously, in his prepared statement, he had read sentences, also very much in character in their spirit no less than in the polish of their phrasing, pointing out that "that which unites us as American citizens is far greater than that which divides us as political parties," and reminding us that "we vote as many, but we pray as one."

The "reluctant nominee" who, in his own words, had not been a "reluctant candidate" was for the moment finished and weary. Thinking back on the campaign some months later, while resting in Barbados and preparing an introduction for his collected speeches,[1] he was to write that he was "soundly defeated," a description justified by Eisenhower's plurality of six and a half millions and the tally of how the states had gone.

Yet Stevenson's failure had about it many of the aspects of success, and a spectacular success at that. He had run a notable race which

[1] *Major Campaign Speeches of Adlai E. Stevenson, 1952,* New York, Random House, 1953.

118

had left him surprisingly little to regret and a great deal of which he —and all Americans—could be very proud. He had captured twenty-seven million votes, a larger number than a defeated candidate had ever received and more than any successful candidate (until 1952) had won, save for Franklin Roosevelt in 1936. An unknown until the boom for him began in January, 1952, except in certain higher circles in Washington, abroad, and at the UN, and in his own state as a successful reform governor, he had by election day emerged not only as a national but an international figure.

Stevenson had done this in ways exceptional and because of being exceptional himself. He had done it because of qualities so uncommon that the admiration they commanded was by no means limited to those who had voted for him. His respect for his countrymen being as profound as his self-respect, he had given them his best, realizing that "it can never be good enough" and apologizing only because "in the fever and haste of the campaign" he "could not better express what was in my heart and head." He had shown his belief to be complete "in democracy and the collective reason of properly informed people." As a man of the highest intelligence and conscience, he had been publicly faithful to both his intellect and his moral sense. He had dared to leave his wisdom undisguised and even to brighten it with wit. Moreover, in his eloquence he used a vocabulary and a range of literary and historical references which assumed universal literacy.

Many of his opponents were pleased, many of his adherents alarmed, because it had often seemed that he would rather be bright than President. But had he really talked over the people's heads, this amazingly articulate fellow who never hid the fact that his head had a brow? "No," wrote he in his stock-taking mood in Barbados, "and that's about the only aspect of the campaign I am sure of!" More than doubting if he could have talked over people's heads had he foolishly wanted to, he agreed with Franklin P. Adams that "the average man is a great deal above the average." This was, and remains, the measure of his faith in democracy and explains why he, at first a shadow, gained such substance.

"Let's talk sense to the American people," he had said in his acceptance speech in Chicago. And sense is what Stevenson had talked during those days and nights of incessant talking which were the campaign. To be sure, in the heat of the conflict he was for a brief interval pressured by circumstance, the tactics of the opposition, and the urging of some advisers into stooping to the overstatements and simplifications synonymous with campaigning. But his major speeches, and even most of his minor ones, were pitched at a level unique in contemporary politics.

The key to them—and to Stevenson—is to be found in the passage from William James that he printed opposite his introduction. In it James, after likening reason to "a small sandbank in the midst of a hungry sea ready to wash it out of existence," states his absolute belief that this sandbank is bound to grow until "bit by bit it will get dyked and break-watered." Stevenson's faith is equally strong. It was as reason's champion and spokesman that he had ventured to approach the irrationalities of politics. Looking back on the campaign, he could write, "I am not downhearted or even disappointed, and I believe more than ever that our 'sandbank of reason' in major political campaigns is bound to grow." Few could question that he had added to it by the caliber of his speeches.

As October came around and the campaign entered its second phase without the reasoned exchange of ideas he had hoped for, Stevenson had felt more and more that "people cared little about the issues and party records or about precise definition of positions." He had found this discouraging though not surprising, because he knew they were "weary of conflict, impatient and eager for repose." Even so he did not lose his belief either in reason or in the people and, having made his stand clear on domestic issues, he tried in the final weeks "to stir deeper waters and talk more and more philosophically about faith and fear and about the mighty and wondrous powers for good of free and independent-thinking Americans."

Throughout the campaign Stevenson had made it abundantly plain that to him a candidate is more than an office seeker. He is a teacher with a huge and challenging "responsibility for public education." His high mission is "honestly to help man to know, as St. Thomas Aquinas said, what he ought to believe; to know what he ought to desire; to know what he ought to do." Stevenson's hope and prayer, as he confessed in his acceptance speech, had been that his party, win or lose, would see in the campaign "a great opportunity to educate and elevate a people whose destiny is leadership, not alone of a rich and prosperous, contented country as in the past, but of a world in ferment." This was the task to which he had devoted himself.

In his speeches a speaker of uncommon ability had used the language with a writer's skill and affection, and a mind, probing and cultivated, expressed itself with delectable precision. In them the philosopher's voice had made itself heard above the politician's. Not since Woodrow Wilson had a Presidential candidate written so well, stated issues with such clarity, or enunciated principles more nobly. But there was a difference. Wilson's public prose, classical in its elevation, was often chilling in its austerity; Stevenson's was infinitely more varied and achieved its eloquence in contemporary terms. It was warm, flexible, and human. Stevenson had not hesitated to be colloquial in his approach to the lofty, to edge into an earnest passage with a hilarious anecdote, or to win laughs in order to win attention for his important points.

Shaw, one of the wittiest of sages, revealed that in his days as a drama critic he had taken the theatre seriously "as a factory of thought, a prompter of conscience, an elucidator of social conduct, an armory against despair and dullness, and a temple of the Ascent of Man." Stevenson, one of the wittiest men ever to run for the Presidency, had taken his job with the same seriousness and could have borrowed Shaw's phrases to explain his concept of a candidate's obligations.

He had spoken to the common man as the Great Uncommoner, and his listeners had eaten it up, feeling uncommon themselves because they discovered that he and they had so much in common. He had treated Mencken's "boobletariat," to its delight, as if it were the intelligentsia. He had talked up, not down, and the individuals who composed his audiences had followed him, each included, not excluded, by his unfaltering reliance on intelligence. No one expressed the untraditional appeal of his speeches better than the late Jan Struther when, in a poem for which the Governor has an understandable affection, she wrote:

John Doe, he heard a speech.
It didn't plead, it didn't preach.
It wasn't loud, it wasn't wild,
It didn't treat him like a child.
It even carried one or two
Words he hadn't known he knew.
John Doe scratched his head:
John Doe smiled, and said:
"Richard wouldn't understand—
But as for me, I think it's grand."

Richard Roe, he heard it too;
Listened hard the whole way through.
It made him feel he wasn't dense—
Addressed him like a man of sense.
It made him feel, "I'm not a fool—
I still remember stuff from school."
Richard Roe, he rubbed his eyes
With a kind of proud surprise.
" 'Tisn't quite in Johnny's line—
But as for me, I liked it fine."

Doe and Roe met face to face
Just outside the polling-place.
"Well, what's new?" said Doe to Roe,
"Nothing much," said Roe to Doe.
"Whaddya know?" said Roe to Doe.
"Not a thing," said Doe to Roe.
In they went, and out they came,
Looking just about the same.
He, and he alone (thought each)
Had *really* understood that speech.[2]

On election day Stevenson had spoken in a fashion unmistakably
and irreplaceably Stevensonian to a group of children outside their
school, which was being used as a polling place. "I would like to ask
all of you children to indicate," he began,[3] "by holding up your

[2] Poem quoted in introduction to *Major Campaign Speeches.*
[3] *Ibid.*

hands, how many of you would like to be Governor of Illinois, the way I am. (*Show of hands.*) Well, that is almost unanimous. Now I would like to ask all the Governors if they would like to be one of you kids. (*Whereupon Governor Stevenson cheered.*)

"I don't know whether you understand what is going on here this morning very well," he went on. "I am not sure I do myself! . . . Here are a lot of your parents and your neighbors going over to the schoolhouse there to cast their vote. That means they are deciding for themselves . . . who will be their officers and who runs their Government, all the way from the county up to the United States. In other words, what that means is that we decide who governs us. It is not everybody in the world who can do that. These are the things you read about in the history books, that your ancestors have been struggling for for generations—not only to get the right to govern themselves, but to keep it. . . . What I hope, as time goes on and you go further along in school, is that you will study more and more about what you have seen here this morning—this business of voting—why we vote and what we vote for. The more you study about it, the more precious it will become to you. The more you do it, the better and more intelligently you will vote, and the better government you will have. Does everybody understand that? (*Chorus of yeas.*) One of the highest degrees of intelligence in the whole United States is political intelligence."

This was the kind of intelligence Stevenson had been exercising and illustrating during the long, draining, elucidating months before he walked wearily into his Springfield headquarters to read the congratulatory telegram he had sent Eisenhower, to make his statement, and to tell his Lincoln anecdote.

The Loyal Opposition

Stevenson had described the possibility of being President as one of the risks faced by every American boy when he grows up. Being a defeated Presidential candidate is another risk, involving hazards, labors, and agonies of its own. With these Stevenson has lived since that night in Springfield when the returns condemned him to them.

He had lost not only the election but his privacy, too. He was the titular head of his party and, therefore, inescapably in the public domain. He had not lost, however, and fortunately could not lose, the qualities which had made his campaign distinguished. These guaranteed that, though politically jobless, he would undertake in his own way the tremendous job he felt he had to do.

Jacob M. Arvey, Chicago's key Democrat who backed him for the governorship, had told Stevenson on reading the draft of his first political speech in 1948, "Don't ever let anyone change a word of it or of any speech you ever write. . . . You've got a new approach to politics entirely." [4] His race for the Presidency four years later proved that he did have. So did the campaign he was forced to keep on running as his party's nominal leader.

To be titular head of the defeated party is to head a government in exile that happens to have remained at home. It is to be the leader of an underground movement which is permitted to operate in the open. It is to be the spokesman for a party that can work with the administration, though never be for it entirely if it hopes to come into power again. It is to face the obligations incurred by a past honor without any guarantee of future trust. It is to be the marshal of former followers who, as the next choice approaches, are free at any moment to turn to a new leader. It is to invite the danger of having ingratitude offered as the only reward and of being treated as shabbily as Willkie was in 1944 when he was not asked to address the Republican convention, or as shockingly as Dewey was in Chicago in 1952 when, as already noted, in addition to not being asked to speak, he was publicly insulted by Dirksen.

Stevenson was well aware of the difficulties confronting him in this "very ambiguous" role. As he says in his introduction to his new collection [5] of speeches and articles written between 1952 and 1955, "the titular leader has no clear and defined authority within his party. He has no party office, no staff, no funds, nor is there any system of consultation whereby he may be advised of party policy and through which he may help to shape that policy. There are no devices such as the British have developed through which he can

---

[4] *Adlai E. Stevenson of Illinois,* by Noel F. Busch, New York, Farrar, Straus & Young, 1952.

[5] *What I Think,* by Adlai E. Stevenson, New York, Harper & Brothers, 1956.

communicate directly and responsibly with the leaders of the party in power."

Nonetheless the titular leader has heavy responsibilities that Stevenson felt strongly and was zealous in meeting. At the campaign's end the Democratic party had a debt of $800,000 which, since it had been incurred in his name, Stevenson characteristically regarded as a personal obligation. By speaking the country over at dinners ranging from $100 to $25 a plate he had, by the beginning of 1955, come within striking distance of paying this off single-handed, a feat as revealing about his drawing power as his probity.

As Stevenson saw it, his duty was to rebuild and reanimate his defeated party. It was to travel extensively around the world in order to develop an informed opinion on our foreign policy. It was to present to the people "considered assessments" of the administration and its performance. Above all, it was to play a part comparable to what in England is known as the leader of the loyal opposition.

To say, as Stevenson does, that all this added up to "a staggering amount of writing and speaking" is to indulge in a major understatement, particularly when one remembers the numerous magazine articles about his travels that he also found time to write and the three brilliant and deeply reflective Godkin Lectures on foreign affairs, delivered at Harvard in the spring of 1954 and published under the title of *Call to Greatness*.[6] Few professional writers in such crowded years could have produced so much, fewer still so much of excellence.

On election night a reporter had asked Stevenson if he would run again in 1956. His answer had been, "Have that man's head examined." It is Stevenson's head that can be examined in his two volumes of collected speeches and the Godkin Lectures, and the mind for which they speak is a fascinating one, at once wise and dexterous, witty and profound. It is the mind of a man, unmistakably big at the moment of his welcoming speech in Chicago in 1952, who has grown bigger because of his ability to keep pace with the experiences the years have brought him.

It is a questing mind, unpedantic though steeped in knowledge,

[6] *Call to Greatness,* by Adlai E. Stevenson, New York, Harper & Brothers, 1954.

that takes its learning for granted, hence shares it without self-consciousness. It is a hungry, hurrying mind, quick to perceive and no less quick to react in phrases mirroring its perceptions. It is also a contemplative mind that broods no less than races. Clearly it has roamed far in its reading, never looking upon books as strangers yet never estranging itself from life because of them. It does not reach for a quotation; it releases one which has become part of its own thinking.

The gaiety of Stevenson's mind is shining. Its wit has conscience. It is corrective and, when need be, chastising, but it is not cynical or mean. Beneath the laughter lies the Lincolnian sadness so often, because so unavoidably, noted. This melancholy is not the sadness of surrender or the whine of futility. It comes from the recognition of human wrongs and follies and the splendor of an ideal that must be reached for even if it can never be realized.

Instead of being downed by actualities, Stevenson is haunted by possibilities. When he describes himself as an optimist, he is accurate. He is, however, a thinking not an unthinking optimist and is able to be one only because his faith is greater than his doubts. His is an analytical mind that weighs long and often painfully before it acts or judges, but that those close to him say can be resolute to the point of stubbornness once it is made up. It is a mind fighting for its own freedom and determined to preserve it in its fight for the freedom of others. Its moderation is the expression of its dislike for cant and its belief in reason, and not the result of any lack of strong convictions.

A friend tells [7] how one day in Chicago, when he was driving down Michigan Avenue with Stevenson, their car stopped at a traffic light and the driver of a truck alongside called, "Hiya, Adlai." The two men talked pleasantly until the light changed. "Where did you meet that man?" asked Stevenson's companion as they drove on. Stevenson admitted he did not know. "Well, you two seemed friendly enough." "Oh, he wasn't being friendly with me," said Stevenson, "he was talking to Adlai."

Stevenson's ability to disassociate his public from his private self, and to appraise both with detachment, is the same analytical gift

[7] *Newsweek,* November 14, 1955.

that he has brought to his consideration of issues and policies both as his party's candidate and titular head. He has explained his understanding of the latter role by saying in *What I Think,* "If 'the duty of a loyal opposition is to oppose,' I cannot see how anyone can offer effective opposition without giving reasons for it and these are, of course, criticisms." He knows that "in many minds political 'criticism' has today become an ugly word," conjuring up "pictures of insidious radicals hacking away at the very foundations of American life." He is well aware that "it suggests nonconformity and nonconformity suggests disloyalty, and disloyalty suggests treason," and this process has all but "turned political criticism into an un-American activity instead of democracy's greatest safeguard." Stevenson firmly believes that "it is better to discuss a question even without settling it than it is to settle a question without discussing it." To him "criticism, in its fairest and most honest form, is the attempt to test whether what is, might not be better."

The staunchest Republicans would find it hard to maintain that Republicans themselves have not rendered Stevenson more than yeoman service in supplying him from time to time with materials begging to be criticized. No silver platter could be large enough to hold some of the bloopers which the administration, in spite of its achievements, has handed him.

The Republicans, being mortal, were bound like the Democrats before them to make their mistakes, and Stevenson, being mortal too, as well as the titular leader of the opposition, was no less bound to pounce upon them. Doing so was his duty; doing so in decent terms and with unusual fairness was his contribution.

Arthur Krock shrewdly observed in the *New York Times,* when Stevenson spoke at a fund-raising dinner in Philadelphia late in 1953, that "the temptation is strong to a defeated Presidential candidate to make the welkin ring, whatever that may do to the Liberty Bell." As Krock states it, "the rule is you must never concede that what is wrong can possibly be righted without adding that this can be achieved only by turning out the party in power." This is a rule Stevenson has seldom obeyed and then with obvious discomfort. Although he has hit hard and laughed hard as a partisan, he has never blinded himself to the fact that errors can be bipartisan, and when speaking has managed to speak for more than his party. If he does not think in the expected terms, it is because he cannot. His mind is of a kind new to contemporary American politics. So, for that matter, is his personality.

"The Way of the Egghead"

Our government is apt to be served by men whose personalities are either elective or appointive. This is by no means a division into sheep and goats. Most of the ablest Cabinet members in any administration belong in the second category. That by type they are not vote getters does not mean that by endowment they may not be brilliant performers. Yet the very traits which underlie their usefulness when heading a department can subtract from their appeal at the polls. Though they may be charming individually, they often do not have the attributes which are crowd-catching because of being too shy or aloof, or because of having minds, impatient from their strength, which do not suffer fools gladly. Lacking the needed public manner and being more at home with large problems than local committeemen, their only hope of performing distinguished services for their country is to be appointed to public office by those who have captured the votes which they themselves cannot attract.

To a unique degree Stevenson combines the best characteristics of both types. He does not possess, as Ike does and FDR did, the sort of personality which can turn a stadium into a den. He is an intellectual who by choice seeks out the company of other intellectuals. Being a writer with skills that professionals envy, he is not suspicious of "word men" but speaks their language as they do his, regardless of his misgivings about their publishers. Contemplation with him is a habit, privacy a principle. In short, he is an egghead unashamed, although he was not aware of it until his aides in 1952 told him what the word meant. Since then he has laughingly referred to the label, as he did in his first Godkin Lecture at Harvard by saying, "I am uncomfortably reminded of the abiding truth of those classic words that never occurred to Horace: *'Via ovicipitum dura est,'* or, for the benefit of the engineers among you: 'The way of the egghead is hard.' "

It has not been hard for him, in spite of the fears of some of his supporters and the hopes of all his adversaries. Seemingly a campus or State Department type, he might (until he speaks) be thought to have an appointive personality. Yet nationally and in his own state he has proved that his appeal can be astoundingly elective. To be sure, he lost Illinois to Eisenhower in 1952, but in 1948, entering politics in the *Chicago Tribune* area as an internationally-minded Democrat with three years' experience with the United Nations among his recommendations, this green and supposedly hopeless candidate defeated his rival for the governorship by 572,000 votes, while Truman edged out Dewey in Illinois by a slim 34,000. It was this that won him Truman's attention and the nation's.

Certainly not compulsive as a political personality in the hearty, earthy, or extrovert fashion of Teddy Roosevelt, FDR, Truman, or Eisenhower, Stevenson has nonetheless won not only warm admirers but millions of partisans "madly for Adlai." These are not limited to those fellow "doubledomes" to whom he once said, "Arise, ye eggheads of the world. You have nothing to lose but your yolks." They include farmers, mechanics, labor leaders, and in every profession and walk of life the uncountable John Does and Richard Roes of Miss Struther's poem. To picture him as cold and withdrawn merely because he is an intellectual and reflective is to misrepresent both him and his mind utterly. In Louis Kronenberger's phrase, "man cannot live by head alone." Stevenson does not and never has.

His heart is as large as his intellect, his interest in people genuine, and his affections and loyalties are strong. Though no back-slapper, he is gregarious, outgoing, and friendly, quick to put others at ease and to be at ease with them. In spite of being complicated and often at odds with himself, he is simple and direct in his manner, a modest person, more truly a man of humility. Since his nomination he has been inundated with praise. But, when still Governor, he said, "I suppose flattery hurts no one; that is, if he doesn't inhale." Stevenson has not inhaled the flattery public life has heaped upon him. The words of self-deprecation in his acceptance speech, startling when coming from a candidate, were sincere in the way Lincoln's were when, upon being told he was being considered for the Presidency, he said, "I hope they will choose someone abler than myself." Stevenson's modesty remains unchanged, though his confidence has grown, and grown markedly.

Stevenson is a Chicago Ivy Leaguer by head and a southern Illinois farmer by heart. A journalist by early initiation, a politician by inheritance, and a gentleman by background no less than by every instinct of his being, he has the midlander's sense of a United States that, instead of facing one ocean, looks in every direction. In a phrase he has quoted from Elijah Lovejoy, this country's first martyr to freedom of the press, his heart beats "thick and proudly" when he contemplates America's achievements, its resources, and its possibilities.

Recognized as a superior talker, Stevenson is no less gifted as a listener. One of the things that made his trip to the Far East in 1953 successful was his frankness in saying he did not know and his being equally frank in saying he wanted to learn. As Barry Bingham, who traveled with him, observed,[8] it was an amazing lesson in democracy for Orientals to discover that Stevenson, a defeated candidate, had lunched with Eisenhower at the White House on friendly terms before he left. It was invaluable to have him point out to Japanese students, who talked about Communism, that democracy is the right to disagreement and the heat of men's minds rubbing against each other, sending out sparks. It was just as important to have him point out to Indonesian intellectuals in Jakarta that we, who seem to them soft in our prosperity today, have not always been rich and powerful, and that we came into being through revolution, with meager resources and few friends, against what was then the world's dominant power. Stevenson's zest for inquiry has not left him. He is an incessant and absorbed questioner. This is why he has so much in the way of information and stimulation to offer to others.

Noel Busch accurately pictured him early in 1952 as a hard-working, self-driving, austerely conscientious Spartan whose whimsical choice was to appear, in spite of his successes as a lawyer, a troubleshooter in public life, a diplomat, and a state executive, as a carefree, casual hedonist fond of telling stories at his own expense. This impression, so carefully cultivated by him before his nomina-

[8] *The Courier-Journal,* May 3, 1953.

tion, was contradicted by his campaign, and since then has nearly disappeared.

Stevenson's daily schedule as titular head of his party was almost Presidential in its burdens. His law office in Chicago became a minor White House. His callers from the world over were endless, his mail was enormous, and the number of his telephone calls staggering. Moreover, wherever he went, except when trying to steal a little rest, the same demands were made upon him. Needless to say, the rigors of his schedule have only increased since in November, 1955, he announced his candidacy for the nomination.

Truman notes wistfully in his memoirs that "a President has little enough time to meditate." The titular head of a defeated party or an announced candidate for the nomination has scarcely more. Since his defeat, most of Stevenson's days must have seemed to him as unhalting and scattering as the months of the campaign. Yet, from the chaos of his schedule as nominal leader, he somehow snatched the time, essential to his mind and temperament, to reflect on, appraise, dig deep into, and clarify political issues as a thinker uncrowded by crowds, and to produce a work of the meditative calm, the historical insight, and unhurried lucidity of *Call to Greatness*.

Stevenson stated his purpose in these three Godkin Lectures as being "to attempt to defrost a tiny segment of the opaque window through which we see others and others see us—and to do it briefly, having listened to many lectures myself!" The result of his efforts at Harvard in 1954 was an achievement, not an attempt. If what he said was in essence seldom new, it had the virtue of seeming new, because it was newly and memorably phrased and its ideas were newly associated. It could claim another novelty. The forgotten is new when rediscovered, and Stevenson was speaking of values almost forgotten then because of the confusing immensity of new circumstances and the fears which these had created.

There are people, too many, who have tongues but not ears, or if they do have ears hear only their own voices. Stevenson, whose eloquence is undisputed, not only listens to others but has the rare gift of hearing nations speak above the blur of their citizens' voices. In *Call to Greatness* he spoke as one who had long known Europe and the world intimately, and had traveled the previous year through thirty countries along the free side of the Iron Curtain from Seoul to Berlin. He did not speak as a person who has taken his body abroad but left his mind at home as many returned travelers do, including some junketing Congressmen and Senators. Instead, he spoke as an intuitive and trained observer, with a mind as open as his eyes, who saw the present's problems in relation to a changed past and the future's need.

His subject was large, and so was his approach to it. At his ease with history, he reviewed the "cluster of frustrations" which since V-E and V-J Days has brought us to the predicament of the present. He indicated "our difficulties which are the price of our blessings," and then turned to the great new problems of "the awakening of continents" and the "sudden redistribution of sovereignty," when "the Western ideas which we have so long taken for granted . . . are now brutally beleaguered."

Unfrightened by the prospects though fully aware of the changes which have brought them about and the hazards they present, Stevenson gave a fresh urgency to familiar facts by pointing out that "in the air age the whole United States is no larger than a county fifty years ago, or, indeed, no larger than a Greek state 500 years before Christ," and by stressing too that all of us, the world over, at least so far as danger is concerned, are "standing shoulder to shoulder—with a hydrogen bomb ticking in our pockets."

It was as an explorer that Stevenson spoke, an explorer in that newest New World, the world itself as it now is, in which people everywhere, regardless of their nationalities, find themselves no longer citizens but strangers. With abhorrence he spoke of the Soviet annihilation of liberty within Russia and the absorbed countries, and with bleak realism faced its menace to our own. Yet, while recognizing our need for military might, Stevenson pleaded for another source of power which is ours—the ideas and ethical values for which America has stood. To him they were—and are—our ultimate strength even as persuasion by example is our final weapon, though both are often overlooked by those who in their alarm think only in terms of armaments, intrigue, or purchased good will. Accordingly, Stevenson spoke as the defender of the free mind, reasoning, thinking, challenging, disagreeing, pliable, and unimprisoned by passions.

As is now easy to forget, when in these lectures he talked as an intellectual in defense of the free mind, he did so the month before Oppenheimer faced the Gray Board and the Army-McCarthy hearings began, when McCarthyism was at its ugly height, when unreason threatened to be epidemic, and when the United States was in the throes of anti-intellectualism, "that swinish blight," as Senator Fulbright described it, "so common in our time."

Though welcome and health-restoring, there was nothing surprising from Stevenson's viewpoint in the stand he then took or the level at which he stated his position. He had spoken in just such terms as Governor of Illinois. He had spoken in the same terms in 1952, at whistle stop after whistle stop, and more particularly in his major addresses. He had persisted in doing so when Eisenhower's advisers during the campaign were plainly cowed by McCarthy. He had done it during the first years after the election when these same advisers continued to be intimidated by McCarthy. He had done it in defeat as the titular leader of his party. And he has continued doing so as a candidate for the nomination, and without question will in whatever position he finds himself after the next convention.

Stevenson Today

Oscar Wilde once said that he sometimes thought God in creating man somewhat overestimated His ability. The average American professional politician, though he would never think of questioning God's ability, manifestly has his doubts about the mentality and decency of the voters to whom he appeals. Not so Stevenson. He does not have to be at a university to address an audience as if it were educated, its ideals schooled, its reason trained. He has lived up to his promise of talking sense to the American people, because his belief in their basic sense is the basis of his belief in America and a major reason for his entering politics in his own way, on his terms, and becoming the very special kind of politician he is.

To be sure, politics is in his blood. The first Adlai E. Stevenson, in his grandson's words, was a Democrat "who flourished politically in Republican Illinois," was elected Vice-President with Grover Cleveland in 1892, was nominated again with Bryan in 1900, and, "as a feeble old man, was a reluctant but very strong candidate for

Governor in 1908." His father, "whose Democratic allegiance and activity ended only with his death in 1929," served at Springfield as secretary of state of Illinois. And his maternal great-grandfather was Jesse Fell, a leader in founding the Republican party, an early and tireless advocate of Abraham Lincoln's candidacy for President, and the man who persuaded Lincoln to write the priceless three-page autobiography that was used in his campaign.

If politics comes naturally to Stevenson, so does his addiction to reading and the habits of gracious living and thinking which are his. His is a family with its roots deep in the soil of Illinois, an old family, the midlands counterpart in position, comforts, wealth, transmitted talents, and inherited sense of public duty of the Adamses, the Lodges, or the Roosevelts.

The charm of a vanished way of American life in which Stevenson was brought up, with its security, its elegance, its cultivation, and affection, is vividly evoked by Elizabeth Stevenson Ives in *My Brother Adlai*.[9] His sister tells how in the informal library of their large, somewhat stately home in Bloomington their mother used to read aloud to them, making "the big doses of the classics so exciting that they never had for us the bitter medicinal taste of compulsory education."

She tells us also how when he was a little boy Stevenson made his first political appearance. Properly slicked up and wearing an Eton collar which he hated, he was taken to sit on the speakers' platform at a Democratic rally and, while William Jennings Bryan was orating, he went peacefully to sleep. That kind of speaking, all sound and fury and oboe notes, has never appealed to him and he has not been guilty of it.

When Stevenson speaks, it is from his heart and head, and not merely from his throat and lungs. The growing "sandbank of reason" remains his concern as he faces 1956, the heads of hearers continue to be his target, and his unaltered hope is to find the right word to say exactly what he wants to say.

Though inevitably far more experienced in national politics than he was four years ago, and possessed of a greater knowledge of the

[9] *My Brother Adlai*, by Elizabeth Stevenson Ives and Hildegarde Dolson, New York, William Morrow & Co., 1956.

world, he is in essence and by endowment the same. He is as moderate as he was before, to the dismay of those Democrats who believe
that the abandonment of reason which is immoderation is the function of their party. He is as much the true hater of dulling conformity as he ever was, and the champion of the free and uncoerced
mind. Though the welfare of the average citizen and small businessman is as genuine an absorption of his as peace, he cannot bring
himself to attack Big Business merely for the political gains he might
make, because he is convinced that Big Business and Labor are twin
essentials to America's health that must, and can, find peaceful
means of coexistence.

He believes as he did before that too much government is dangerous, and does not want a warmed-over version of the Fair Deal.
The proof to him that the New Deal and the Fair belong to the
past is that they served their purposes so well that the Republicans
have felt safe in appropriating many of their major programs. Because of all this, some Democrats, yearning for war whoops and the
good old days, have convinced themselves that Stevenson has
changed since 1952 and that the rattled youth who greeted him
then in Spokane by screaming, "Hooray for Stevenhower!" must
have been right after all. But to try to blend him with Eisenhower,
and interchange their gifts, is in all fairness to misrepresent both
men.

Stevenson has changed in certain respects. He has grown in confidence and authority. He has not lost his admiration for Eisenhower,
though he is no longer inhibited by it as some say he was in the last
campaign. He has become convinced that Eisenhower has often been
ill-advised, ill-used, and ill-served by those who have protected themselves by relying on the magic of his name. He knows also that any
Democratic candidate in 1956 is the gainer because of his party's
loss in 1952, since "time for a change" is a slogan the Democrats can
now adopt instead of having to combat. The house cleaning needed
after twenty years of one party rule has been done. The nominee, if
elected, would be free to form his own administration rather than
obliged to inherit another's.

James Reston reported [10] soon after Stevenson had announced his

[10] *New York Times,* November 20, 1955.

candidacy in 1955 that he "is still brooding over his typewriter like a frustrated poet." His habit of shutting himself in to perfect his speeches won him in the previous campaign the criticism of those who contended he would have done better to go out and polish up his acquaintanceship with the local committeemen instead of staying in to polish his phrases. But words mean much to Stevenson just as his words mean the more to others because of the fastidiousness with which he uses them. Reston notes, however, that, though Stevenson has not lost the harried look of a writer trying to meet a deadline, he is devoting more time to "the little courtesies and the big bull sessions that mean so much to the smoky-room set," and that both he and his organization are now professional. To some liberals this is upsetting, because, though they admired Franklin Roosevelt and Truman for being pros, in general their distrust of professionals in politics is as great as their contempt for amateurs in the arts.

In Defense of Laughter, Learning, and Language

Stevenson's admirers run into millions and remain both grateful and enthusiastic, but he continues to be eyed with suspicion by a large number of Republicans and even some Democrats. These suspicions are interesting, quite apart from Stevenson, because of the paradoxes they reveal in the American credo. They have their origin not in his faults as an individual but in the endowments he brings to public life. He is witty and delights in laughter. He is educated and does not hide the fact. And he is a master of words, fluently and brilliantly articulate. These are the charges, odd and contradictory, as seriously brought against Stevenson by some people as if they were Articles of Impeachment to disqualify him for the Presidency.

It seems strange, indeed it is strange, to have to defend laughter in America, for Americans are a laughter-loving people and our ability to laugh is supposed to be the guarantee of such sanity as we have. It is strange to have to defend wit and humor in the land of Abraham Lincoln, Mark Twain, and Will Rogers. But there are those, not always witless themselves, who believe that anyone aspiring to the Presidency must forget that even the Declaration mentions happiness as a proper pursuit.

Dullness is the kind of brightness they want Presidentially, pomposity their notion of the proper. They seem convinced that because a man can be gay, he cannot also be serious. Quite rightly, they no more want official Presidential utterances to read like Ludwig Bemelmans or James Thurber than James Thurber and Ludwig Bemelmans want their books to read like official Presidential utterances. But the law of gravity of these sobersides does not stop with state papers. Let a man away from the White House be entertaining while hoping to talk himself there, and they brand him as being no more than an entertainer.

They were quick to do this with Stevenson in 1952, and they have not stopped. Unable to respond in kind, they have frowned on his gaiety. Because he is an exception to their non-gag rule, they have tried to paint Stevenson as a George Gobel or a Bob Hope. Forgetting that Churchill's wit has added to, not subtracted from, his weight, they have tried, sincerely or for political reasons, to damage Stevenson by picturing him as a professional funnyman. In the process they have also forgotten that when speaking humorously Stevenson is speaking the language of his listeners. To be instructed or even uplifted, American voters do not have to be bored, though many have been bored so long by the speeches of their political leaders that they have apparently come to associate boredom with leadership.

Stevenson's wit, delightful and irrepressible as it is, is more than an expression of gaiety. It speaks for his reason and also his strong sense of right and wrong. "Man," said Hazlitt, "is the only animal that laughs and weeps; for he is the only animal that is struck with the difference between what things are, and what they ought to be." It is by this gift for laughter that Stevenson shares his awareness of this difference with his listeners, and leads them into the long serious passages of his speeches.

Most Republicans who admit the merits of these passages know that Stevenson is a profoundly thoughtful man. But ask the Republican who dismisses him as a buffoon if he has read the *Major Speeches, Call to Greatness,* or *What I Think,* and his reply, honest though not open-minded, is apt to be either "No" or "Of course not." If he has read them, he usually retreats from the "buffoon" or "gagster" charge and attacks Stevenson for being an egghead, a doubledome, and too intellectual a type for the Presidency.

Here another oddity in the American credo comes to light. No country has ever spent so much (however inadequate) on education as the United States. None has ever built so many schools or colleges, accepted public schooling more ardently as a principle, or on the elementary levels sent out so many truant officers as dogcatchers to round up the recalcitrant young. None has ever given more honorary degrees or held class reunions more ubiquitously and noisily.

Yet for a man in high office to let his education show is held to be an act of indecency. The Venus de Medici is not more precautionary in shielding her charms than the wise political aspirant is supposed to be in masking the fact that he has been exposed to an education that has left him cultivated. Life-wisdom, business experience, and a "diploma gained at the school of hard knocks," as James M. Cox used to say, that is one thing—acceptable, respected, and vote winning. But any betrayal of such life-wisdom, augmented by too much reading, except for certain books, is another matter.

In that hucksterdom for power which is American politics, the belief seems to be widespread that a little learning is a dangerous thing, and that it is wisest to lay off even touching the Pierian spring. The Founding Fathers, unnamed individually but mentioned as a package deal, are held to be safe references. Patrick Henry is good for seasoning, and Benjamin Franklin for leavening if not cited on the subject of thrift. Democrats can quote from Jefferson, Jackson, and Wilson while praising FDR and Truman, and Republicans from Lincoln and Theodore Roosevelt while extolling Ike. In truth, Lincoln by now is as serenely bipartisan as Washington, and hence interchangeable as a party reference. But let a candidate for high public office, or a public official of importance, buttress a point by turning to literature (with the exception of Shakespeare and the Bible) and he is taking a calculated risk. According to the myth, Texas would be lost by a mention of Kafka, the Corn Belt by a quotation from T. S. Eliot, the Solid South by a borrowing from Santayana, and New England by an admission of being familiar with Baudelaire.

That is the myth, not the truth, as Stevenson has proved by referring to more authors while campaigning than most college professors do in their classrooms during a year. The point is that he has not referred to them as most college professors would. Instead, he has done it so naturally that millions have been pleased by it, admiring him for being himself and flattered by his assumption of their knowledge. Only those who have forgotten they have read other things than newspapers have resented it.

Stevenson is more than an intellectual. If he were not, his intellect would have scant popular appeal or be of little public value. He is life-wise as well as steeped in literature. Without meaning to do so, he best described his special, unashamed and joyous type of cultivation when in 1954 he spoke at a senior class banquet at Princeton. Confessing then that what a man knows at fifty that he did not know at twenty is, for the most part, incommunicable, Stevenson said:

"What he knows at fifty that he did not know at twenty boils down to something like this: The knowledge he has acquired with age is not the knowledge of formulas, or forms of words, but of people, places, actions—a knowledge not gained by words but by touch, sight, sound, victories, failures, sleeplessness, devotion, love—the human experiences and emotions of this earth and of oneself and other men; and perhaps, too, a little faith, and a little reverence for the things you cannot see."

In addition to being witty and an educated man whose knowledge is a verb in his living, Stevenson has another mark against him in the demonology of American politics—his incredible way with words. Deeds are words in the vocabulary of many good, stolid, practical Americans, and silence is admired among certain businessmen, perhaps because they have heard it is golden. Indeed, silence can often create a reputation for wisdom, as it did in the case of Coolidge, and in spite of that, still does. Strong men, masters of things but not of ideas, find it easy to convince themselves that their inarticulateness is an indication of their strength. Theirs is a natural distrust of the gift which is transparently Stevenson's and not theirs.

Right as they are in their awareness of how close gaiety can be to glibness, fluency to mere facility, and facility to foolishness and the unreliable, they are on dangerous ground when they look with suspicion on the responsible leader who includes the use of words among his responsibilities. The leader's voice is more than his own. It is the echo to a people's needs and dreams. And these are worthy of the best statement they can have.

As the months dragged by between the election and inauguration of Warren Harding, Woodrow Wilson is supposed to have said, "I look forward to the new administration with no unpleasant anticipations, except those caused by Mr. Harding's literary style."

One may agree or disagree with Stevenson politically, or like or dislike him personally, but to have a political leader able to bend the language to his will as Stevenson can must be counted among our national resources. The fight to keep free minds informed, issues clear, and ideals aglow is the truceless battle of democracy. The shot fired by the embattled farmers at Concord would never have been heard round the world if it had not been supported in time by the verbal artillery of the Declaration of Independence, the pamphlets of Tom Paine, and *The Federalist* papers. For democracy, being itself an idea and one always in danger, includes in its arsenal no weapons more powerful than these.

Because of using them and himself as he has and because of believing in the best and giving of his own best, Stevenson has already made his invaluable contribution to American politics, regardless of his ultimate fate politically.

VII

LODGE OF THE UNITED NATIONS

Man with a Mission

Of all the housing developments along the East River the greatest, since it is the home of man's hopes for peace, is the United Nations. The General Assembly and the Secretariat are buildings aggressively untraditional in their architecture. In form and detail they are as bold as the dream they shelter. The one is low with a roof line that, though interesting, is curiously sway-backed. The other is a towering rectangle, all marble on its narrow ends, all windows on its broad sides, which by its singularity catches the eye at once.

There were people, and plenty of them, who at first did not like the shaft of green glass and Vermont marble which is the Secretariat. But they have grown accustomed to it. They have come to see why, in a world threatened by war, a structure devoted to peace should stand up like an exclamation point. Perhaps they have sensed, without being aware of it, the rightness of those acres of windows in a day when many fear the light. Perhaps, in the same fashion, they have come to appreciate the assurance of survival that a house of glass represents in the age of the atom.

The missions of the member nations are not housed in the UN buildings. Instead, they are scattered throughout New York, a city so large, bustling, and self-absorbed that it has become a world capital without its citizens' being aware of the change or seeming to care. The United States mission is located at No. 2 Park Avenue. There Henry Cabot Lodge, Jr., as our Chief Delegate, occupies the same corner office on the twenty-third floor which was Warren Austin's when he was our Ambassador.

Although many of the UN's representatives can doubtless see the Secretariat from their headquarters, none has a view of it more emphatic in its contrasts than Lodge. Plainly visible to the northeast from the windows behind his desk is that soaring tower which is dedicated to peace. Yet in the immediate foreground, and diagonally across from his office, Lodge looks down on the Seventy-first Regiment Armory and the army trucks which sometimes choke 33rd Street. Sharp as this contrast is between the beckoning hopes and the bitter truths of the present, it is as realistic as Lodge's approach to his task. The sight of an armory and army trucks in the foreground below him would not strike Lodge as an incongruity. Peace is the world's dream and Lodge's too, but he does not work for it as a dreamer.

If he believes in the UN, as he does wholeheartedly, it is not because he thinks it needs us but because events have convinced him that we need it. This unflinching acceptance of the changed facts of a radically altered universe is what has turned Lodge, an ardent nationalist, into a no less ardent internationalist in the national interest. A realist in public life does not waste his time or imperil his country by thinking of the cards he wishes he held. His job is to play the hand history has dealt, and play it as well as he can.

Lodge is essentially such a realist. When he was a year old, Henry Adams, a close friend of the family, smilingly suggested that he resembled St. Thomas Aquinas. Time seems to have lessened the resemblance. There is nothing of the visionary in either the appearance or the thinking of this remarkably handsome, dark-haired man of fifty-three who, being six feet two and three-quarters inches tall, stands out as something of a skyscraper himself both at the UN and among the members of his own mission. His features are clear-cut. His mouth is firm and his chin has some of New England's granite it it. His lightish-blue eyes sparkle with animation. He holds himself well and moves with the same decision with which he thinks and talks.

When relaxed, Lodge smiles with his whole face; when serious, he concentrates with his whole body. From long years of political experience, he can turn on at will a professional smile which, though winning, comes near to being mechanical in its good humor. His real smile and the earthy, cannonading laugh which often follows it are as contagious and genuine outbursts of gaiety as a human throat can release.

His habit, while listening, of jiggling his right foot or snapping his right thumb against the index finger is not so much a gesture of impatience as an indication of his eagerness to get at the core of the subject under discussion. Most frequently at a party, or even among intimates, he is careful to wriggle out of final opinions stated in quotable form. Cagey no less than discreet, he enjoys evasion as a conversational game. He likes to pretend that, if only he were not interrupted, he would be able to give a definite answer, all the while that he is provoking interruptions, indeed making them inevitable, by challenging questions or deliberate overstatements so that he will not have to give the answer sought.

Lodge's evasions in private talk and his alertness to expediency in public action are not to be confused with timidity. He is plainly a man to whom fear is unknown and misgivings are uncommon. The sheen of success is on him. Ideally happy in his marriage and family life and free of financial worries, Lodge has the assurance of a person born into "a social position unconscious of dispute or doubt" (to turn to Henry Adams again and borrow a phrase he used about Lodge's father, the poet George Cabot Lodge).

This assurance was often mistaken for arrogance in his Harvard days and at the beginning of his career. It still is, though not so often—due to his own maturing, to his sincere interest in people, and, above all, to the Maggie Shand-like wisdom and sunny natural-ness of his wife. The confidence Lodge continues to exude creates confidence not only among those working with him but also among those who see and hear him at the UN.

When he speaks at the General Assembly, he strides toward the podium, carried forward by an idea. Clearly he is thinking not of himself but of what he is going to say. By birth one of the most Brahmin of Bostonians, Lodge is neither a Brahmin in manner nor a Yankee in accent. His speech is precise without being clipped or flat and, except for a few inescapable throwbacks, is cosmopolitan rather than regional. His gestures, though forceful, tend to be tight and jerky, but his voice is deep and vigorous and his language bless-edly bereft of the gaseous ambiguities of traditional diplomacy.

Since his first appearance as our Chief Delegate at the UN, Lodge has been widely and properly praised for talking straight from the shoulder. His speeches have been refreshing in their brevity and have avoided oratory for pungency. They have made their points sharply in terms simple enough to be understood by everyone everywhere. An example was the way in which Lodge pounced upon Vishinsky's statement in March, 1953, to the effect that the United States was going to lose Asia anyway. "That astounding remark," said Lodge, "made me realize how far apart his view of humanity is from mine. The United States is not trying to get Asia. We have never thought of Asia as some sort of object inhabited by slaves which was to be won or lost by outsiders. We believe that the people of Asia, like the American people and like all other people, have the right to live their own lives and to develop themselves in their own way."

Four years in the Massachusetts Legislature and thirteen in the United States Senate have trained Lodge in the ready give-and-take of debate and the ability to detect and expose at once a weakness in an opponent's argument. The ten years he spent as a journalist before entering politics taught him that tomorrow morning's headlines are made from today's news. Hence his instantaneous answers to Gromyko, Vishinsky, or Sobolev, in order to win for the American point of view the press attention which a night's delay would have given to the Soviets.

It is characteristic of Lodge that his first statement in the Security Council was a neat marshaling of "ten facts" which proved that the Russians, in spite of all their claims to the contrary, had given specific aid to the aggressors in Korea. Lodge has a healthy fondness for facts. Among the facts he has long faced is that military strength is one of our best guarantees of peace. Few now question such a belief. Lodge, however, championed it in those almost forgotten times when most Americans thought that peace could be achieved by decent wishes and sacrificial gestures and when any mention of preparedness was anathema to liberals and intellectuals.

In 1932 he published *The Cult of Weakness*, his only book. Its title explained the then popular attitude in this country which Lodge deplored. Although it was an indifferent tract and one for which its author now has little affection, it made its valid points. Lodge maintained we were living in a "softie" era and emphasized the dangers of peace through unpreparedness. He was for disarmament provided all the great powers would live up to their promises and disarm equally. Having observed the results of the Washington, Geneva, and London Conferences, however, he was opposed to having us face an armed world with inadequate or disproportionate arms. Never a militarist and too practical to be a pacifist, Lodge was prompted by his hatred of war to fight for the building up of our military forces before and after his election to the Senate in 1936.

He hated the idea of war long before he saw combat himself. Today he hates war as only a man can who has experienced its horrors first hand in Libya, Italy, southern France, the Rhineland, and central Germany, and has had a son in Korea. Known as a non-interventionist before World War II and thought by many as an out-and-out isolationist, Lodge never permitted his hopes of our remaining at peace to blind him to the need of our readying ourselves to resist attack. His voting record prior to Pearl Harbor may, in certain respects, have been elusive in its consistency, to put it mildly, but on measures aimed at strengthening our defenses it followed a path as straight as a thruway.

He favored naval expansion in 1938 and an increase in army planes in 1939. The next year he was one of the earliest and strongest advocates of compulsory military service. In 1941 he voted for both Lend-Lease and an eighteen-month extension of military service. Our neutrality was Lodge's ideal but, as he once stated in the Senate, the notion that we could be neutral and unarmed had always seemed to him false and dangerous.

First Meets Eisenhower

Believing adequate preparedness was our best peace insurance, Lodge practiced as an individual what he preached publicly. Summer after summer since 1924 he had interrupted his vacation to train as an active reservist. As a matter of fact, it was in the heat and turmoil of the Louisiana maneuvers in 1941 that he had his first meeting with an officer who has since confessed that the popping of photographers' flash bulbs was at that time a fairly novel element in his daily life. Inasmuch as the officer was Dwight D. Eisenhower, that novelty was soon to wear off. Eisenhower, however, was then so unknown outside the Army that when a picture was taken of him with two higher officers their names were correctly given but he was identified as "Lt. Col. D. D. Ersenbeing."

Eisenhower, a temporary colonel, was chief of staff of Krueger's Third Army during the maneuvers, and the senator a captain in

Patton's Second Armored Division in Lear's Second Army. Although the two men were for the moment "strategic enemies," Lodge grew accustomed to having regulars speak of Ike as "a smart one." When he heard Patton, already a major general and as flamboyant and daring as he was to prove in Europe, say, "I'll give fifty dollars to anyone who takes prisoner a certain s.o.b. called Eisenhower," Lodge realized the colonel's special value to the Third Army. Their first conversation convinced him Eisenhower was the bright officer he was reported to be.

They were to meet three times again before Lodge traveled from Washington to Morningside Heights to warn the former colonel, by then the president of Columbia, that in the interest of a "modern-minded" Republican victory in 1952 it might be his duty to run for the Presidency of the United States. When Lodge said "duty" on that June afternoon in 1950 he meant it as surely as he knew that it, of all words, would have a special meaning for a soldier.

For Lodge himself, as for his family, duty has always been a summoning word. Public service, civilian or military, has been very much in the blood of the Cabots, the Frelinghuysens, the Davises, and the Lodges. The present Henry Cabot Lodge is the eighth United States senator to have come from a strain which has produced a Secretary of the Navy, a Governor of Massachusetts, a Governor of Connecticut (John Davis Lodge, the Ambassador's younger brother, now Ambassador to Spain), sent several members to the House of Representatives, and played its part in most of America's wars from the Revolution to Korea.

By actions exceptional in the Senate's history, Lodge was to demonstrate in the years following the maneuvers how urgent was his own sense of duty. The earthquake of an event, remote by the map yet so near in its impact and effects as to shake the foundations of the loneliest American home in the most serene of American landscapes, struck at Pearl Harbor soon after Lodge's first meeting with Eisenhower in Louisiana. A little more than a month before that permanently dislocating tremor, when tensions in our relations with Japan were increasing daily at an alarming rate, Lodge had voted against lifting the restrictions which kept our merchant vessels from entering belligerent ports.

His vote was in the nature of a delaying action. He knew from the maneuvers that we were not yet ready for war, and saw clearly (again as a realist) the dangers of declaring a war we would not be able to fight for six months. Although he recognized our neutrality had vanished, he still hoped our serving as an arsenal would be service enough and that young Americans would not have to be sent overseas. Pearl Harbor put an abrupt end to such hopes.

Pearl Harbor and Ike, Vandenberg, and Lodge

None of us old enough to understand the implications, national, international, and personal, of the news with which our radios assaulted us that Sunday will forget that afternoon or the sudden plunging finality with which what we heard shattered the world of our private living, planning, and dreaming. All of us can tell where we were, what we were doing, and what we were thinking as vividly as if that December 7 in 1941 were today.

That same afternoon at Fort Sam Houston, Texas, Eisenhower was taking a well-earned nap. He was exhausted from the duties of the past months, which he had carried out so vigorously and well that he had been made a temporary brigadier at the end of the maneuvers. He had worked in his office until noon. Then he had gone home, saying he was dead tired. After lunch he went to bed, with orders that under no circumstances was he to be disturbed.

In no time he was dreaming about the two weeks' Christmas leave he and Mrs. Eisenhower were going to have at West Point with their plebe son, John. He had slept perhaps an hour when the telephone rang and his wife heard him say, "Yes? . . . When? . . . I'll be right down." As he hurried to the front door, he told Mrs. Eisenhower that the Japanese were attacking Pearl Harbor and she had better turn on the radio. He added he was going to headquarters and did not know when he would return. "Well, boys," he said to the officers tensely waiting for him, "it's come."

And come it had—everywhere and to everyone. Some eighteen hundred miles away, in the little Massachusetts town of Groton, Senator and Mrs. Lodge stopped for gas in the late afternoon of this same December day. They were heading for Boston after a happy visit with their elder son, George, then fourteen and a third-former at the nearby Groton School. "Can you beat what the Japs have done!" exclaimed the attendent at the gas station.

This was the first word the Lodges had of Pearl Harbor. Mrs. Lodge recalls how white and grim the Senator's face was as they sped toward Boston, listening to the radio in their car. Before leaving for Washington on the midnight train, Lodge went on the air, urging all Americans, regardless of their politics and no matter how isolationist their thinking might have been, to unite and fight as one.

In Washington Arthur H. Vandenberg, whose career in the coming years was to be intimately linked with Lodge's, also found his life and thinking changed by the news his radio brought him that fateful Sunday. His son has revealed [1] that this kindly man from Michigan, with twinkling dark eyes, emphatically drawn black eyebrows, gray hair, a plump pink face, and a wide, balding forehead, was taking his Sabbath ease in a way he enjoyed. He was seated at a desk in his bedroom, which reeked of cigar smoke and mucilage, proudly pasting in his scrapbook clippings that recorded his long and vigorous fight against our involvement in the war.

Vandenberg had been the favorite choice of the isolationists for the Republican nomination in 1940. Now in December of the next year he was the leader, symbol, and internationally recognized spokesman of isolationism ("insulationism," he preferred to call it) in this country. At least he was until 4 P.M. on December 7. At that hour his isolationism ceased. He knew we were in it. Nothing mattered to him as of that moment except victory. He immediately issued a statement to that effect, then telephoned the White House and spoke to "Steve" Early, Roosevelt's press secretary, asking him to tell the President that, in spite of their many deep differences, he would support him without reservation in his answer to Japan. "In my own mind," Vandenberg wrote later, "my convictions regarding international cooperation and collective security for peace took firm form" that same afternoon.

The war, so violent in its coming, was to change Lodge's thinking about international cooperation and collective security as much as it did Vandenberg's. They had known each other since 1937 when Lodge, at thirty-four, first took his seat in the Senate. From the start they had agreed about the need for altering the Repub-

[1] *The Private Papers of Senator Vandenberg,* edited by Arthur H. Vandenberg, Jr., Boston, Houghton Mifflin Co., 1952.

lican party even as in the years ahead they were to agree about the altered needs of the Republic in a transformed world.

When Lodge assumed office, he was one of only seventeen Republicans in the Senate. They were a lonely group, a minority so minor as to be without practical effect. They voted mainly for the record and sometimes, when insignificant measures were coming up, they did not bother to vote at all. Instead, they went bowling in the late afternoon in the alley above the Center Market, where at least they carried some weight.

Although Lodge was eighteen years younger than Vandenberg, they had much to draw them together. Both had been newspapermen, the one having been the successful editor and Jack-of-all-trades on the *Grand Rapids Herald,* the other an energetic reporter, with a flair for scoops, and a vigorous political commentator on the *Boston Transcript* and then the *New York Herald Tribune.*

Both had stories to tell. Both liked to laugh. Both had done battle as "Young Turks," those insurgent Republicans ("the sons of the wild jackass," Senator George Moses of New Hampshire branded them) who had rebelled against the Old Guard's domination of their party. Both at the outset had overestimated the protection offered by the Atlantic and Pacific Oceans. And both at the time they first met had been slow to recognize the extent to which air power had revolutionized warfare. Before the outbreak of the war, however, Lodge had become keenly aware of the change and Vandenberg was to concede it little by little because of the frequent talks he had in Washington with his nephew, a junior officer, Hoyt S. Vandenberg, who was later to be chief of staff of the United States Air Force.

In spite of their friendship and the undoubted influence each had on the other, Lodge and Vandenberg did not always vote or think alike. Lodge, for example, voted for Lend-Lease, Vandenberg against it. Neither liked what he was called upon to do and both were fully aware of the meaning of what was being done. Lodge's vote meant he had accepted the inevitable; Vandenberg's was his last protest against it.

This protest recorded, Vandenberg was determined to support the future measures the bill's passage would demand, notwithstanding his feeling, when the result of the ballot was announced, that he "was witnessing the suicide of the Republic." Both Lodge and Vandenberg knew, as the latter confessed to his diary, that when we chose sides and committed ourselves to all-out aid for Britain and her allies we had "torn up 150 years of traditional American foreign policy," "tossed Washington's Farewell Address into the discard," "taken a first step from which we can never hereafter retreat," and linked our fate inseparably with Europe, Asia, and Africa.

Until the Japs struck, Lodge though he had done everything in his power to build up our military strength and recognized we were already participants in all but name, still hoped we would supply arms, not men. Vandenberg railed against the administration's "opportunist" policy of "war by proxy," and condemned as cowardly the idea of America's being half in, half out. He wanted us wholly out, though he was as sure as Lodge that we were being drawn in.

Both men accepted at once the new challenges and responsibilities created by Pearl Harbor. Within a week Vandenberg wrote to Roosevelt, overlooking the "active dislike" each felt for the other, to urge the creation of a Joint Congressional Committee on War Cooperation, and received a friendly answer. The champion of isolationism, a man big enough to change his mind and with a big mind to change, Vandenberg was already beginning to emerge as the apostle of bipartisanship.

A Note from FDR

As for Lodge, the idea of "war by proxy" was one he found intolerable when applied to himself. His struggle to keep his country out of the war did not mean, once it had come, that by temperament he could keep himself out of combat. His opportunities for service in the Senate were such that there were no obligations for his getting into uniform and many good arguments for his staying out. Yet by May, 1942, he had flown to Libya with one of the first American units to arrive in North Africa. There as a major in the first American tank detachment he saw action under General Auchinleck with the British Eighth Army in operations near El Adam and in the disastrous retreat from Tobruk to El Alamein when, for a dark interval, it looked as if Rommel and his Afrika Korps would sweep straight on to Cairo.

When ordered back to Washington in July, after he submitted what Stimson praised as a "most valuable personal appraisal of the military and diplomatic factors influencing the campaign currently under way in that theatre," Lodge expressed his eagerness to continue his military service. The Secretary of War, however, directed that he should be returned to inactive duty, explaining he could be of greater use to his country as a United States senator than as a junior officer.

Some Democrats, mindful in both Massachusetts and Washington of the strategies of other than military campaigns, suddenly realized that Lodge's army record would not hurt him when he stood for re-election that fall. Accordingly, they saw to it that a ruling was passed forbidding a person to be in the Senate and the armed forces at the same time. This ruling, though sensible in practice, was political, even personal, in motive since there were no other senators in the armed forces. Lodge fought against it as hard as he could, making clear his desire to stay in the Army and his resentment at being compelled to become a civilian again. He was the more irked because, though he could play politics with the toughest of them, making political capital of his uniform was a trick to which he would never have stooped and an idea which would never have occurred to him.

The ruling did not settle Lodge's problem for him. He continued to be torn in his thinking. After his re-election (he polled 721,239 votes, defeating his Democratic rival by 80,197) and still in doubt as to where his real duty lay, he went with four other senators on a 41,000-mile tour across five continents from July to September, 1943, investigating the conduct of the war. This tour made up his mind for him. He was forty-one and far healthier and more vigorous than many of the young men or those his own age he saw in uniform.

He decided an older man could do his work in Washington. To the surprise of everyone (except those who knew him) he resigned from the Senate and went back into the Army, insisting that no announcement of his resignation be released until he was on his way overseas. After he had gone, Vandenberg praised his action

highly in a speech in the Senate. And before he left, prompted by a
sense of courtesy which it is pleasant to be reminded does exist in
the higher echelons of politics, Lodge called at the White House to
tell the President, whose policies he had often opposed, of his decision and was cordially welcomed by him.

That afternoon (February 1, 1944) he received a letter from
Roosevelt which read, "Dear Cabot, I want you to know I am
awfully glad that you came to see me this morning. And I am
writing you this note to tell you that I would do just what you are
doing if I could. I missed being with the guns in 1917–18. It's too
late now. I envy you the opportunity that is yours and I congratulate
you on the decision you have made."

When Lodge returned to the United States after having served
in Italy as deputy chief of staff, Fourth Corps, and chief of the
Combat Liaison Section with General Devers in the Southern
Group of Armies in France and Germany, he was a lieutenant
colonel entitled to wear a campaign ribbon with six battle stars and
one arrowhead. He had been awarded the Bronze Star for bravery,
the Legion of Merit medal, the *Légion d'Honneur,* and the *Croix
de Guerre* (with palm). It was as inevitable, considering his career
before the war, that he would go back into politics as it would have
been unthinkable in 1941, or for that matter when he was at
Harvard, that he would ever be our representative at such an
organization as the United Nations. But the Lodge who came back
and was elected to the Senate for the third time in 1946 was not
the Lodge who had gone overseas.

Proper Bostonian

The Lodge some of us first met at Harvard in the early
twenties was already absorbed in politics. He was a smiling young
man of positive opinions. The fight over the League of Nations was
still in the air, which meant that Lodge, though popular, was a
center of controversy in the Yard inasmuch as he not only bore his
grandfather's name but had inherited his convictions. Lodge did
not duck the issue. He made himself heard in no uncertain terms,
and it was just as certain that he would be heard from in the future.
He was quick of mind, quick to laugh, and quick to plunge into an
argument.

He was an extrovert, cocksure in a community of youths many of whom were equally confident, yet he had depths, even as they did, which he took pains to hide. Although seldom seen studying, he always had the required knowledge. No one would have guessed from his relaxed manner and his undergraduate activities that, in order to complete the usual four years in three, he was carrying extra courses. But he was. And, though he chose to wait until 1924 to be graduated (*cum laude*) with his class, he was already at work as a reporter on the *Boston Transcript* during what would ordinarily have been his senior year.

Among his classmates who were to become well known were such authors as Ogden Nash, Oliver La Farge, and Van Wyck Mason; such an editor as *This Week*'s W. I. Nichols; Bobby Jones, the golfer; and Corliss Lamont, whose disputes with Lodge, since they already disagreed about almost everything, used to set fire to the talk at Harvard's conversational paradise, the Signet Society.

Lodge was known to his contemporaries as a person who liked or disliked people with the same intensity with which they liked or disliked him. He had his other likes. He liked to row on the Charles with his class crew. He liked parties and dances. He liked to act, especially in French with the Cercle Français. He liked to write occasionally, as when in his final year he attacked starry-eyed idealists in an article, called "Political Sentimentalists," which he wrote for the *Advocate*. He liked to sing (he still does), solo or in close harmony, there being a Whiffenpoof side to him more native to New Haven than Cambridge. Above all, he liked to talk. Talking was his favorite exercise. In this he was not alone. Bull sessions were his meat, political arguments his delight. In the course of them he hit hard and took hard hits, and had the ingratiating quality of enjoying the hits he received as much as those he gave.

Although politics were his preoccupation, Lodge did not have a political career in mind when he turned journalist. Instead, he sought that blessed immunity of the press which guarantees the right to air opinions without assuming the responsibility of action. During his first months on the *Transcript* his was the young reporter's eternal excitement at seeing parts of a city and sides of life hitherto unsuspected.

A letter written me in November, 1923, tells about his "having scooped all the Boston papers on a story about the Ku Klux Klan which was run on the right-hand column of the front page." Because of this story Lodge was flattered to receive a note from a Klansman, warning him he had better keep quiet, or else. Lodge's answer was to make some more investigations, to pretend he wanted to join the Klan, to interview some of its members who were jealous of each other, and then to print three more articles denouncing it. In the midst of such heady experiences he had editorials to turn out and stories of all kinds to write. He even strayed into the realm of aesthetics when H. T. Parker, the *Transcript*'s famous drama and music critic, so approved of Lodge's first-night review of Pavlova that he assigned him to cover her for a whole week.

Busy as he was on the *Transcript* and pleased as he was with journalism, Lodge was already beginning to speak on political subjects. In this same letter he describes in detail a speech he delivered to a Young People's Club in the parish house of a church in Roslindale. The audience consisted of sixty girls and forty boys nineteen and twenty years old. It was his first speech, and to his surprise he had no tremors and never faltered or stammered.

He talked first about the tariff and then against the League. At one point he walked slowly across to the right side of the platform and, pointing his finger at the audience, said quietly, "All of us here tonight are very young but the time is not so far when all the young women here will have children. I sincerely hope so." Then, raising his voice, he continued, "I ask any of you here whether you would be willing to send your boy to a distant province to fight for the crimes which some Oriental potentate may have committed." The speech apparently was a success, and Lodge confessed he enjoyed doing it as much as anything he had ever done. He added, "I received four dollars for it, so now I am a professional."

At the time Lodge turned pro as a speaker he was seeing a great deal of his grandfather, who was one of the outstanding professionals in the annals of American politics. The young Lodge had never known his grandfather when he was not a United States senator, a person who was a personage, an individual who was a part of history, and a headliner in the world's news that one talked to about family matters. Naturally he was proud of him. He was fond of him, too, because the old gentleman, so formidable in pub-

lic and implacable as an opponent, could be beguiling. No less
naturally, having grown up listening to his grandfather's arguments
and sharing his interests, he was influenced by him.

If his father had not died suddenly at thirty-five when Lodge
was seven, he would have come under another, very different, but
no less strong influence. For George Cabot Lodge, by all accounts,
was an extraordinary man. "Bay," as he was called, was a rebel at
heart. He was a proper Bostonian who had chosen poetry as a
career—in itself an act of daring in those days. Though death denied
him fulfillment as a writer, he was a poet of far more than promise
when he died. A creator, he was also a scholar, and among his
many gifts was a phenomenal aptitude for languages.

George Cabot Lodge's letters, like his poetry, make clear the heat
of his perceptions and the dazzling prowess of his intellect. "Abundance" was the word which came to Edith Wharton whenever she
tried to describe him. He was one of the lucky, tortured, joyous,
questing spirits who are born with a surplus of energies and endowments and give of them freely. When he died, even Henry Adams
could not speak of him "with the smallest calm." "Bay," wrote
Adams, "was my last tie to active sympathy with men. He was the
best and finest product of my time and hopes." And Theodore
Roosevelt, in his introduction to Lodge's *Poems and Dramas,* said,
"Of all the men with whom I have been intimately thrown he was
the man to whom I could apply the rare name of genius."

After the death of Lodge's father it was his mother, Elizabeth
Frelinghuysen Davis, a woman of remarkable character and distinction, who made, and made wisely, the decisions affecting the
lives of her three children, Cabot, John, and Helena. She gave them
a serene and happy childhood, with summer after summer spent
in the pillared house on the cove at Nahant near the secluded point
on which the old senator lived. In spite of her dignity, she giggled
like a girl at their jokes, granted them full rein in pursuing their
ideas, and treated the wildest youthful talk as if it were conversation
worthy of a salon.

In those days, when the radio had not yet taken over, she encouraged reading aloud after dinner, and liked to have young people
gather around the piano to sing songs of all kinds, including Gilbert
and Sullivan and the *Cautionary Tales.* It was she who shaped the

education of her children, she who sent the boys to Middlesex, and made the decision, later to prove so contributive to Lodge's effectiveness with the Army, at NATO, and the UN, to take her daughter and two sons abroad for the winters of 1912 to 1914 and put them in school in Paris, where they learned to speak fluent French.

Oddly enough, considering his father, Lodge admits he draws a blank as far as poetry is concerned. He revealed this rather publicly when, in a speech at the UN, he quoted

> But those behind cried "Forward!"
> And those before cried "Back!"

and, to the polite amusement of the London *Times*, attributed these lines to "John Gilpin" rather than to "Horatius." From his father, however, he did inherit much—his physique, a good deal of that "abundance" Mrs. Wharton mentioned, the same boyish relish for life, and to some extent his gift for languages. In addition to French, Lodge speaks more than fair German, fractional Spanish, and reads Italian.

Wilson and the Elder Lodge

Politics absorbed Lodge as they had never attracted his father, and his politics, while he was in college and for the first years thereafter, were his grandfather's. The old senator died in 1924, nine months after Woodrow Wilson. During his last three years, when he was reviled or revered for his successful fight against Wilson's League of Nations, the first Henry Cabot Lodge's relations with his namesake became closer and closer. An austere man, small in size but commanding in manner, he thawed completely when with his grandson. His eyes lighted up at the sight of him and his face, so often haughty in expression, creased into a hundred smiling wrinkles above his pointed beard and flowing mustache. His was the final flattery of treating his grandson not as a grandson but as an equal in knowledge and experience, and talking with him man to man about national and international affairs.

The young Lodge had good reasons for being proud of his grandfather, reasons which have been obscured or forgotten by those unable to forgive the senator for having won his battle against the League. Many disagreed violently with his policies, but none could deny his courage, his skill as a strategist, and the multiplicity of his talents. More than being a practical politician, he was a scholar-author-historian. As such he belonged, even as Wilson and the earlier Roosevelt did, to a race of public servants, now almost extinct in this country, of which Churchill in contemporary England has been the most glittering example.

Considering the crowded life he led, the elder senator's literary productivity was incredible. His biographies of Hamilton, Webster, and Washington were much admired. He turned out work after work on American history, produced countless monographs, and found time to edit, among other things, *The Federalist,* André's *Journal,* and a nine-volume collection of the works of Alexander Hamilton. The bitterest of his books, though an able presentation of his own position, was *The Senate and the League of Nations,* a subject which the old gentleman and his grandson discussed by the hour.

The struggle between the elder Lodge and Wilson left its permanent scars on history. Although it turned everyone into a partisan, few could have followed it with a keener interest than young Lodge. It was a battle royal from which, in a ringside seat, he learned much about the infighting of politics, the sorry fate of the highest of ideals when those who fight for them disregard the political means essential to their realization, and the Senate's adamant determination to preserve its constitutional rights.

In spite of their irreconcilable differences, the elements of greatness in Wilson, and Wilson's far larger role in history, Lodge and Wilson had many things in common. Both were brilliant and both scholars. Both were zealots in the beliefs they held and acted in good faith. They were equals in their arrogance and in their unwillingness to compromise. Lodge fought his case with the technical precision of a lawyer; Wilson championed his cause with the dedication of a prophet. This meant the President enjoyed an advantage in the eyes of his contemporaries no less than of the future. He held the trump card, an appeal to the most radiant of man's hopes—lasting peace.

The senator paid dearly for his victory. His reputation continues to suffer because he felt obliged to oppose the President's global program by mentioning anything which seemed so mean and petty to the idealists of that moment as our national interest. Wilson was talking in terms of moral grandeur, Lodge in cold hard facts. The senator was, therefore, cast as a villain in the minds of many who did not care about the details by which peace was achieved so long as it seemed guaranteed. Although Lodge rightly resented having the covenant and the treaty presented as a package deal, he was not against the League, as some were. He was for it, but with reservations. Wilson, however, wanted all or nothing and, rather than accept the treaty with reservations, urged Democratic senators to vote against it when it came up a second time on March 19, 1920.

Many have pointed out the irony of having the United States represented at the "new League" by the grandson and namesake of the man who in the popular mind is supposed to have done most to keep us out of the old League. The real irony lies elsewhere. It is to be found in the UN charter. It was presented to the Senate unattached to any treaty, and its provisions include equivalents of some of the reservations which created such bitterness when Lodge proposed them. Among these are the UN's guarantee not to intervene in a domestic question; the denial to small countries of equal voting power with the large countries in the making of "action" decisions; and—shades of Article X—the stipulation that each member nation can ratify its participation in military actions according to its constitutional processes. In other words, in theory at least, the United States cannot be involved in a war or requested to send men overseas without the consent of our government.

By the time the senator died, four and a half years after the defeat of the treaty, young Lodge had cleared a major hurdle. He was never to be the scholar his father was in literature and his grandfather was in history, politics, and government. But, due to his intimacy with the senator and his daily stalking of political events as a reporter, he had grown up to his grandfather. His next hurdle was to outgrow him, as all young people must outgrow their elders. This took longer.

Lodge Enters Politics

As he became more expert in journalism, Lodge became less and less satisfied with it as a lifelong career. He had learned a lot about this country from covering City Hall and the State House in Boston, and then national affairs for the *Herald Tribune* in Washington. He was to learn more when in 1932 he was persuaded to run for the Massachusetts Legislature. Lodge, brought up in the protected and compartmented society of Beacon Hill and Nahant, remembers this first local campaign as a turning point. His years as a reporter had exposed him to places and people in the news—in short, the exceptional. The simple act of ringing doorbells while seeking votes introduced him to the average. His eyes were opened to the needs, the ways, the standards of life, and the dreams of the vast majority of Americans. As a result, he played an active part in the passage of the Massachusetts Workmen's Compensation Law, and later in the Senate he was a resolute supporter of the Wages and Hours Bill.

The war was the second major turning point in Lodge's professional maturing. All men learn things terrible and wonderful from war. But the middle-aged and the young are not apt to learn the same things. Understandably the young tend to think of war in personal terms, hating it the more because of what it has denied them. The middle-aged, having already tasted life, are different. If they have heads, hearts, sensibilities, and vision—and survive whole—they can count themselves a "found" rather than a "lost" generation.

Lodge found himself in World War II. As surely as politics had made him see the realities of American living, the war opened his eyes to the realities of the world which it had almost brought to ruin. It made him aware that countries, like individuals, need friends and gain by working together as communities. Peace was now his concern even as the war had been. His experiences overseas convinced him that the sturdiest safeguard of our continued independence lay in our recognizing the interdependence of all free people.

Before the war, liberals were apt to be suspicious of Lodge, thinking him too cunning, too wedded to expediency, and blaming him for the policies of his grandfather which they had loathed. After the war it became manifest, however, that Lodge had reversed the usual pattern of a career. Instead of starting as a progressive and freezing with the years into a conservative, he had commenced as a conservative and thawed into a progressive.

When Lodge was re-elected in 1946, no senator could have been more pleased to have him back than Vandenberg. He recognized that in Lodge he had an ally as well as a friend. It was Vandenberg who saw to it that Lodge was put on the Foreign Affairs Committee. It was Lodge who stood with Vandenberg on the Marshall Plan (that "heroic adventure," Vandenberg called it), on the Rio Pact, on Greek and Turkish aid, and NATO.

If Lodge and Vandenberg saw eye to eye on the role we should play internationally, they were no less close in their conviction that the Republican party stood in need of being rejuvenated. In his maiden speech at the parish house in Roslindale, Lodge had urged his audience to remember they were approaching their sovereignty when they could vote and make themselves felt. Two years later, and one year after his grandfather's death, he was working feverishly as Nahant chairman of the Republican Associates of Massachusetts to get out the young vote, convinced that the "G.O.P. was threatened with old age and was in the position of a club which has taken in no new members for thirty years." Ever since, though his position was not always clear or recognized, Lodge has aligned himself with the younger and more liberal Republicans, working for Willkie in 1940, having Vandenberg as his first choice in 1948, and finally winning (with Dewey and Brownell) a victory over the Old Guard at the Chicago convention by securing Eisenhower's nomination.

With that peak of victory in mind, Lodge was to reveal his ardent professional respect for the intricacies of politics by writing, "A national convention has the same meaning to me that an operating room has for a surgeon." This enjoyment of political skirmishes has long been his, and is part of the equipment he brings to his job at the UN.

Typical of Lodge was the strategy he indulged in when, as chairman of the Resolutions Committee in 1948, he wanted to gain acceptance of a foreign policy plank drawn up by Vandenberg. Before presenting it to his committee, Lodge added four or five extreme statements against isolationism and desertion of the peace plan. He was counting on the isolationists on his committee to strike these statements out, which is precisely what they did. In this way Vandenberg's platform was adopted intact and unanimously by the convention.

Vandenberg stated his regard for Lodge in his diary. In 1949 he wrote, "He is one of my most precious friends. He has been of great assistance to me. He is a superb public servant. I fully expect him to be a Republican President of the United States—and I hope I live long enough to have the chance to help put him in the White House."

Urges Eisenhower to Run

Lodge was to think long and often the next year about the White House but not for himself. He was searching for a Republican candidate most certain to win the election at the same time that he represented the "modern-minded" element in the party. The decision he reached led him to Columbia that June afternoon in 1950. Lodge does not recollect whether Dewey and Brownell had called on the General before him. He does remember that Eisenhower, who had been courted by both parties since the war and had repeatedly stated his unwillingness to run, was still reluctant—truly reluctant. In the course of their two-hour talk he paced his office restlessly, as he listened or answered. When Lodge used the word "duty," the General said, "It would be the bitterest day of my life if it ever became my duty to run. But if my duty I would not flinch from doing it."

Lodge had met Eisenhower three times since the Louisiana maneuvers, twice in Washington and once in France when the General visited Devers's headquarters. Although he had come out for him publicly in October, 1950, he did not see the General again until July of the next year when he went to Paris on one of his several trips in the interests of NATO. On this visit they lunched together at the Astoria Hotel and, though they discussed politics only in passing, it was plain that the General was still reluctant. When Lodge said, "You will have to make up your mind, and not later than January," Eisenhower's answer was, "Thank God, I have until then."

On November 17, 1951, before Eisenhower had consented to run, Lodge was chosen as his campaign manager. It was not till the following April, when Lodge saw him again in Paris, that the General's mind was made up. This time their talk was entirely political, and the trip was paid for by the Eisenhower Committee. Lodge was met by General Wilton B. Persons in civilian clothes in an old car. Lodge's task was to give the General an initial briefing on the political situation at home. He presented his brief in five parts, according to staff office procedure at the Pentagon.

It is encouraging to see that good morals can be good politics. Certainly they proved so at the Republican convention in Chicago. When Lodge seized upon the shadiness of the contested Southern delegates as a pivotal issue, he may not have been thinking only in terms of ideals. Yet his tactics helped to secure Eisenhower's nomination. This is not to say that Lodge was not in full agreement with the General's conviction, as stated in his acceptance speech, that he was leading a crusade. Lodge's belief in that crusade remains strong.

Lodge had frequently attacked the Old Guard and pleaded for the rebirth of his party in such magazine articles as "What's Wrong with the Republicans?" "Think Anew and Act Anew," and "Let's Face We Are in a Jam." He had never stated his constructive (really reconstructive) attitude more clearly, however, than he did in "Modernize the G.O.P." in the *Atlantic* of March, 1950, three months before his conference with Eisenhower at Columbia. Running the political risks of being definite, Lodge offered many specifications about civil rights, social legislation, health, old-age retirement, and labor for a new and vital Republican program. He wanted to have the Republicans put back on a competitive basis with the Democrats. He felt this could be done without either "me-tooism" or negation. In his phrase, "Instead of scolding the darkness, let us light a lamp."

The autobiographical sketches most college graduates contribute to the volumes published at the time of their twenty-fifth reunions are human documents dazzling in their dullness and frightening in their smugness. As a rule, they read as if John P. Marquand had decided to combine and rewrite the *Kinsey Report, Middletown,* and *Babbitt.* But Lodge's report to his Harvard classbook in 1949 contained its interesting revelations. "Life as a legislator," he wrote, "has on the whole made an optimist out of me—about both the United States and human nature." His experiences, he said, had proved to him that "the interests which men have in common are more numerous and important than those which drive them apart," and that "the really evil politician is he who seeks to stress the things which divide." Among the convictions he had reached was "the absolute refusal to take counsel of one's fears."

In this mood of optimism and faith Lodge worked and campaigned for Eisenhower, giving so unstintingly of his energy, time, fervor, and politician's skill that he had little energy and less time to conduct his own campaign for the Senate, and lost his seat to his young Democratic rival, John F. Kennedy. After Eisenhower's election there was much speculation as to what Cabinet post Lodge would receive. Rumor had it that he would be made either Secretary of State or Secretary of Defense. Even Republicans close to the administration were surprised by Lodge's delight when he was offered the Ambassadorship to the United Nations, a post which was given added importance by Eisenhower's inviting Lodge to attend Cabinet meetings regularly.

As Ambassador at the UN

Lodge's belonging to the party in power, having Cabinet status, being close to the President, and seeing him at least once a week in Washington give him a prestige at the UN which Warren Austin did not have. The Russians and all other members are not unmindful that when he speaks he is speaking for the President and the Secretary of State. He enjoys the advantage of having "Cabinet presence," which is a real advantage.

The UN is not exactly new territory for him since, in the fall of 1950, he served for two and a half months as an alternate delegate, appointed by Truman. Lodge's present position is different. Its responsibilities are enormous. But even while he was feeling his way, he brought new vitality to the operations of his mission. When he wants something done, he wants it done quickly; and when he needs information, he does not hesitate to have Brass Hats in Washington wakened in the middle of the night to get it for him.

He drives himself as hard as he drives his staff. He is usually at the mission at nine, where, before leaving for the morning session at the UN, he catches up with his mail, discusses plans for the day with his long-time secretary Francis McCarthy, confers with his staff, and sometimes meets groups that have come to see him in the conference room off his office. His daily schedule varies, of course, according to what committees he must attend and whether the General Assembly or the Security Council is meeting.

While Lodge is apt to be at the U.S. mission or the UN until late in the afternoon, his work does not stop then. Parties are very much a part of it. They may be fun or they may be as boring as only protocol can make them. Nonetheless, they are essential and can be valuable. Lodge, who is almost a teetotaler, sometimes has to go to three cocktail parties in the late afternoon and give or go to formal dinners night after night and week after week. He submits to this wearing routine conscientiously because, as he sees it, his duty is to win as many friends as possible for the United States and the American point of view. Within his first few months in New York he had made forty-seven forty-five-minute calls on delegates, of small countries no less than large, and had seen all the representatives from the smaller Latin American countries.

Ambassador and Mrs. Lodge live at the Waldorf Towers in the same forty-second floor apartment, provided by the government, where the Austins lived. When they moved in, the chill of an embassy was on it, but, since they have occupied it, it has taken on the warmth of a home. The many official parties the Lodges have given in it have been far from stiff. After dinner the Ambassador often breaks the ice and solves the problem of the many unshared languages of his guests by drawing upon his endless repertory of songs —old or new, ballads or blues, sweet or hot, French or British but usually American—and singing them lustily alone or with his old friend and closest harmonizer, James J. Wadsworth, Deputy United States Representative to the UN. As examples of folk art, these duets are instructive. They may bewilder delegates from Pakistan and Saudi Arabia, but over the years they have created good will, reduced Sir Gladwyn Jebb (who was not easy to reduce) to tears of laughter, and prompted Trygve Lie to say that if only everyone would sing like these two men there would be peace in the world.

In ordering his social life at the UN, indeed in aiding his whole career since their marriage in 1926, Lodge's wife, Emily Sears, has played a part that cannot be overestimated. Mrs. Lodge is a tall, slim blonde who somehow manages at all times and under all circumstances to be chic. She has great style of spirit as well as of appearance. Nothing seems to worry her. It is part of her charm that, though she knows much, she likes to ask questions as if she knew little. She loves people of all kinds and is incapable of pretentiousness. Like all good wives, she has functioned as a steering committee without ever seeming to steer. She has relaxed and humanized Lodge, and brought him the counterbalance of her happy casualness and gaiety. Never scolding, never nagging or interfering, ready for everything and at ease everywhere and with everyone, she has helped him incalculably, as he is the first to admit.

The lighter sides of Lodge's life as our Ambassador to the UN have not kept him from realizing the seriousness of his task. He brings to it the same optimism and faith that he brought to campaigning for Eisenhower. Ever the realist, he cannot understand Americans who attack the UN as an expensive indulgence. He used to be fond of pointing out that, whereas to build such a battleship as the *Missouri* in 1953 would have cost us more than a hundred million dollars, the UN, upon which the world's hopes for peace are built, had cost this country only sixty-six million at that time.

Lodge knows that the insults and verbal slugging which have often passed for diplomacy at the UN represent a dangerous interlude in international relations and are poor substitutes for statesmanship. Facing facts as usual, he has described the UN as "a novel, primitive, exasperating, essential contrivance," the charter of which is by no means perfect. The UN's faults and failures, however, do not keep him from recognizing its virtues and successes.

To him it is "the world's greatest adventure in building collective strength"; an open forum for the world, which exerts a powerful influence on the thoughts of peoples everywhere; an organization the creation of which, if it had not already been created, would be the first concern of men of good will in all countries. His strong conviction is that the UN offers the one hope of world order. Without that order it is "painfully and incontrovertibly clear" to him that "our ultimate destruction is only a matter of time." He feels, therefore, that all Americans and all peoples must be willing to surrender a little in order to gain a lot.

Lodge sums up the present and the future of the United Nations in these terms: "When the Wright Brothers in 1903 at Kitty Hawk, N.C., made an airplane that flew only a short distance, they did not thereupon rush out and destroy it simply because it had not been able to fly a thousand miles. Instead, they set about to improve it until we have the airplane of today."

Quick as he has been in his answers at the UN, Lodge has naturally had to keep in constant communication with Washington on matters involving his government's general policies. These policies, and his maneuverings to win support for them, have on occasion come in for sharp criticism. Our votes at the UN, like our abstentions, have at times appeared short-sighted, inconsistent, or misguided to some well-informed observers. At no time, however, have the protests against our stand and strategies been bitterer than they were in December, 1955, when the debate over the package deal admission of sixteen new members, and the exclusion of Outer Mongolia and Japan, was in full swing. Then the Republican *New York Herald Tribune,* usually strong in its support of Lodge, said that at the UN we had been "outmaneuvered" and "outplayed"; declared that the Soviets for the moment had "seized the initiative," and lamented that the United States was "left in the position of being neither practical nor principled." Subsequent developments proved this attack to be based on a misunderstanding of the real problems, but the feeling was at first shared by several columnists, including Lippmann.

Though both errors and criticism have been inevitable, no one has questioned the diligence with which Lodge has labored as our spokesman at the UN and as the UN's spokesman in the United States. Whenever his overcrowded schedule has permitted, he has hit the sawdust trail for it up and down the country, explaining our need for it—and the world's—on countless television and radio programs, and before organizations as different as a Kiwanis convention, the Executives Club in Chicago, the American Bar Association, the Overseas Writers Club, a New York chapter of the D.A.R., the Naval War College, and the Governors' Conference.

If, in working for the UN and at it, Lodge has functioned more like a foot soldier than a knight, it is not surprising. Such an approach is with him a matter of professional habit no less than character. The *panache* of Cyrano is something for which, by temperament, he has never reached. The stars in the eyes of the traditional idealist do not shine in his eyes at all. Those who have accused him of corralling votes at the UN as if he were rounding them up in the Senate cloakroom are not wrong. Statesmanship with Lodge continues to be practical politics in a different assembly. Yet, as a man firm in his personal and family loyalties, he has loyally embraced that greatest of ideals, the hope for peace through such a world organization as the UN. His dedication to it is not the less complete because he fights for it in terms of today's actualities rather than tomorrow's dreams, or if, without heightening the splendor of the vision, his struggle has been to secure the effectiveness of the reality.

VIII

FRANKFURTER AND THE UNIFORM OF JUSTICE

The Big "Little Jedge"

Justice is a principle, and a great one; a Justice is merely a man who may or may not be great. By convention a member of the Supreme Court, wherever met and even when not wearing his robe, is addressed as "Mr. Justice," as if the principle in some miraculous though very cozy way had taken human form.

Quite rightly, the building which houses the Court is anything but cozy. Its every emphasis is on the principle rather than the persons who are its guardians. Seeking to give physical expression to an ideal older than the Greece and Rome with which it is linked by the Corinthian columns on its portico, its façade is deliberately austere. Its lines are serene and strong and high-minded in their simplicity; its matching wings have the balance of scales.

The acres of white marble, inside and out, continue the symbolism. They speak for the purity of justice as a principle and are as cool as reason. Architecturally, the room in which the Court sits is less successful. It is hard to see in, hard to hear in, poorly planned, and poorly lighted. With its oppressive display of Ionic columns, bronze, mahogany, and red velvet, it sinks to the gaudy in reaching for the grand. Yet, in spite of itself, it does succeed in suggesting the majesty of its purpose.

This majesty is also expressed in the ceremony enacted each day in this room at the stroke of noon whenever the Court is sitting. A warning gavel raps for silence, everyone present rises as the curtains part, and the Chief Justice and his associates enter, dressed in their black gowns. In tones appropriately awesome the marshal chants, "Oyez, Oyez, Oyez! All persons having business before the Honorable, the Supreme Court of the United States are admonished to draw near and give their attention, for the Court is now sitting. God save the United States and this Honorable Court."

Upon the reading of these words, with their firm assertion of present power in terms of phrases from the past and their coupling of the nation's safety with the Court's, the gavel raps again, the Justices take their seats as do those facing them, and the day's business begins. During these preliminary moments it is easy to believe that, instead of nine men coming into a room, "Justice" itself has made an entrance. The black gowns contribute to the illusion. They are vestments which set their wearers apart. Although similar to the gowns worn by judges in courts high and low throughout the country, they take on a special significance in this, the highest Court.

Perhaps it is the number of them that makes them here the more insistent as symbols. Perhaps it is the awareness of the authority and finality of this Court, and its terrible responsibility. Whatever the explanation, the gowns, like the building, are reminders of a noble concept.

Even before the marshal has finished reading, the illusion of justice as an abstraction has vanished (or almost vanished, because it never quite vanishes in this courtroom), and visitors, no matter how impressed, have become aware that beneath these black gowns are men, very mortal men. They are men whose only assured uniformity is the color of their robes; men known for their records, and liked or disliked for being "liberal" or "conservative." Spectators either recognize them at once as excitedly as if they were movie stars or are eager to have them identified.

They are men who vary in their regional accents, and other more important accents too. Different in their personal and professional backgrounds, fed on different philosophies, and fired by different dreams, they can—and many times do—come up with opposite conclusions after reading the same precedents and listening to the same arguments.

Regardless of the outward imperturbability they either possess or have been careful to cultivate, their annoyance with each other, no matter how controlled it may be in the conference room or in the Court, is often sharply stated in their written opinions. Frequently it spills over into their conversations or letters, and has been known on rare occasions to swell into expressions of anger which have found their way into newspapers. Above all, these nine stand-ins for justice are no more able than other men to escape completely from themselves. In spite of the white marble, the black gowns, and the respect they share for the law and the Court, what they are as individuals determines what they are as Justices and is bound, therefore, to change the history of the Court, hence of the country.

No one is more conscious of this than Felix Frankfurter, affectionately called the "Little Jedge" (behind his back) by his law clerks. And none of the "Mr. Justices" is more colorful as a personality or has been more controversial as a figure. Some twenty years have passed since, because of his closeness to Roosevelt in the early days of the New Deal, he was called "the most influential single individual in the United States" and damned as an "alien-minded mentor from Vienna." Still unforgiven by political enemies he made then, still feared by conservatives who think of him as a dangerous radical, and now accused by liberals of having become a conservative, Frankfurter, after more than seventeen years on the Court, remains a figure of enormous influence. The controversies involving racial tolerance, civil liberties, and suspicion of the foreign-born, of which he was the storm center, have not disappeared. They have merely moved on in all their ugliness to involve others, and in the process given a renewed significance to Frankfurter's career and the part he has played as one of those nine individuals, dressed as judges, who have taken a solemn oath to administer justice "agreeably to the Constitution and laws of the United States."

Frankfurter recognizes the mystical and transforming significance of the black robes, and when asked, as he frequently is, "Does a man become different when he puts on a gown?" he answers, "If he is any good, he does." To Frankfurter the gown is very definitely the uniform of a principle. As such, it is something to make all members of the Court, in spite of their human inadequacies and limited insights, remember that disinterestedness is their obligation and that, in interpreting the Constitution, they owe "allegiance to nothing except the search" for EQUAL JUSTICE UNDER LAW, those noble words of promise carved large above the portico of the Court building.

Yet the same Frankfurter who has maintained that ultimately men are governed by ideas or by ideas about ideas is well aware there can be no government of laws except through men. To him the Court is not an abstraction. It is an institution, the actions of which have always been determined by the character of the "fallible creatures," responsive or resistant to the spirit of their times, who happen to have been on it.

Frankfurter cannot understand why anyone in his senses should be surprised when the Justices disagree. For that matter, he cannot understand why, chosen as they are for their special capabilities, they should be expected to agree any more than scientists, historians, or critics. The Court, like the law, as he sees it, draws its juices from life. He has pointed out that "the inclination of a single Justice, the buoyancy of his hopes or the intensity of his fears, may determine the opportunity of a much-needed social experiment to survive, or may frustrate for a long time intelligent attempts to deal with a social evil."

So ardent is his belief in the importance of the individual that it once tempted him to write, "There is no inevitability in history except as men make it." Although such a generalization invites challenge, few would question Frankfurter's contention that "it would deny all meaning to history to believe that the course of events would have been the same if Thomas Jefferson had had the naming of Spencer Roane to the place to which John Adams called John Marshall, or if Roscoe Conkling rather than Morrison R. Waite had headed the Court before which came the Granger legislation." In his opinion an understanding of what manner of men the Justices are or have been is crucial to an understanding of the Court.

Trying to understand what manner of man Frankfurter is, is a fascinating but tantalizing task. To describe him is easy enough, and made the simpler because there is not too much of him to describe. He stands a mere five feet five. He is the shortest of the Justices, this bantam who sits two down to the right of the Chief Justice. When seated in the smallest of the black leather chairs, with his head just peering above the bench, he faintly suggests the Dormouse. In scale only, of course, because the Dormouse slumbered through the Tea Party and drowsing is the last thing Frankfurter's confreres, his former students, and his friends or enemies would ever associate with him. His manner, which is jaunty to the point of cockiness, has no slumber in it. He is one of the most utterly awake and completely alive of men. Everything about him proclaims this, including his fine bluish-gray eyes which are forever flashing and sparkling behind his pince-nez.

Although most of us would not choose the faces we have, Frankfurter has no reason to be dissatisfied with his. It is decisive and handsome; an intellectual's face, quizzical, sensitive, and worldly, yet not disillusioned. Its eagerness counterbalances its sophistication; its friendliness softens its penetration. It is the face of a performer, not a spectator, and its mobility should be the envy of actors.

Many have noted the Justice's birdlike expression. But there are birds and birds, and Frankfurter complicates this comparison by refusing to remain within one species. He does tilt his head with the questioning alertness of a robin, and in a robin's fashion he does tug at life as if it were a juicy worm he had been lucky enough to get hold of and was determined to gulp down. It is, however, with a tern's swiftness that he moves and thinks and dives at an idea.

Had his height been a matter of choice, Frankfurter would undoubtedly have elected to be taller than he is. Jokingly he once said, when speaking at the University of Virginia's Law School, that he thought all Justices of the Supreme Court should be strong, big, powerful-looking men, and added that a jowl also helps. His being small should not bother him. He is a proof that bigness is not a matter of stature. In the opinion of many Americans this littlest of the Justices is one of the largest figures on the Court, and some would say the largest.

Such is his excess of energy that a friend of his told me he could only liken him to a golf ball dropped from a considerable height onto a cement floor. The trouble with this image is that, whereas a golf ball's bounce diminishes, there is no end to Frankfurter's. Or almost no end. This is as true today when he is over seventy-three as it was when at fifty-six he was appointed to the Court. His mind is never still, his tongue seldom, and his gestures and movements are agile enough to keep up with both.

Many men rely on sports to tame their energies. The Justice does not and never has. If, when summering at his somewhat sunless old house at Charlemont, Massachusetts, he spends most of his time indoors, he has his reasons. One is that he agrees with his close friend Wilmarth S. Lewis that nature is supposed to be looked at through glass; the other (and the better) is that being Felix Frankfurter is in itself a violent form of exercise. He does like walking and in Washington continues to walk to work as he did in Cambridge during the twenty-five years he was on the faculty of the Harvard

Law School. One of the sights of the capital must be seeing him and
another of his old and dear friends, Dean Acheson, striding—the
short and the long of it—the good half mile from Acheson's Georgetown home to his law office, where the Justice is picked up by his
car and driven to the Court.

His Mutinous Inner Selves

The inner Frankfurter is infinitely more complex than
the spruce, confident, and bustling outward Frankfurter seems. Some
of those who know him best deny this. They insist he is simple and, as
Wesley McCune pointed out, when trying to prove it became complicated themselves. It is easy to see why. Compact as he is in his person, Frankfurter is markedly diffuse as a personality. If his interests
are many, so are the contradictions in his nature.

Considering how numerous and mutinous these are, it would seem
that he is an outstanding Justice because of his gifts and in spite of
his temperament. The judge's dispassion must often come hard to a
man whose zeal as an advocate is instinctive. Regardless of the
detachment Frankfurter achieves intellectually, emotionally he is a
participant. His heart is as warm as his head can be cool. Though
his mind, a brilliant one, is a Catherine wheel always twirling and
sending off sparks, his ability to concentrate is no less marked than
his mental restlessness. His mastery of large ideas and intricate legal
problems is equaled by his relish for small talk and gossip.

One of the most gregarious of people, he is a scholar who over
the long years has been on intimate terms with the loneliness scholars
must know. He neither shuns pleasure nor avoids drudgery, and in
conversation is as gay and indiscreet as he is serious and judicial in
print. Just as the Court gains because of his presence, so do parties.
He enjoys them, "makes them," and is one of the last to leave them
even as he is among the first of his colleagues to reach the Court
each morning. At once a worldling and an idealist, he is a lover of
comfort and the delights of good living who has never been interested in money or tempted by it.

Tolerant of ideas, he is intolerant of dunces, and his voice, usually
amiable, can still "crackle under a fool's complacence like dry wood
under an empty kettle," as Archibald MacLeish remembers its doing
when he studied with Frankfurter at the Harvard Law School. The
Law School is a reminder that the Justice has never quite got over

being a professor, and infuriates some of his fellow Justices by heckling lawyers who appear before the Court as remorselessly as if they were students. Incidentally, though Frankfurter excels at reason, he is subject to exasperation, even petulance. But since he cools off with the same speed that he warms up, his secretary Alice Pratt says his impatience means nothing because, if he sends her or his law clerk a sharp note, he follows it up instantly with a friendly one.

Childless, he has a way with children which is the envy of parents. A major figure in the New Deal, he is an Anglophile with a profound reverence for English manners, the traditions of England, and the ritual and practice of her law. Modest and vain, a man of tremendous sincerity at the same time that he is a performer with a touch of the ham in him, he is a doer and a thinker whose love of power is almost as great as his passion for the law and whose aptitude for intrigue matches his capacity for affection.

Perhaps the simplest clue to Frankfurter's character is to be found in his own explanation of why history has not properly honored Morrison R. Waite. Waite, a Grant appointment, was the first Chief Justice who, in Frankfurter's phrase, "had to respond to the impact of current social legislation." Frankfurter's esteem for him is such that he has bracketed him with Marshall and Taney. Why then has the memory of Waite's contribution dimmed? Because, according to Frankfurter, he lacked what these other men possessed, "that spark of the divine gift which lent excitement in any company," and that "aesthetic sensibility [which] gives to personality the touch of charm that makes the difference. . . . In a word, the stuff of the artist was not in him."

This elusive and this sparking stuff, absent in Waite and most others on the bench, is abundantly present in Frankfurter. His personality has the flamboyance of the artist. He is an artist, too, in his living, his tastes, his conversation, his aesthetic sensibility, and his approach to his profession. He brings to his work the proud consciousness of a craftsman exercising his skill. He loves the law and the great concepts of freedom and justice with the same passion that an artist loves his medium. Even government for him involves aesthetics. As he sees it, "It is neither business nor technology nor applied science." It is an art, and "one of the subtlest of the arts . . . since it is the art of making men live together in peace and with reasonable happiness."

In no respect does the stuff of the artist show itself more strongly in Frankfurter than in his mastery of the gentle art of making friends. Although few contemporaries have been more violently attacked, few have been so cherished by so many. Even those who have tried to paint him as a sinister and conspiratorial radical may have deplored but have not been able to deny his genius for friendship or doubt that, so far as living is concerned and making others the more alive, he is blessed with a "green thumb."

When Holmes described him years ago as having "walked deep into my heart," he used a phrase that, since then, could have been used by countless others. His friends are an army drafted by his charm. Ranging as they have from A. N. Whitehead to Herbert Croly, from Einstein to Bernard Berenson, from FDR to Robert Frost, from Henry L. Stimson to Harold Laski, from C. C. Burlingham to Reinhold Niebuhr, from Holmes to Sidney Hillman, from Tom Corcoran to Sir Frederick Pollock, and from Al Smith and Charles Curtis to the Hands (Judges Learned and Augustus), they have had interests of all kinds and come from far-flung places. They have included the poor as well as the rich, the obscure along with the famous, and the young no less than the old.

And why not? There is a lilt to Frankfurter's personality that has about it something of the quality of the Strauss waltzes and the Vienna in which he was born in 1882. Hardheaded realists who are fond of him point out that it is doubtful if a boy, particularly a Jewish boy, who left Vienna when he was twelve, was fed on champagne, brought up on waltzes, and exposed to the gaieties of Sacher's Restaurant or the Hofburg. Nonetheless, others in their attempts to explain Frankfurter start off with this "Blue Danube" theory, recognizing it is only a theory but relying on it as a clue.

Gay at heart Frankfurter unmistakably is. His is a dancing spirit, possessed of that supercharge of zest which generates gaiety in others. In human relations he is one of those lucky ones who makes his friends lucky by being a giver, not a taker. His interest in what is happening to people is genuine. He has the gift—a rare one—of immediate intimacy, and a flattering memory for the smallest details of past encounters which puts those who have met him only casually at ease at once. When he comes into a room many agree it is as if all the lights had suddenly been switched on and a match put to the logs on the hearth. "Wherever Frankfurter is," wrote Matthew

Josephson in his admirable "Profile" of the Justice in *The New Yorker* in 1940, "there is no boredom. As soon as he bounces in— he never walks, he bounces—the talk and laughter begin, and they never let up. . . . His mind is endlessly adjustable rather than specialized."

MacLeish in *Life* earlier that year caught the essence of Frankfurter when he described him as "that rarest of God's creatures, a simon-pure, unmitigated intellectual with a limitless relish for living in a human world . . . a disciplined and learned man of books—a man who reads in automobiles and at lunch and at night late and on sidewalks walking—who also loves the fat stews and the wifely breads and the honest cheeses and the common wines of Austrian cooking," and an "outward-turning scholar [who] hunts men out . . . loves the touch of people . . . stands near them when he talks . . . holding them above the elbow with a gripping hand [and] turns the talk of two or three at one end of a self-conscious dinner into a drama of the whole table in which self-consciousness is lost."

Absorbed in others, Frankfurter is fond of saying, and may even believe, that he is not interested in himself. If he is not, he is all the more exceptional because the number of men who are not interested in themselves must constitute a band smaller than Henry V's "happy few." On occasion he has been mortal enough to show signs of self-interest, as he did at the dinner given at the Century Association in honor of his seventieth birthday.

The private dining room was awash with camaraderie; the wine, the food, and the company were excellent; and the Justice was understandably touched and excited. When introduced by Judge Learned Hand, Frankfurter is reported to have launched into the story of his life, a story which proved to be a long-playing record that got stuck in his youth. After twenty minutes had passed and the Justice had progressed no further than a schoolteacher who had had a profound influence on him at the age of eight, Acheson, who loves him dearly, was heard to call out, "For God's sake, Felix, get beyond that schoolteacher."

In spite of such indulgences in autobiography among friends, Frankfurter has shown a resolute unwillingness to talk about himself for publication and has adhered to the policy, as he puts it, of "abstaining from any share in anything that may be written about

me." I know that three times when I asked him personal questions
his reply was, "I'm not really interested in myself." And Louis
Jaffe, his successor as Byrne Professor of Administrative Law, has
told me that, when he saw Frankfurter in 1952, three years after he
had written a brilliant appraisal of him for the *Harvard Law Review*, the Justice said, "I have never read your article because I'm
not interested in myself."

To a dramatic critic such declarations may bear a suspicious
resemblance to the insistence of certain actors that of course they
never read their notices. But if the Justice is an uncooperative
witness on the subject of himself, he is far too courteous to deny all
aid to those writing about him. "Go see my friends," he urges, adding, "they know much more about me than I do."

A Green Thumb for Friendships

Being the all-embracing kind of person he is, Frankfurter
has not only many friends but many "best" friends, and all of them
like to talk about him. They find him good copy in addition to being
good company. To a man they start off by praising his courage and
integrity, his brilliance, charm, and knowledge, the altitude of his
standards, and the purity of his motives. A few continue in this vein,
admitting no faults in him or leaving them unmentioned. Yet even
these do not feel about Frankfurter as he did—and does—about
Holmes. They admire him unstintingly. They love him. He aston-
ishes and delights them. But they do not push admiration to the
point of veneration, no doubt because, high as they know the reaches
of his thinking to be, they recognize that he belongs most decidedly
to this earth, while Holmes appeared to be earthy on Olympus.

Most of Frankfurter's friends (at least those I saw), after speaking
from the heart about his virtues, showed a disconcerting tendency
to touch upon his frailties. Though when they did this it seemed to
me that the buglers had turned snipers, this was not the case. The
best of men are not expected to be perfect except by their enemies,
who are also imperfect. Frankfurter's intimates, instead of being
annoyed by proofs of his mortality, are pleased by them. When they
refer to his quirks and foibles they do so with affection, not mean-
ness, and also with a twinkle. He amuses them, and the fun which
at times they appear to be making of him proves, in part at any

rate, to be their way of thanking him for the fun he has given them over many years by being what he is.

They may hint at his flamboyance by remembering how, when a professor at Harvard, he used to appear as a host at dinner parties wearing a crimson dinner jacket, which in those sober days and in that academic setting seemed a little startling. They may indicate his love of things English and amiably suggest vanity by wondering why, in the portrait his students presented to the Law School after his appointment to the Court, he chose to be painted in the scarlet robes which came with his honorary degree at Oxford instead of the simple black gown of a Supreme Court Justice. But they are happily aware that if he has his touches of vanity Frankfurter, unlike many vain people, has a great deal to be vain about.

Proud as they are of his incredible learning, his friends may laughingly recall the time he held forth knowledgeably on Thomas Mann until he was finally badgered into confessing that he had never read any of Mann's novels. One of the Justice's friends may have seemed to be implying that he is an opportunist with a zeal for cultivating the right people when, in answer to how Frankfurter gets along with Warren, he replied, "Oh, naturally, since he is Chief Justice, a love affair at first sight." It was this same friend, however, who in the next breath stressed Frankfurter's brave and dangerous fight for such "wrong" people as Mooney and Sacco and Vanzetti, and commended him for his loyalty in appearing as a character witness for Alger Hiss.

Beyond question the Justice entertains his friends because his life has about it the elements of a performance. Yet clearly they are grateful to him for the show he puts on since it so heightens their own living that they could say of him, as Agnes de Mille did of Pavlova, that he "makes our lives less daily."

They are most voluble when chuckling over Frankfurter's volubility, when fondly noting that he is "a terrible talker," or likening him to Bacon's "Overspeaking Judge." They make these points with relish, yet in order to make them they have to interrupt their tributes to the Justice's prowess as a conversationalist, his remarkable versatility of mind, his gift for keeping table talk in a state of happy ferment, and his surprising talent for listening. When they smile at his flow of language, they do not intend to deny that he can be eloquent and witty, pungent and concise. They mean only to emphasize that in or out of print he is never at a loss for words.

Francis T. P. Plimpton caught the spirit of their comments in the verses he read at the twenty-fifth reunion of the Law School class of 1925:

> And Felix—ah, that conversation!
> Just nothing could impede it
> Or slow that verbal animation—
> But *now* we have to read it!

> Ah, F.—it's fine when you expose
> Your lesser brethren's low licks,
> But can't you make your deathless prose
> Not quite so rich and prolix?

Two or three of those close to Frankfurter are harsher in their judgments. Although they cherish and respect his many dazzling endowments, they miss certain final attributes. While acknowledging he is a big man, they wish he were bigger than he is. But even the lonely carpers among his friends, after having emptied their guns, are as quick as the others to reach for their bugles and salute the Justice as "*primus*—unquestionably *primus*"—among the present members of the Court.

Dissenting Opinions about Him

Inevitably, not all who have worked with Felix Frankfurter or been acquainted with him feel about him as do his hosts of friends. Among the lawyers, judges, and teachers of law with whom I have talked there are those who, though by no means bitter in their enmity, are most certainly qualified in their admiration. A few are allergic to his personality, others take a dim view of his brightness, and all are as frank to state their misgivings as they are ready to grant that he is a remarkable individual who has done remarkable things.

Some distrust his facility, holding it to be dangerous. Others accuse him of assuming that he knows everything or, if not that, something about everything, except science. Several maintain that he lives on a plane of heroes and villains, that he plays favorites, or that, in spite of being resolutely above party politics, he sometimes indulges in "politicking" in his attempts to influence members of the Court. One, who is grateful to him and fond of him in an unenthusiastic way, insists that Frankfurter's most endearing quality and worst vice is loyalty to his friends. Frankfurter, he writes, "cherishes their foibles, encourages their self-development, and stimulates their work with undeserved praise. His creativity is personal not intellectual. In short, he wins and loses on the grand scale of what I am tempted to call a feminine nature."

This opinion is contradicted by some of those whose warmest praise for Frankfurter is tepid. They deny him the intuition which is supposed to be feminine and contend that he is curiously imperceptive about himself and others. Such a contention is also open to dispute. It exceeds and wearies credibility when one remembers the number and quality of his friends, the intensity of his friendships, and the unflagging consideration shown by him in maintaining them. It likewise ignores the unanswerable evidence supplied by the late Judge Augustus Hand when he wrote, "For years Justice Frankfurter [when he was at Harvard] selected the law clerks of Justice Holmes, Justice Brandeis, Justice Cardozo, Learned Hand, and myself with a rare skill in meeting our various desires and aptitudes. He possesses imagination and practicality to an unusual degree in appraising the value of various personalities."

Notwithstanding such divergent verdicts, almost all of those who neither love nor hate Frankfurter appear to agree in certain important respects with those who dote on him. They admit he is very serious about the grave business of being a Justice, that he labors mightily to be disinterested, and that he has disciplined a mind which needed disciplining because of its irrepressible activity and ranging curiosities.

So devoted a friend of Frankfurter as Harold J. Laski was well aware of his needed control as long ago as 1916. From Cambridge that year he reported to Holmes,[1] "Felix of course is a world in himself and he lights up dark places. . . . To talk of Felix reminds me to put some thoughts to you. I think he badly needs some kind of settling influence. He is always nervously restless, dashing here and there in a kind of creative fertility that drives me to despair. I don't find him able to sit down solidly to a single thing. He wastes the time that ought to be given to the permanent work that is in him in writing fine letters to antiquated New York lawyers with doubts

[1] *Holmes-Laski Letters,* 2 vol., edited by Mark DeWolfe Howe, Cambridge, Harvard University Press, 1953.

about the Constitution. I wish he were a little more concentrated—and I get afraid for his health."

That "settling influence," or as settling as any could hope to be in his case, was found a little more than three years later when Frankfurter, then thirty-seven, married Marion Denman, the Yankee-born daughter of a Congregational minister. At that time, with her rich red hair, her shining blue eyes, and the radiant tranquillity of her expression, she reminded Laski of a Luini.

Though her hair is now white, neither her beauty nor her outward calm has left her. A Phi Beta Kappa graduate of Smith, for a while a journalist, an incessant and selective reader with an excellent critical mind, a coeditor of *The Letters of Sacco and Vanzetti,* and a person who, in the words of one of her husband's ex-clerks, does not listen to as much music as the Justice does but "hears it better," she has not only been very close to Frankfurter but has given a stability to his life which it would otherwise have lacked.

Their happiness makes itself felt at once. So does their pride in each other. Seeing them together in the serenity of their book-lined living room in Georgetown calls to mind Frederic William Maitland's description of Leslie Stephen, "He was very good to live with, though he may have required a little of that sort of management which is gladly bestowed by the affectionate upon the affectionate."

No individual, however, and not even the Supreme Court with its rigorous routine can curb Frankfurter's energies. Many people never touch life at all, choosing to turn their backs on it. Others either take dips in little side eddies or hug the banks and wade in timidly. Few men of our time have plunged into the main current with greater joy and have been swimming in it over the decades with more vigor than Frankfurter.

A century hence readers, hazy about his legal opinions and other writings, will be amazed to see how often he appears in memoir after memoir, including those that have nothing to do with law or politics. They will wonder about this man who touched so many lives and events. And they will be left wondering, because the best of his own writing and the best writing about him have never quite captured those dynamic personal qualities which explain him as a force and are more importance than any single thing he has ever done or written.

In an address on Jefferson, Frankfurter pointed out that "there are creators of ideas and creative translators of ideas into the habits and institutions of society." Frankfurter himself belongs in the second category. He, too, in spite of his love and command of language, has not been content to rest with the mere enunciation of noble ideas. He has always wanted to see them converted into deeds.

This is one of the reasons that he and history have not been strangers. Among Frankfurter's earliest recollections in Vienna is his family's being deeply moved on reading at breakfast of the death of the Crown Prince Rudolf at Mayerling. He was six when history touched him in this fortuitous fashion. In the years ahead, in a different century and a totally different world, he was not merely to hear about history already made but to have a hand in its making.

F.F. as Teacher and "Mr. Fixit"

Frankfurter was still twenty-three when, in the fall of 1906, Henry L. Stimson, then United States Attorney for the Southern District of New York, chose him as an assistant in his prosecution of the trusts. He was twenty-seven, and traveling with Stimson as his adviser during his unsuccessful race for governor of New York, when he heard Theodore Roosevelt exclaim, "Darn it, Harry, a campaign speech is a poster, not an etching!" [2] He was twenty-eight when Stimson, as Taft's Secretary of War, took him to Washington and made him law officer of the Bureau of Insular Affairs. He was thirty-four when in 1917, as a member of the President's Mediation Commission, he was told by Wilson at the White House, "Mr. Frankfurter, as the lawyer of the Commission, it will be your special task to charge yourself with inquiring into [the Mooney case]." Frankfurter's answer was, of course, "Very well, sir," though until then he had never heard of the case and did not know whether the name was Mooney or Muni.

The dates of these forward steps and Frankfurter's age when each of them was made deserve to be stressed in his career as they would not in that of a bright native-born American drawn to government and the law. Such progress, certainly not average in the rise of most young lawyers, was phenomenal in Frankfurter's. At the time that

[2] *On Active Service in Peace and War*, by Henry L. Stimson and McGeorge Bundy, New York, Harper & Brothers, 1948.

he attracted Stimson's attention he had been in this country twelve years, which is another way of saying he had spoken English only that long.

A boy from a cultivated Jewish background in Vienna, he was in his twelfth year when his family, traveling steerage, followed his father to New York. Although the Frankfurters faced immigrant hardships on the East Side, by the time young Felix was approaching twenty-four he had completed not only grammar school, high school, and college (standing third in the class of 1902 at C.C.N.Y.), but had worked for a year as a municipal clerk and earned enough ($1,200) to underwrite his going to the Harvard Law School, from which he was graduated in 1906 as a top student and an editor of the *Law Review*.

Following his graduation Frankfurter was employed for two months by a large law firm in New York, the only period in his life when he was engaged in private practice. The job he gave up to join Stimson was pleasing in its prospects and lucrative offers were to come his way in the future. They were to leave Frankfurter untempted because, after his experience with Stimson, public service was very much in his blood. He learned much about the law's relation to government during the years he spent in Washington from 1911–14 and 1917–19, and proved his spectacular gift for friendship by becoming the intimate of men at the highest levels. Among these the ones who were to mean most to him and history were Justice Holmes and a handsome young man with whom he had first become acquainted in New York, the Assistant Secretary of the Navy, Franklin D. Roosevelt.

In 1914 Frankfurter had been appointed to the Harvard Law faculty and was no doubt delighted to return to Cambridge when his wartime work was done. The excitements and pleasures of Washington had never blinded him to the fact that teaching was in itself a public service if it prepared and persuaded capable young men to go into government who might otherwise devote their talents to amassing fortunes. Loving this country with that extra ardor of the immigrant which has about it the convert's zeal, he wanted the government he believed best to be served by the best. In his twenty-five years at Harvard, MacLeish estimates that Frankfurter taught 4,500 men. Though this is forgotten, he sent many of them to Washington in the Harding, Coolidge, and Hoover administrations, long before the capital, with the coming of the New Deal, suddenly seemed overrun, if not taken over, by an army of his "Happy Hot Dogs," as they were sneeringly labeled.

By the common consent of his quicker-witted students, Frankfurter was a great teacher. Unorthodox in his means, impatient with the dull, at his best "as a small club man, not a big club man" with his handpicked advance course, he was superbly stimulating to those who could keep up with him and his dartings down the byways of the points he discussed. Holmes once described him and Roscoe Pound as the "soul" of the Law School.

A few of his colleagues complained that, though he gave courses in public utilities, administrative law, and federal jurisprudence, what he taught was Felix Frankfurter, not law. To most of those who studied with him, however, Frankfurter was the kind of law they liked. He returned their liking and their loyalty, going to great pains to place them. He liked teaching, too, and the stimulation and delight that "only the young can give to a teacher." He also liked Cambridge. He liked it so much that after his return in 1919 he remained there, at least officially, for the next twenty years (some say the happiest of his life) until Roosevelt appointed him to the Supreme Court.

To pretend that he was chained to Harvard by his duties would be to ignore the truth and misread Frankfurter. During those years at the Law School he was all over the place physically as well as mentally. This was bound to be because, intense as his now more disciplined interests remain, he was then a man who could not find enough pies to have his fingers in. Laski playfully touched on this side of his nature when, after a visit to Washington in 1917, he wrote Holmes,[3] "Mr. Wilson has charge of foreign policy and Felix seems to sponsor the rest of the Government. To my certain knowledge he directs the War Department; Mr. Baker is the pale wraith that Felix casts before him in his progress. I saw that he had almost annexed the Shipping Board; there are similar rumors from the Department of Justice."

Though written by an imaginative friend in a smiling mood, this sketch (so close to what Frankfurter's detractors would like to believe true) suggests the characteristic wholeheartedness with which he continued to hurl himself at life after his return to Cambridge.

[3] *Holmes-Laski Letters.*

He was writing pieces, signed and unsigned, for *The New Republic* and the *World*; exposing what he held to be the injustice of the Sacco and Vanzetti trial in an article which catapulted him to national fame; lecturing widely at other universities and culling from his lectures and his journalism an impressive number of distinguished books on the law, government, and the Supreme Court; making trips to Albany to give advice to Franklin Roosevelt, by then his warm friend; and later spending more and more time in Washington and Hyde Park, so trusted by FDR that he was recognized as a major factor in the New Deal.

According to Ickes, in 1933, when ranking members of the administration met at the White House with leading operators and union officials to discuss the coal code, Frankfurter was seated "a little to the rear, as an interested auditor." Two years later Ickes reported that Frankfurter "has been spending the better part of every week at the White House for some time recently and he sees the President on occasions when the President can talk freely." Even before then, when Frankfurter stayed with a friend in Washington, his host was amazed to find people queued up all day long outside his house, hoping to see Frankfurter about jobs. No wonder John Gunther said he "served as a kind of recruiting officer for the whole administration," especially in finding young lawyers for the ever-multiplying government agencies. No wonder James A. Farley is said to have grumbled, "I don't see why I am here as Postmaster General since Frankfurter seems to hand out all the patronage." Or that General Hugh Johnson, in words already quoted, resentfully described him as "the most influential single individual in the United States."

One reason for Frankfurter's influence was his uncommon talent as an emissary, a troubleshooter, a go-between, a "Mr. Fixit," call it what you will. Since his elevation to the bench he has, of course, exercised this talent rarely. To be sure, he did help persuade Roosevelt to send Harry Hopkins to confer with Churchill in London at the beginning of 1941. To be sure, Stimson's presence as Secretary of War in Roosevelt's Cabinet may have been in part due, as Stimson believed, to Frankfurter's intimate relationship with the President. But once on the Court his relations with the White House changed and were bound to change because, with his fastidious regard for the Court's dignity and his own role as a Justice, he was thereafter (as he later described himself) "out of party politics and party attachments."

In the preceding decade the reverse was true. He was so involved in politics that at times his confreres in Cambridge must have wondered if he were not a visiting rather than a resident professor. With Frankfurter's formidable knowledge of the law, it was not surprising that Roosevelt, before and after his election, turned to him as an increasingly trusted adviser or that members of the Cabinet, such as Miss Perkins and Ickes, sought him out when they needed an expert legal opinion. Though invaluable in the counselor's role, Frankfurter was no less valuable, because of his way with men, working behind the scenes like a stage manager. Again and again he demonstrated that, as an emissary or go-between, he could placate, coax, persuade, or reconcile persons who were angry, hostile, stubborn, or seemingly irreconcilable.

Were Roosevelt and Al Smith at odds in 1932? Frankfurter was instrumental in patching up their disagreements, at least temporarily. Was Hoover in the last months of his Presidency unwilling to have Stimson brief Roosevelt on the affairs of the State Department? It was Frankfurter who telephoned Stimson about such a meeting and finally made it possible by getting FDR to write Hoover the letter requesting permission, which Hoover insisted must be sent before the two men could meet. Was Ickes hurt and on the verge of asking to be relieved of further responsibility for the Public Works program because he thought the President "had gone a little sour" on him? It was Frankfurter who calmed the "old curmudgeon," a considerable task, by assuring him he still had Roosevelt's high regard.

Although countless other instances of Frankfurter's skill as an oil-dropper and negotiator could no doubt be supplied, in the fashion of wallpaper they would be repetitions of the same design. All of them would illustrate one thing—the power possessed by this Harvard professor, not appointed or elected to any official position, who performed offstage, and whose brilliance and charm were his sole warrant to influence at the highest level.

That Frankfurter had power no one can deny. It was quite different from the power he was to have as a Supreme Court Justice, but fabulous nonetheless, and therefore deeply resented. There were thousands who eyed him with misgiving or alarm. To them Frankfurter was the Rasputin or Iago of the administration, as the hostile press did not hesitate to call him. To some his being a New Dealer and a member of the "Brains Trust" stamped him as a Pink, if not a Red. Others accused him of following the Communist party line and even of hoping to seize and overthrow the government by placing his men in key positions.

That was in the thirties. Surely few reasonable people, whether they approve of him or not, think of Frankfurter as a conspirator today. This may explain why Westbrook Pegler still does, and when writing in 1954 about our recognition of Soviet Russia, said, "This deed was done by an arbitrary personal decision of Franklin D. Roosevelt, encouraged by Felix Frankfurter, who soon was to slip onto the Supreme Court bench and begin organizing a secret political machine within the bureaucracy which included Alger Hiss and other actual Communists."

Prejudices Aroused by His Appointment

The shaming reasons for much of the opposition to Frankfurter did not show themselves until Roosevelt, who had already elevated Black and Reed to the Court as his first appointments, suddenly sent Frankfurter's name to the Senate early in January, 1939. "Honestly, I think Felix's nomination," wrote the President, "has pleased me more than anybody else in the whole country." Although many shared his pleasure and many did not, no American, proud of his country and believing in its promises, could be pleased by the prejudices, hatreds, and slanders that floated to the surface in the Senate hearings.

The hearings lasted only three days, compared to the month-and-a-half ordeal which Brandeis endured twenty-three years before. This much was good about them. Among their other cheering aspects were these: that most of the senators acquitted themselves admirably; that Frankfurter did, too, as the second nominee to the Supreme Court to appear before the Judiciary Committee in its entire history; and that those who testified against him, instead of being prominent and responsible citizens like Brandeis's opposition, were mainly crackpots and fanatics. One's horrible suspicion is, however, that the views expressed in public were privately shared (and still are) by too many who should know better.

The hearings make frightening reading today because, though presumably a blemish on the past, they have a sickeningly contemporary ring. They have their interludes which would be hilarious if laughing at them were not like having fun at Bedlam. The eleven witnesses were on the whole a sorry lot. They included a man who identified himself as national director of the Constitutional Crusaders of America, an organization which, in spite of claiming to represent almost everybody in the United States except the C.I.O., the A.F. of L., Dr. Townsend, and Professor Frankfurter, turned out never to have had a meeting, much less a convention, and to have a membership of one. The climax in this crusader's testimony came when he read into the record a telegram which asked, "Why not an American from Revolution times instead of a Jew from Austria just naturalized?" and Senator Neely answered, "An American from Revolution times would be too old."

Another witness was Elizabeth Dilling, later the author of *The Red Network,* who insisted Frankfurter's being a member of the national committee of the American Civil Liberties Union was a proof of his Communism, apparently forgetting that this same A.C.L.U. had once defended her right to broadcast her opinions. There was even "a Seneca Indian from the State of Indiana" who, speaking for the American Indian Federation, said she opposed Frankfurter because the Civil Liberties Union (she could only guess it was with Frankfurter's knowledge) had supported a bill which "communized" Indian living.

Freakish and contemptible as most of the statements were, the hearings had their high points. One came when Senator Borah thundered at a witness, "So far as I am concerned, I do not propose to listen to an argument against a man because of his religion." Another was supplied by Frankfurter. When asked by Senator McCarran if he would agree with Harold Laski, had Laski in one of his books advocated Marxism, Frankfurter replied, "Senator, I do not believe you have ever taken an oath to support the Constitution of the United States with fewer reservations than I have or would now, nor do I believe you are more attached to the theories [he later added that by "theories" he meant "principles"] and practices of Americanism than I am. I rest my answer on that statement."

Inevitably, the often-quoted letter Theodore Roosevelt wrote Frankfurter in 1917 was again quoted; the letter in which T.R. condemned the attitude taken by Frankfurter in his report to Wilson on the Bisbee deportations as being "fundamentally that of Trotsky and other Bolsheviki leaders in Russia." Fortunately, Frankfurter's little-known answer, in which he denied the views attributed to him and wondered if the ex-President might not have had the letter of another correspondent in mind, was also included. Moreover, Frankfurter was granted permission to introduce his widely misinterpreted reports on the Bisbee and Mooney cases.

What Frankfurter deplored in the deportation of the striking war workers from Bisbee, Arizona, to New Mexico was that the action "was wholly illegal and without authority in law, either State or Federal." In the San Francisco dynamitings he held no brief for Mooney, whom he described as "a well-known labor radical," "associated with anarchists," and "a believer in 'direct action' in labor controversies." He was disturbed by the prejudicial atmosphere in which the trial was held, and appalled to find that Mooney's first conviction was based on the flimsy evidence of dubious witnesses. Accordingly, he recommended a new trial at which Mooney's guilt or innocence could be "put to the test of unquestionable justice."

In both cases, as cannot be emphasized too strongly, Frankfurter wrote not as the friend of labor, capital, or any special interest, but as the champion of law and justice. Though overlooked by those who testified against him at the hearings, it was precisely in this spirit that Frankfurter undertook his famous article for the March, 1927, *Atlantic* about the Sacco and Vanzetti case. This article, written after the case had dragged on for six years, was referred to constantly at the hearings to prove that Frankfurter was not only the friend of anarchists but a dangerous agitator himself.

It is hard to understand, reading that article today as expanded into book form, why it should have created such a furor, scandalized proper Bostonians, imperiled Frankfurter's position at Harvard, and won him an adhesive reputation as a radical. It is a courtroom chronicle told as simply and engrossingly as any ever recounted by William Roughead or Edmund Pearson. The miscarriage of justice is its one flaming theme. Its strength lies in the skill with which Frankfurter mobilizes the facts and, by citing instance after instance of rigged identification, unreliable testimony, misleading questions, and the reprehensible conduct of the presiding judge, creates terrible and abiding doubts.

Facts, by the time Frankfurter wrote his *Atlantic* article, were not the major interest of the more alarmed among Boston's Brahmins. They thought they had the facts anyway. Whatever misgivings they may have had were removed, five months after Frankfurter's piece appeared, when the report was issued by the advisory committee Governor Fuller had appointed. After all, such outstandingly "right" people as Harvard's president A. Lawrence Lowell, Judge Robert Grant, and Samuel W. Stratton, president of M.I.T., composed this committee and they upheld the verdict of guilty and did not question Judge Thayer's conduct of the trial.

The fact which seemed to matter most to some was not whether Sacco and Vanzetti were murderers (the evidence never proved conclusively that they were) but that they were radicals (as they freely confessed) and foreign-born. That their trial was held in a period when the country was facing a Red scare, less dangerous by far than the menace it now faces but terrifying enough, helped neither them nor justice.

This is where Frankfurter stepped into the picture. The paradox was that, though it caused him to be thought of as a radical, his position was in a final sense more conservative than that of the conservatives. Where some were not above wanting to make an example of these two Italians, he battled only for an honest verdict. No defender of order for the old order's sake, his belief was that a breakdown of law endangered all order. As in the Mooney case, it was "unquestionable justice" for which he fought.

There were many, however, who missed the point. They were enraged by the interference of an outsider. It was as if the boy David, instead of attacking Goliath, had intruded upon the playing fields of Eton and dared to take on singlehanded Wellington, Palmerston, and the Prince Consort. To the "old guard" Frankfurter's presuming to protect Massachusetts against itself was impudence, just as his daring to defy the pack was proof enough that he must be subversive.

The resentment against him was immediate and formidable. Although as a teacher one of the Law School's greatest assets, he became for a while a financial liability. Some Harvard graduates demanded his removal and others threatened never to give a penny to the Law School while such a Red was on the faculty. Lowell and the Corporation stood firm, however. Twelve years later, when no longer Harvard's president, Lowell wrote to Frankfurter, in spite of the difference of their views, to congratulate him on his appointment to the Court, saying, "Although I suppose I might not always agree with all the decisions you will render, I know you will be no man's tool but stand squarely upon your own principles. I suppose this has been the worthy ambition of your life, and I wish you all success therein."

What had been unyielding though misguided in the attacks of sedate reactionaries on Frankfurter just before and after the execution of Sacco and Vanzetti became vituperative and demented in the crackpot testimony at the Senate hearings on his nomination. Scratch a Russian, we used to be told in Czarist days, and you will find a Tartar. Scratch an American in moments of local or national hysteria and all too often you will still find a vigilante. This spirit was humiliatingly vocal in the objections raised against Frankfurter.

Those against him were out to get him by any means. Of course, the self-elected patriots, riding as a posse on wooden horses, accused him of being a Communist, offering prejudice for proof, rumor for fact, or lies for truth. This is the familiar pattern that occurs with disquieting frequency. It is the same pattern followed in 1953 by those who, without a shred of evidence, charged Earl Warren, when he was nominated Chief Justice, with having had "a 100 per cent record" of following the "Marxist line."

There was, however, a difference between the opposition to Warren and to Frankfurter. The madness dug deeper and was more wounding in the earlier hearings. Warren was native-born and a gentile; Frankfurter, foreign-born and a Jew. The feeling against him on both counts runs through the testimony like a polluted stream. Needless to say, several of the witnesses pretended they had no race prejudice, and one showed his friendship for Jews by advancing the slimy argument that the appointment of a Jew would increase anti-Semitism in this country. The final prejudice, or more precisely the ultimate un-American activity, was indulged in by the citizen who pointed out that the only previous foreign-born member of the Supreme Court had been Justice Sutherland, who apparently was all right because he "came from the mother country which also gave birth to our Bill of Rights."

Radical or Conservative?

Notwithstanding such nonsense, Frankfurter's nomination was swiftly confirmed. He had every cause to be delighted and for reasons not altogether personal. He was right in feeling, as Ickes reported, that his appointment was a "symbol" which meant "much to the liberal cause," as indeed it did and still does. Yet within two and a half years of his becoming a Justice the man who had been assailed as a radical (which he never was except in the hopes—they called them the fears—of his enemies and in the minds of crackpots) was being described in *Harper's* as a conservative. Most conservatives must have read this article by the Yale Law School's peppery Professor Fred Rodell with disbelief, and not a few New Dealers with dismay. For in it, instead of being painted as the firebrand they had fondly imagined, Frankfurter was presented not even as a moderate extremist but as an extreme moderate, indeed a conservative.

If this picture was then novel, it soon lost its novelty. "Comment on his record most often centers on whether he has 'become a conservative,'" wrote Louis L. Jaffe in the *Harvard Law Review* on the tenth anniversary of Frankfurter's elevation to the Court. It still does. The assumption that the Justice has turned conservative, said Jaffe, is "announced by liberals sometimes sadly, sometimes with the malicious pleasure of the self-righteous," and "by the conservatives with smug satisfaction."

Rodell's claim, when he had neatly pigeonholed the Justice as a conservative seven and a half years earlier, was that as Roosevelt's adviser Frankfurter had spent most of his time in Washington "urging caution and more caution." He had gagged on such New Deal acts as the NRA and the AAA; had tried in vain to block the rushing through of legislation which he knew would not be upheld; and had been confronted, in spite of his loyal silence, with "the most painful dilemma of his career" by Roosevelt's Court-packing plan, a plan the President had not told him about in advance, perhaps because he sensed Frankfurter would disapprove of it. Unquestionably he did, ·having stated his position in print three years before (1934) when he said, "Experience is conclusive that to enlarge the size of the Supreme Court would be self-defeating."

As a Justice, according to Rodell, Frankfurter's conservatism became increasingly clear. He may have dominated the Court for a term or two, but within two and a half years, Rodell contended, it was passing him by. Liberal and labor circles were "wide-eyed" as Frankfurter spoke again and again for the Court's conservatives. New Dealers in the know had first begun to suspect, then to denounce him. And in the late spring of 1940 he had dumfounded his admirers by writing for the Court (with Stone alone dissenting) the "most anti-liberal decision in years." This was the decision involving Jehovah's Witnesses in which Frankfurter upheld the right of the school board in a small Pennsylvania town to compel two children to salute the flag, though their doing so was contrary to their religious training. Why this sudden critical barrage against Frankfurter? Not, Rodell maintained, because the Justice had changed, as some angrily complained he had, but because as a person "strangely misunderstood" he had stuck "steadfastly by the ideas and philosophy" which he had held and lived by for more than thirty years.

When Professor Jaffe, then dean of the University of Buffalo School of Law, sought to chart "The Judicial Universe of Mr. Justice Frankfurter," the Justice had been on the Court for a decade. Naturally, the additional years had enlarged the territory Jaffe covered, and the territory itself could be mapped with much more detail and far greater certainty in 1949 than when Rodell surveyed it in 1941.

The Frankfurter who emerges from Jaffe's technical, and therefore from this layman's point of view often elusive, pages was a judge with a high sense of his duties, though torn by understandable contradictions. He had shown he felt intensely that the Supreme Court plays an exalted but self-moderating role in the "great secular trinity of the executive, the legislative, and the judicial." He was reluctant to abuse the judicial power by using it to produce political results, however desirable. His first impulse was to defend the rights of the individual state in whatever form they were attacked. Regardless of how on occasion he may in practice have reversed his theory, his conviction was that a judge should not write his own views into the law.

In at least two broad fields of conflict between state power and the Constitution, Jaffe maintained Frankfurter had shown "decision, doubt, and reconsideration." One was the Commerce Clause as used to invalidate state regulation; the other, civil liberties. A passionate champion of these and a zealous enemy of wiretapping, illegal searches and seizures, and almost "obsessive in his compulsion to cite the English stand against third-degree police methods," he had made clear his belief (as in the Jehovah's Witnesses case) that "the Court must occasionally reconcile 'the conflicting claims of liberty and authority.' " His fear was not of authority, but of the breakdown of authority. One of the "deepest impulses in his judicial philosophy" was his agreement with Brandeis that "the right to be let alone" was "the most comprehensive of rights and the right most valued by civilized men." This, added Frankfurter, is not "an outworn bit of eighteenth-century rationalism, but an indispensable need for a democratic society."

Jaffe did not answer the common question—Had Frankfurter become a conservative?—as did Rodell, who contended the Justice had always been one. To Jaffe, Frankfurter was no more a conservative than he was a liberal. Moreover, Jaffe objected to the misleading oversimplification of having a mold marked "liberal" and a mold marked "conservative" into which judgments are automatically poured. He did not stop with damning these as "molds." He called them "coffins." And coffins they often are for thinking that has no life in it, for ideas which are stillborn, for knowledge stifled because unwanted, and for truths and subtleties which have died of malnutrition.

Jaffe's article was written in 1949. The lawyers and judges with whom I have talked about Frankfurter do not question his liberalism. They seek to explain how, in spite of it, in a very special sense he is a conservative. As a proof of where the real emphasis of his spirit continues to lie, they point out the large part he is said to have played in the Court's reaching a unanimous decision against segregation in the public schools. They do not deny that, with age, he may have grown more conservative than he once was, but at the mere mention of the word "conservative" they insist upon defining the area in which his conservatism has increased.

They describe him as a man who grew up fired by the progressivism of the elder Roosevelt. Unlike Rodell, however, they do not feel his liberalism stopped there or that he has fallen out of step with the times. They admit he may be lonelier on the bench than he formerly was, particularly now that he has lost so close a friend as Justice Jackson. Some complain that he came on the Court as a captive of the views of such of his heroes as Brandeis, Cardozo, and, above all, Holmes. Others contend that he quotes them too often and has never advanced beyond them. But, when cornered, all agree that a Justice could not choose better heroes and that, as often happens in the choosing of one's idols, Frankfurter's choice explains much about him.

Where Frankfurter has always been conservative, according to experts in the law, is in his punctiliousness in demanding that its processes be followed. Although he may have become, as some object, overfussy in such matters, one of the unbroken consistencies of his career is his conviction that "the history of liberty has largely been the history of observance of procedural safeguards." Since justice has been his objective and the law his means of guaranteeing it, it seems odd that he should have been branded a conservative, by those who use the word as a term of abuse, merely because in his eyes the rightness of a cause is never an excuse for the wrongness with which justice is administered. A traditionalist, a ritualist, a perfectionist in legal matters he may be, but surely as a member of the Court he has been right in struggling not to be a partisan (a hard struggle in his case), and to put strict observance of the law above the strongest of his personal biases.

No one is more aware than Frankfurter that "you cannot tell the quality or importance of a man on the Supreme Court solely from his opinions." When writing them the Justices as a rule deliberately lose themselves in a cold and impersonal style. In their concurring or dissenting opinions, however, they are freer to let their personalities come through. On at least one occasion Frankfurter the Justice spoke movingly for Frankfurter the man. This was in 1942 when, on the matter of compulsory salutes to the flag, the Court reversed the majority opinion he had written some two years earlier. Frankfurter's dissent was stated with passion as "one who belongs to the most vilified and persecuted minority in history." He continued, "Were my purely personal attitude relevant I should wholeheartedly associate myself with the general libertarian views in the Court's opinion, representing as they do the thought and action of a lifetime. But as judges we are neither Jew nor gentile, neither Catholic nor agnostic. We owe equal attachment to the Constitution and are equally bound by our judicial obligations."

Though as a defender of civil liberties he was on debatable ground, he was stating his gratitude to the United States as he had in 1938 when he said, "I can express with very limited adequacy the passionate devotion to this land that possesses millions of our people born like myself under other skies, for the privilege this country has bestowed in allowing them to partake of its fellowship."

"Those Wise Restraints"

If Frankfurter has seldom written so directly from the heart for publication, it is because his writings, before and after he became a Justice, have been largely on legal subjects. This has imposed its inevitable limitations. For neither warmth nor wit nor sprightliness nor beauty of style is among the law's first concerns. Peace lies in obeying the law, but comfort can be had at times from leaving it to lawyers to read. To laymen, in addition to being a foreign language, it is apt to be a dead one.

Justice Holmes's father felt this way. When his son chose the law as his profession, the "autocrat" was reminded that an English barrister had said to a young aspirant, "If you can eat sawdust without butter, young man, you will be a success in the law." Some jurists, such as Holmes, Learned Hand, and Cardozo, have produced literature in spite of being judges. But, as Frankfurter has admitted, "of the many mansions in the house of literature law is not one." He explains this by blaming "the dull qualifications and circumlocutions" which, though necessary, would "sink any literary barque or even freighter."

Cardozo, a master of "the right style," once said with a bow to Polonius that in the higher legal writing he had discerned six types or methods: "the type magisterial or imperative; the type laconic or sententious; the type conversational or homely; the type refined or artificial, smelling of the lamp, verging at times upon preciosity or euphuism; the type demonstrative or persuasive; and finally the type tonsorial or agglutinative, so called from the shears and the pastepot which are its implements and emblem."

Close readers of Frankfurter must have observed that he has employed all six types, notwithstanding his ability to achieve his own "right style." His prose is variable; at its best, light and direct, be-

cause simple; at its worst, ponderous, not only because of its con-
volutions and prolixity but because of its addiction to such words
as "eschew," "bifurcate," "aliquot," "eventuate," "adumbrate," and
"effectuate," which are ugly words, the blood relatives of govern-
mentese and too heavy to keep a sentence afloat.

In his poorer passages he may have proved himself, as he said of
Chief Justice White, "a master of speech, though a master of too
abundant speech," and "made three words grow . . . where there
was appropriate room for only one." But with his clarity of mind
and formidable fluency he has seldom been guilty of the "shrouded
exposition" which he complained of in Waite. His best writing is
very good indeed, and is all the more remarkable when one remembers that he, like Conrad, employs a language he did not know as a
boy. Although his sentences at times are as baroque as the architecture of the Vienna in which he was raised, they are often vivid in
their imagery and can be wonderfully clean and precise in their
thrust.

Some lawyers think that his opinions are too long and his arguments fortified with an eternity of references and dulling appen-
dices. Many lawyers, however, believe that Frankfurter is a far
better craftsman than Cardozo was and that he has written some
superb opinions which they use as models. A few, to be sure, are
irritated, as Chief Justice Stone was, by the impulse which so often
compels Frankfurter to write an opinion even when he concurs.
"Why does he do it?" Stone asked. "Is it a form of vanity?" The
truer reason would seem to be that articulateness, in addition to
being among his talents, is one of his most urgent needs.

That he talks better than he writes does not mean that Frankfurter cannot write extremely well. Those who have heard him, and
then read him, may echo his regret about Charles A. Beard's prose
and wish he had "smuggled into print the luminous gaiety" of his
conversation. But few pens could hope to keep pace with such a
racing mind and anyway, as Frankfurter recognizes, the law as
literature is "restricted by its responsibility."

When he does not face these restrictions, Frankfurter's writing
lifts at once. His letters are sparkling and joyously uninhibited out-
pourings. His journalism, collected in *Law and Politics,* reflects the
rich variety of his knowledge and the vigor of his thought. *The Case
of Sacco and Vanzetti* is a fascinating story told in uncluttered and

fast-moving terms. His insight into people is revealed in his charac-
terizations of Marshall, Taney, and Waite in *The Commerce Clause*.
Yet nothing he has published so captures his own charm, so completely radiates his warmth or displays the agility of his mind, as
the transcript of the extemporaneous talk he gave at the University of Virginia Law School in 1953 on "Chief Justices I Have
Known." The source of its delight is that Frankfurter comes through
on the printed page as the virtuoso conversationalist he is.

Has he become different since putting on the gown? He would
not be the good Justice he is if he had not. Of course, Frankfurter
remains the complex character he has always been. Nonetheless,
certain unexpected simplicities in his nature and beliefs have become
clear. Among these count his attachment to tradition. Firmly convinced that the Court is an implement of progress, he has never
forgotten the past in considering the present or looking to the
future. His courage has never been in doubt, but on the bench he
has shown a new independence, as when he said, "What judge
would be worth his salt if it made any difference to him that the
President who appointed him . . . disagreed with him?"

Ever a brilliant rationalist, he has come to recognize "how slender
a reed is reason," and as a progressive has dared to insist that "we
are desperately in need not of new truths but of passionate devotion
to old truths." "Unquestionable justice" has been the goal of his
whole career. Though an idealist, he has approached both justice
and government as a realist, warning that "two notions exert powerful and destructive sway over us—the assumption of a Golden Age
and the hope of a Utopia: a Golden Age that never was and a
Utopia that never will be. These beliefs are powerful because they
are rooted in romance, and for the same reason they are destructive.
They provide the satisfactions of fairyland, but cloud the mind and
debilitate the will in facing the grim realities of an intractable
world."

Indifference is a crime of which Frankfurter has never been
guilty, caring a virtue which has won him friends, enemies, and admission to history. Turbulent by nature, he may at times have lost
the hard battle he has fought to achieve disinterestedness, but as man
and Justice he has given his full faith to "those wise restraints that
make men free."

IX

A PREFACE TO LIPPMANN

Philosopher-Journalist

The philosopher-king was an ideal in the *Republic* of Plato; the philosopher-journalist is a fact in the person of Walter Lippmann. No one can read his column, "Today and Tomorrow," without sensing that his approach to the contemporary scene is different from that of the countless other newspaper commentators here and abroad whose province is national and international affairs. Their eyes may be equally sharp, their search for the significance of passing events no less constant. They may be as well, if not better, informed in this or that particular field. They may write with a color and vivacity which he neither commands nor attempts. But none of them brings to his task the same background, the same concerns, the same sustained calmness of tone, the same lucidity of style, or the pitch of mind that Lippmann does.

He stands apart from his profession in his looks and living no less than in his thinking. Meeting him, one would never guess that he had seen the inside of a newspaper office, so much closer does he seem to a library, a drawing room, or a campus. He is a lean, dark-haired, fastidiously dressed man of sixty-six who takes scrupulous care of himself, appears ten years younger than he is, and lives and works in Washington in a charming house on Cathedral Heights which is as beautifully ordered as his daily routine. When young, he was nicknamed "the Boy Buddha." He has not lost that Buddha look. His is a contemplative face, ascetic in addition to being thoughtful, which is dominated by his somewhat protuberant brownish eyes. More than being unblinking and bright, they are uncommonly alert and give the impression of seeing far beyond what is immediately at hand, which indeed they do.

Though one of the best-known and most widely syndicated of present-day journalists, Lippmann is in character when he confesses he has never considered journalism his real calling. In spite of

the millions of words he has written about current issues for newspapers, his truest interest lies in the dateless subjects he has pursued
in the more important of his twenty books. For the past four decades
he has lived a double life professionally, giving most of his time, but
never all of his mind, to questions of the day. Beyond the ephemeral
particulars of the present, other problems, ethical, general, timeless,
occupy him; problems upon which the contemplative have brooded
over the centuries; problems dealing with the inward meaning of
events rather than their outward appearance; problems involving
the nature of the ideal society and the spiritual no less than political
values by which the individual must live.

Most people in Washington, including those who write about it,
live only in the present. Quite understandably, the Republic which
occupies their time has no more conscious connection with Plato's
than their Politics with Aristotle's. Lippmann, though immersed in
the conflicts and issues of the day, does not forget the past. He is
haunted by the problem Aristotle raised in the seventh book of his
Politics—how to find a bridge between man's environment, which
is complex, and his political capacity, which is simple. His best
columns betray in this style and tone the philosophical bent
of his mind. His mentors in journalism were Lincoln Steffens and
Frank I. Cobb, vivid figures who would have left their mark on
almost anyone else. Yet it is such teachers he knew at Harvard as
William James, Santayana, and Graham Wallas who gave Lippmann's thinking its direction and whose clear, calm voices can still
be heard in his calm, clear prose.

His followers sense this offbeat quality in Lippmann and are
grateful for it. They do not expect reporting from him. They turn
to him for an analysis of what has happened rather than an account.
They do not want him to cover the news; they rely on him to uncover
its significance. They know that, instead of treating the issues and
happenings of the day as if they stood alone in time, he will endeavor to relate them to yesterday and tomorrow, giving the long
view, not the short one. They realize he seldom indulges himself or
his public by writing about personalities.

Ideas, not people, are news to him, and Lippmann makes them
news for others. He never descends to gossip, is above name-calling,
and seeks to think rather than to feel his way to his conclusions.
He sees his job as a serious one and performs it seriously, denying

himself and his readers the entertaining cajoleries by which a writer can win and hold attention. His austere assumption is that those who turn to him care, as he does, for logic and enlightenment. Accordingly, he comes to grips at once with the core of his subject, dispensing with nonessentials, however tempting. Dispassion is in itself a kind of passion with him. No matter how heated his convictions, the chill of reason is on his copy. So detached is he in tone and attitude that often, when he writes of history in the making, it sounds like history already made.

Lippmann was already well known as an author and journalist when, on the morning of September 8, 1931, the *New York Herald Tribune* began publishing the column that has made him famous here and abroad. He had written ten well-received books, the last of which, *A Preface to Morals,* was a best seller in 1929. His contributions as an editor of *The New Republic,* in the days before and after our entry into World War I, had established him as a leader of liberal thought. His editorials for and ultimate editing of the *New York World* during the decade before 1931 had won him a wider public and an even greater reputation. It was not, however, until that incomparable paper had folded and he at forty-two had started his syndicated column for the *Herald Tribune* that he emerged as a national and international figure.

Success to Eminence

"Today and Tomorrow" caught on at once. Free of all sensationalism, it was a sensation over night. Within twelve months Lippmann's name up and down the country was almost a household word. In him the United States had discovered its own Delphic oracle. He was acclaimed not as *a* pundit but as *the* pundit. He was quoted everywhere and with special gratitude by those uncertain of what they thought until he had done their thinking for them. There was as much truth as humor in Perry Barlow's *New Yorker* cartoon (prized by Lippmann and even now hanging in his study) which showed two dowagers in a dining car, one of whom, buried in the *Herald Tribune,* was saying, "Of course, I only take a cup of coffee in the morning. A cup of coffee and Walter Lippmann is all I need."

The Lippmann fever raged among people of every kind and profession. In the *American Magazine* of September, 1932, Beverly Smith, after describing Lippmann as writing "in language which is precise enough for a Supreme Court justice, simple enough for a ward-heeler, and entertaining enough to woo a magnate from his grapefruit," saluted him as "the Man with the Flashlight, the Great Elucidator." The epidemic reached out to include historians. In January, 1933, in *The Saturday Review* two months before Franklin D. Roosevelt took office, James Truslow Adams ran a risk few historians would choose to run by hailing Lippmann as "the only national leader who has appeared in these postwar years." Nor did Adams apply the brakes there. He added, "What happens to Walter Lippmann in the next decade may be of greater interest than what happens to any other single figure now on the American scene."

There were those who were immune to the Lippmann fever and those who reacted to his rise from "success" to "eminence" with a heat which was itself feverish. Among these none was more violent or vocal than Amos Pinchot. No broadsides aimed at Lippmann (and there have been many during his long career) have been more blistering than the four articles Pinchot published in *The Nation* in July and August, 1933. The editors explained that, "since the creation of an informed public opinion is indispensable to the functioning of democratic government, the factors which tend to mold that opinion require vigilant scrutiny." They did not deny that Lippmann was probably "the most influential journalist of our time."

It was this very influence which whipped Pinchot into a Peglerian frenzy. To him "the Great Elucidator" was an "Obfuscator de Luxe." He admitted Lippman's excellence as a writer but accused him of being a "salesman of plutocracy" and an equivocator who could be "quoted on either side of almost any question." He dubbed Lippmann "our Merlin of journalism," an "ambassador of good-will to the philistines," and "a David with a smile instead of a sling." He described him as "once a votary in the house of Marx" who "now worships in the house of Morgan."

In his serialized excoriation Pinchot insisted that Lippmann did not believe in democracy. He charged him with having done an immense amount of harm, with having confused the thinking of his readers, with soothing them to sleep where the public good required vigilance, with telling them what they wanted to be told, and confirming them in unconscious Bourbonism. On important policies, Pinchot contended, Lippmann "is rarely ahead of his time.

And as a good pragmatist, who avoids being right at the wrong moment, his opinion is generally the postscript of the least illiberal group in Wall Street."

During the years that have followed Lippmann has had his other detractors. No self-respecting man could fail to who writes regularly about public figures and issues. Among the most withering was Fred Rodell, a member of the Yale Law School faculty since 1933. In the *American Mercury* for March, 1945, Professor Rodell enumerated Lippmann's errors as a prophet and his political inconsistencies with the relish of a cannibal dining off a plump enemy.

He implied that Lippmann was popular not because he made people think but because he made them think they were thinking. He sneered at him as someone who "was simply living, breathing, writing, of the right people, by the right people, and for the right people." Professor Rodell railed against what he held to be Lippmann's "almost uncanny knack of using words in such an impressive way as to *appear* to be sapient and lucid and even liberal." Lippmann's huge success, he maintained, was due to a mastery of a species of distinguished and high-grade double talk. This, according to the Professor, "has required a complete forswearing, as to himself, of all humor and all true humility. It has required an air of Olympian omniscience coupled with a sort of patient pedanticism that condescends now and then to words of one syllable in order to clear things up for the class." Above all, it has required "the temerity to state the disputed as though it were obvious and to intone the obvious as though it were profound."

Such attacks have done no real damage to Lippmann. The fever of the first months may have subsided but his appeal has continued. Few serious syndicated columnists have commanded so large and steady an audience. Although his position has shifted in popularity polls, for more than twenty-four years Lippmann, without ever catering to mass tastes, has held a place among the top ten commentators. His prestige continues to be as great in his own profession as with the general public. In the fall of 1953 his name headed the list submitted by 111 American editors and editorial writers rating columnists on the basis of their reliability, fairness, and skill in analyzing the news.

About 140 papers carry Lippmann's column in the United States, nearly fifty in foreign countries. In London it can be found in the

Daily Mail, in Tokyo in the *Yomiuri Shimbun,* in Paris in *Le Figaro* as well as the *Herald Tribune* European edition. It is published in such far-spread lands as Canada and Greece, Belgium and Australia, Spain and India, Brazil and New Zealand, Uruguay and Sweden. An accurate count of his readers is impossible, but his syndicate estimates, in a perhaps promotional and therefore over-optimistic mood, that he may have as many as thirty-eight million weekday readers in the United States, and that his foreign papers command a circulation of approximately ten million. In the language of diplomacy, this is quite a sphere of influence.

When Lippmann started his column, free to write (as the *Herald Tribune* expressed it) "what he likes on whatever he likes," he did four columns a week. Now he does only two. His writing, of course, does not stop with "Today and Tomorrow," since between columns he is almost always working on magazine articles, lectures, or books.

The pressure of his schedule does not appear to trouble Lippmann. The philosophic calm which characterizes his prose is also characteristic of his manner and living. In a profession forever in a hurry he always seems unhurried. If he has nerves, he does not show them. His courtesy is indestructible, his quiet friendliness winning. Given infrequently to jokes himself, he responds to the jokes of others. Although he takes a human interest in dinner-table prattle, small talk is not his forte. He is an earnest man whose earnestness is unmistakable without being dampening.

The fault is not his if almost every chair he sits in is turned into a tripod by gushing hostesses or eager guests. Socially, he is the victim of his reputation, a person expected at the drop of a question to come up with an answer and to speak columns instead of writing them. When jockeyed at parties into the role of pontificator, he remains the least aggressive of conversationalists. Definite as his opinions may be, he states them mildly, almost shyly, and is as willing to listen as to talk. He discusses the most controversial subjects in crisp tones without raising his voice. Even in political arguments, where tempers run short, he has mastered the art of keeping his. In speech no less than in print he presents his ideas in a pattern as neat as the planning of his daily routine in Washington. And nothing could be more systematic than that. It is almost metronomic in its regularity.

Lippmann is usually up at 6:45 and breakfasts at 7:15 with his wife, Helen Byrne, and their two French poodles, Coquet and Vickie, in Mrs. Lippmann's bedroom. By eight, being an exceptionally quick and selective reader, he has finished three newspapers (*The New York Times,* the *Herald Tribune,* and the *Washington Post*) and marked those items of special interest to him. Wearing either pajamas and dressing gown or slacks and a sweater, he is then ready to go to his study and begin writing.

Years ago Lippmann insisted that "every man whose business it is to think knows that he must for part of the day create about himself a pool of silence." It is in such a pool of silence that he works even as a journalist in the big house he has owned since 1946. His study, a large handsome room lined with books, is at the end of a long hall on the second floor. Friendly as its feeling is, it is a fortress against noise and distraction. Its quiet and sense of solitude in a home humming with activity are indispensable aids to Lippmann in maintaining the steady pulse beat of his schedule.

Unlike most people, Lippmann has the strength not to look at his mail until he has finished his morning's stint. Nothing or no one is allowed to interrupt him. His secretaries, who work in the neat but file-jammed attic, are under strict instructions not to disturb him until he buzzes for them. Often without notes and sometimes with only three or four guide words jotted on a slip of paper, he settles down at his desk.

Lippmann's columns average 1,200 words and, as a rule, he turns them out in three hours, writing on white paper in a small hand that takes deciphering. Generally he does a second draft before recording the final version on his dictaphone. At eleven or soon thereafter he calls his secretary, Jean Wehner, who has been with him for ten years, and she returns to the attic to transcribe the final version, a process requiring thirty to forty minutes. While Miss Wehner is typing, Lippmann dresses, reads his mail (which is large), and turns to the dictaphone to answer it. By 12:45 he and Miss Wehner have gone over the column she has typed. At one o'clock the *Herald Tribune* calls and Miss Wehner in the next ten or fifteen minutes reads the approved script over the telephone to a girl in New York, a method found less expensive than wiring it.

Meanwhile Lippmann has driven to the Metropolitan Club, where he lunches at one on columnless days, and one-fifteen on column days, mainly with key figures, foreign or American, in search of background for what he will write next. After lunch he returns home between two and two-thirty to sign his letters, catch up with periodicals, continue his extensive reading, take a short walk, or work at carpentry in a room in the cellar.

Every afternoon he consults for half or three-quarters of an hour with Barbara Donald, whose task is to aid him in his research, clip newspapers, keep his copious files, and preside over the reference library, which is also in the attic. In a trunk room, adjoining the office, an AP teletype machine ticks away, a link with the outside world. When a column is dispatched and a chapter or magazine article finished, Miss Wehner types Lippmann's letters, while Charlotte Wallace takes care of social and other correspondence. All three women admit that, genuine as is Lippmann's serenity and courteous as he always is, the pressure is terrific when he is around.

Lippmann's second wife, to whom he has been married since 1938, shares her husband's energy, graciousness, and serious interests. She is an accomplished hostess, hospitable to both ideas and people. Trim and stylish herself, she likes life to be tidy too and has the gift of making it so. She is equally skillful at insulating Lippmann against the world and in bringing him out into it.

With her he often goes to cocktail parties between six and seven-thirty and returns home to dress before either giving or going to a dinner at eight. Although such social activities supply diversion, they also provide invaluable opportunities for brain picking, a favorite Washington indoor sport and one vital to Lippmann's job. When he dines out, Lippmann seldom stays late, leaving as a rule between ten-thirty and eleven unless imprisoned by protocol, that curse and killjoy but necessary evil of Washington society. Before going to sleep he seeks more relaxation by reading something not connected with his work. In general his light is turned off well before midnight. Having finished "today" on schedule, he is prepared to start "tomorrow" on the same schedule even when he is devoting the morning to magazine articles or books rather than columns.

The Civilized Life

Lippmann is selective in his friendships as in everything else. His enemies have attacked him for knowing the well-heeled and the mighty rather than the poor and the unimportant. They have claimed that his liberalism has been subdued by what Beatrice Webb called the "aristocratic embrace." But the charge that he sees only the "right people" overlooks his temperament, background, and the special nature of the role he has made his own. He sees the people he enjoys, the people who stimulate him, the people he needs to see for professional reasons—in other words, the people who are right for him. This does not mean they are politically to the right. They may or may not be. He only hopes they will talk well, and does not mind if they live well, too.

Diogenes, who also had a philosophic turn of mind, elected to live in a tub. This was his prerogative, but his example, though admired by many, has been followed by few. Diogenes' choice would never have been Lippmann's. This does not mean that the ostentatious has any appeal for him or that he is taken in by price tags or interested in them. Worldly-wise as he is, Lippmann is much too wise for that. Much too much of a moralist also, and much too much of a gentleman. He is a man of informed tastes who happens to prize the amenities. A snob, however, he is not and never has had to be.

His parents, Jacob and Daisy Baum Lippmann, were cultivated people. His father was a New York clothing manufacturer and real estate investor successful enough to retire early. Both his father and mother saw to it that the young Walter enjoyed those privileges and protections which go with being the only child of prosperous parents. They sent him to Dr. Sachs' School for Boys, an excellent private day school attended in large part by children of affluent families of German-Jewish descent. They encouraged him to buy books and to read them. They took him abroad summer after summer on vacation trips (once even to St. Petersburg) during which he acquired an early acquaintance with painting, sculpture, architecture, and European history. He was one of those sons who have the sense to take advantage of every advantage given.

The civilized, the somewhat cottoned and cushioned, approach to life Lippmann knew while growing up remains the pattern of his living even now. Undoubtedly his writing would have been different had he had the common touch and spent more time in the company of that mythical entity, the common man. Lippmann, however, is by no means alone among Washington columnists in being on closer terms with labor as an idea than with laborers. He has always worked at the top level; been a captain, so to speak, at home on the

bridge and uncomfortable with the crew. Even in journalism he became an editor without ever having served any real apprenticeship
as a reporter.

If the society he finds agreeable is good society, it is because that
is the environment in which he is at ease. This is not to say, as his
critics have maintained, that he sees the world through a class
darkly (to misapply a phrase of Philip Littell's). A conventional life
may appeal to Lippmann because the very grooves it follows are
expressions and guarantees of order. As a young man just out of
Harvard, where he had championed socialism, he may have fancied
himself for a while as a radical and tried hard to belong to New
York's Bohemia by attending Mabel Dodge's "evenings" at her
home at 23 Fifth Avenue. But, at least at heart, Lippmann was a
fish out of water on the seacoast of this particular Bohemia.

The talk of such young untamed spirits as Hutchins Hapgood, Jo
Davidson, Emma Goldman, John Reed, Max Eastman, Frances
Perkins, Robert Edmond Jones, Lee Simonson, and Margaret
Sanger was bold, free, and provocative. There was apt to be, as
Mrs. Dodge observed one evening when Big Bill Haywood was a
guest, "a great deal of General Conversation but no definition."
This was a lack which Lippmann would have noticed and resented.
He was a short-haired among the long-haired. Most decidedly, he
was not a batik or barricade type. Intellectually he was "thoroughly
free," Mrs. Dodge admitted.[1] Yet she remembers him as being Har-
vardized, well bred, possessed of "a fine poise" and "a cool understanding." Her complaint was that, though she found him "strong,"
"young," and "succinctly male," "there was no incontinence and no
flowing sensuality."

Like many another, Lippmann could appreciate the beauties of
art without being able to tolerate the offstage egotism and eccentricities of artists. For example, he found himself "utterly disgusted"
by Isadora Duncan's behavior one night at Mrs. Dodge's and left
the party early. "If this is Greece and Joy and the Aegean Isles and
the Influence of Music," he scribbled in a note to his hostess when
he had retreated to the propriety of the Harvard Club, "I don't want
anything to do with it."

That Lippmann was out of place in Greenwich Village did not

[1] *Movers and Shakers,* Vol. 3 of *Intimate Memories* by Mabel Dodge Luhan,
New York, Harcourt, Brace & Co., 1937.

mean his friends and acquaintances there failed to stimulate him or appreciate him. John Reed—his classmate and fellow Socialist at Harvard, who was in time to join the Soviets, become one of their heroes, write a classic account of the Red Revolution in *Ten Days That Shook the World,* and be buried beneath the Kremlin's walls— dashed off a vivid portrait of the Lippmann of those days:

> Lippmann,—calm, inscrutable,
> Thinking and writing clearly, soundly, well;
> All snarls of falseness swiftly piercing through,
> His keen mind leaps like lightning to the True;
>
> .   .   .   .
>
> Our all unchallenged Chief! But . . . one
> Who builds a world, and leaves out all the fun,—
> Who dreams a pageant, gorgeous, infinite,
> And then leaves all the color out of it,—
> Who wants to make the human race, and me,
> March to a geometric Q.E.D.

Harvard and the Early Years

Much has been made of Walter Lippmann's socialism at Harvard by those who contend he walked out on it to become a conservative. His link with socialism was in the nature of a flirtation, not a courtship, and a brief one at that. It amounted to little more than a stolen kiss or two with the rector's daughter in the guise of Fabianism, and was never a passionate embrace of the rowdy moll of Marxism. According to Lippmann's recollection, the affair was over before he left Cambridge. For all its seeming daring, this short dalliance with revolutionary ideas was only in the conventional pattern of that period.

In his first speech to freshmen in 1953 Harvard's new president, Nathan M. Pusey, wisely pointed out to his youthful hearers who might be disillusioned or cowed by recent history, "It will be a tragic lack, and a very unwise kind of 'wisdom,' if your generation feels no compelling urge to make the world over after its own heart's desire." By common acceptance in times less intimidating and intimidated than the present, colleges used to be places where young men proved their health by having "scarlet" fever early. That is, if these young men had consciences, eyes, and minds instead of hopes of squeezing through, making the right clubs and friends, and then heading for Wall Street. Lippmann recognized this as an under-graduate. In the *Monthly* he said, "Men who are 'orthodox' when they are young are in danger of being middle-aged all their lives."

The Harvard Lippmann entered in 1906 influenced him in ways apparent even now. He was just seventeen when he went there, and his recent hope had been to become an art critic like Ruskin. Harvard soon changed that hope and gave him new interests and ambitions. Colleges have their fat years and their lean. The four during which Lippmann was in Cambridge were among Harvard's best. Its faculty, especially in English and philosophy, was Olympian, its undergraduate body exceptional. Over both, Lippmann recalls, President Eliot "loomed like Zeus himself, stiff but not unpleasant."

As all colleges do, Harvard attracted students of every kind but, being Harvard, prided itself on making no attempt to fuse these different kinds into a type. There were poor boys and rich boys; those favored because they were Brahmin-born and others penalized because they were not. There were insiders and outsiders, clubmen and mavericks, young men who yearned to succeed at letters and young men whose sole ambition was to win them. Although there was the usual quota of nobodies, the number who would become somebody was phenomenal.

Lippmann's classmates included Heywood Broun, Alan Seeger, Carl Binger, Stuart Chase, John Reed, Robert Edmond Jones, and T. S. Eliot. While Lippmann admired Eliot's poetry, he remembers him as "an exquisite young man—too refined for this world." Among Lippmann's contemporaries in college were Edward Sheldon, Van Wyck Brooks, Samuel Eliot Morison, John Hall Wheelock, Ernst Hanfstaengel, H. V. Kaltenborn, Francis Biddle, Lee Simonson, Hermann Hagedorn, Conrad Aiken, Kenneth Macgowan, Frederick Lewis Allen, and Robert Benchley.

If the number of undergraduates destined to become well known was impressive, so was the number of faculty members already secure in their fame. In the English Department, for example, were Kittredge, Bliss Perry, Barrett Wendell, William Allan Neilson, George Pierce Baker, Irving Babbitt, and Copeland. With Baker, Lippmann took a survey course in the history of the drama. He was at first repelled by Babbitt, the archfoe of Rousseau and romanticism and champion of the New Humanism, because of the arrogance of his defense of classicism, but later conquered by the brilliance with which he stated the case of restraint, order, and the mind as master of the emotions. His fondness was genuine for "Copey," that big little man, part ham, part magician, so self-indulgent in his oddities, so sincere in his love of literature and amazing in his ability to create in his students a respect for writing.

It was, however, the "greats" among the philosophers at Harvard—James, Royce, and Santayana—who cast the most abiding spell on Lippmann. Platos and Aristotles they were not, yet they came as close to being so as members of a faculty are ever apt to. Better shepherds to philosophy one could not ask for than these men, so different in their beliefs and characters. They were not only outstanding philosophers themselves, but James and, even more particularly, Santayana were artists whose mastery of language equaled their command of ideas. They led Lippmann straight to the core of philosophy, accustoming him to think in terms of basic concepts and making him aware, as Plato was and certainly Santayana, of the disparities between the ideal republic and the demagogic dangers of democracy in action. Only Frederick L. Thompson, who fired Lippmann's interest in history and became a second father to him, and Graham Wallas, the British sociologist then a visiting lecturer at Harvard, had as teachers so strong an influence on him.

To this day Lippmann recalls with understandable pleasure how, one November afternoon when he was only nineteen, he answered a knock on his door in Weld Hall to find there a bearded, compact, alert elderly gentleman. It was William James. He had just read in the *Illustrated Monthly* a blistering review by Lippmann of Barrett Wendell's *The Privileged Classes*. He was in full agreement with the attack on Wendell's snobbism and wanted to meet the critic. Though Lippmann never took courses with James, who had retired the year before, he thereafter saw him almost once a week at his home on Irving Street.

He responded to the warmth of James' "come-hither" personality. Indeed, as he once said, he "almost worshiped him." He admired the flexibility of James' vigorous thinking, and was delighted to find a philosopher who was a poet and an intellectual who was truly a democrat. Two years later, after James had died, Lippmann wrote, "He was the most tolerant man of our generation. He would quote Mr. Dooley on God to make himself understood among men."

Lippmann completed his undergraduate work in three years and during his fourth year, while working for a master's degree, assisted Santayana in a course on the history of philosophy. Although he saw him once a week and often had tea with him, Lippmann never felt the same affection for Santayana that he did for James and was never close to him. This was not surprising. All that was warm, friendly, and human in James was cold, disdainful, and detached in Santayana. There was about him nothing of the democrat and everything, at least in attitude, of the grandee. Born in Spain, of Spanish parents, he appeared always in his lectures, according to Simonson's recollection, to be "gazing over our heads as if looking for the sail that was to bear him home."

A cynic and a misanthrope who found much to criticize in others, Santayana seemed to feel his own superiority beyond question. His word for his approach to life was "disintoxication." His spiritual sneer did not keep his prose from being intoxicating in its wit and irony, its clarity and music. No champion of reason was more persuasive than this man of the marble-cold mind who, regardless of his subject, created beauty whenever he wrote. His effect on Lippmann was profound and would have been just as great, Lippmann says, if he had never known him. It was Santayana who kept him, in spite of his fondness for James, from becoming a pragmatist, and he who in *The Life of Reason* wrote what Lippmann still considers the finest philosophical work produced in America.

The abstract problems of philosophy were by no means the only problems which ignited Lippmann's mind as an undergraduate. Government, economics, and sociology came to have an increasing hold on him. As a volunteer at Hale House in Boston, he had a welfare worker's introduction to the poor. But he was to see poverty plain and human misery at its most pitiable when, with some other Harvard men in 1908, he struggled for days in the slums of Chelsea to assist the survivors of a major fire that had broken out on Palm Sunday. Shocked by what he had seen, he joined the recently formed Socialist Club, of which he was later to become president. He also started to write articles about other subjects than books or plays for the college monthlies. In a style already firm and clear he championed socialism, defended the suffragettes, and attacked Harvard undergraduates for their political apathy and irresponsibility. A reader though not a disciple of Marx, and a Socialist whose brand was nearer to Sanka than coffee, he may have become disenchanted with socialism before he left Cambridge, but he was never to lose his interest in politics and public affairs.

A decisive factor in persuading him to devote his life to following them was Graham Wallas, who in the spring of 1910 came over from England to give a discussion course in government. To the knowing, young and old, Wallas's presence at Harvard was an event. This "drooping, scholarly, fastidiously lucid" man, this "rather slovenly, slightly pedantic, noble-spirited" person, as Wells described him, was one of the leaders of London's Fabian Society. He knew— yes, actually knew, and as an equal—the Webbs (Beatrice and Sidney), H. G. Wells, Sidney Olivier (Sir Laurence's uncle), and that incredibly audacious and then red-bearded iconoclast George Bernard Shaw.

By common consent a great teacher, Wallas had an immediate and lasting effect on Lippmann which he has always gratefully acknowledged. Wallas was different. When he talked about government he was no theory-spinning professor. He had been a candidate in five London municipal elections and had helped in several Parliamentary contests. From these conflicts he had gained a realism which was not lost on Lippmann. He introduced him, and many others, to an abundance of new ideas which Harold Laski, in a waspish moment, accused Lippmann and these others of developing to build their own reputations.

From Wallas, Lippmann learned some basic truths, simple enough to be overlooked by theorists—that you cannot know politics without knowing politicians, that persons and principles are vitally related, and that abstractions, however systematized, are valueless unless based on an understanding of motives. In Wallas's reverberating book *Human Nature in Politics,* he found a model expository style, strong, brook-clear, and almost conversational in its ease, and in Wallas himself a friend, in spite of the more than thirty years that separated them. Wallas proved his respect for Lippmann four years later when he published *The Great Society* and in it printed a prefatory letter to his former student.

Another indication of the esteem in which Lippmann was held at Harvard came during the summer of 1910 when, without taking the examinations for his M.A., he had gone to work on a new crusading paper called the *Boston Common.* Lincoln Steffens (that "gentle, little, steel man" in Mabel Dodge's words) had suggested to his fellow editors on *Everybody's* that it would be a good idea if they tried to "find and form" their own cubs. With their blessing he went to Cambridge in search of "the ablest mind that could express itself in writing." Everyone he interviewed there, when he described the kind of man he was looking for, agreed on one person—Walter Lippmann.

Lippmann remained on *Everybody's* for about a year and a half, reading manuscripts, helping Steffens with investigations, writing several articles (among them his moving tribute to William James), and serving as a subeditor during his last six months. Steffens [2] admired his young assistant and his writing. He noted that he was keen, quiet, and industrious; that as an interviewer he asked more questions than he was told to; that he understood the meaning of everything he learned; that he was "ever eager to try new things," and had a way of "searching" people.

The two men were an unlikely pair. Billy Graham and Toynbee could scarcely have less in common. Philosophy was the field in which Lippmann had been trained; muckraking the art at which Steffens excelled. Although he remembers that he never agreed with Steffens, his relations with him were close and affectionate, and he remains grateful for what Steffens taught him about the mechanics of journalism and the art of interviewing.

That Lippmann was not exactly happy on *Everybody's* may be guessed from his use of the word "rescued," in a Harvard Class Report, to describe his leaving the magazine. His rescuer was the Reverend George R. Lunn, an ardent reformer, a Dry, and later prominent in Democratic party politics, who was then the newly elected Socialist mayor of Schenectady. Lippmann was his executive secretary from January to May, 1912. These five months were one of the two interludes in his nearly forty-six years of professional activity when he has chosen to play the participant's role instead of the observer's.

The other, a longer one lasting two years, came after our entry into World War I. Taking a leave of absence from *The New Republic*, he served variously as an assistant to the Secretary of War, Newton D. Baker; on "The Inquiry," a top-secret board that supplied data on which some of the Fourteen Points were based; as a

---

[2] *The Autobiography of Lincoln Steffens*, New York, Harcourt, Brace & Co., 1931.

captain of military intelligence in the Meuse-Argonne sector; as a member of the staff of Colonel House in Paris (with Frank Cobb, his future editor on the *World*), and later on the American Commission to Negotiate Peace. By the spring of 1919 he was back on *The New Republic,* having returned to America and civilian life earlier that year and written *The Political Scene,* a short book on the peace as he then saw it.

Before the war, Lippmann had been interested mainly in municipal and national problems; after it, he gave much of his attention to international affairs. This widening of his concerns was symptomatic of the growth imposed on him—and America—by forces and events which changed the world and our place in it. To think, as we are often tempted to today, that this change once begun and even now continuing has been complete is to delude ourselves.

Many things remain the same. Politics and some politicians, for example. "You have only to look at the Senate of the United States," wrote Lippmann in 1912, "to see how that body is capable of turning itself into a court of preliminary hearings for the Last Judgment, wasting its time and our time and absorbing public enthusiasm and newspaper scareheads. For a hundred needs of the nation it has no thought, but about the precise morality of an historical transaction eight years old there is a meticulous interest . . . enough to start the Senate on a protracted man-hunt. Now if one half of the people is bent upon proving how wicked a man is and the other half is determined to show how good he is, neither half will think very much about the nation."

This uncomfortably contemporary paragraph comes from Lippmann's first book, *A Preface to Politics,* written the summer after he had left Schenectady. The more he had seen there of politics at first hand, he admitted, the more he had respected the indifference of the public. But indifferent to American politics and the operations of government he was not himself, and he was determined that other Americans should not be.

To arouse their interest, to expose the abuses of the day, and to suggest an approach to more responsible action, he hastened to follow *A Preface to Politics* with *Drift and Mastery.* Both books were incredible performances for a man in his early twenties. Both reflected the hopes of a younger progressive inspired by Theodore Roosevelt's New Nationalism and Woodrow Wilson's New Freedom.

Both are written with unmistakable skill and showed Lippmann's extraordinary gift for the assimilation and exposition of ideas. They were the products of wisdom no less than knowledge, yet the thinking of both, realistic though it was about national and local issues, betrayed—in the light of what was about to happen—an innocence about international affairs typical of most Americans at that time.

One-Man State Department

As early as 1910 Graham Wallas had warned Lippmann at Harvard that a great war might soon break out and that, if it did, it would probably smolder on for thirty years. Lippmann, however, could not persuade himself that such a war was imminent or that it would ever touch or involve this country. To indicate how possible it was for an American in those years to be "totally unconscious of the world he lived in," he did not hesitate later to use himself as an example.

In *U.S. Foreign Policy* (1943) he told how he sailed for England a few days after the Archduke Ferdinand's assassination in June, 1914; had a delightful time in London and later in the English Lake Country, where he attended a Fabian gabfest presided over by the Webbs and Bernard Shaw; then crossed to Belgium in the last week of July and bought a ticket for a journey through Germany to Switzerland, expecting to spend his vacation walking in the mountains. "I remember," he wrote, "being astonished and rather annoyed when I went to the railroad station and found the German border was closed because Belgium had had an ultimatum." It was not until he had returned to England and happened to be in the House of Commons lobby on August 4, 1914, when Britain declared war, that he "began to take foreign affairs seriously."

World War I and the following decade demanded readjustments in thinking as difficult for Lippmann as for other Americans. He had to learn how to face the stark facts of power politics, battle, and survival. In spite of his extensive studies, he was, by his own admission no more "mentally prepared" for the new age at hand than were most of his contemporaries brought up in the seeming security of those prewar years, when oceans were still oceans, when birds were the only true masters of the air, and Europe and the Far East were for most Americans pleasant places to visit, not problems for them to live with in order to live.

Little by little he came to see, for example, how the Spanish-American War, by extending our frontiers and commitments far into the Pacific, had reversed our policy and position as a nation. Little by little he began to understand why Teddy Roosevelt was not eccentric in harping on the Panama Canal and the Navy; to realize that the Monroe Doctrine was made operative not by our will but by Britain's strength at sea; and to be ashamed (because, as he put it, he had no excuse for not knowing better) of championing editorially in the *World* such an "exorbitant folly" as the Washington Disarmament Conference. The changes in his thinking, once commenced, have never stopped. Right or wrong as his conclusions may have been in this instance or that, he has faced the realities which the passing years have brought into focus, and kept his mind pliant so as to meet their ever-altering challenges.

Few American career diplomats, and fewer American journalists, have followed foreign affairs so closely for so long. Since that August day in 1914 we have had three changes of party in Washington, seven Presidents, and twelve Secretaries of State, all inextricably concerned for varying lengths of time with our relations with the outside world. Lippmann's preoccupation has been continuous. Indeed, it has grown so steadily that he has come to function more and more like a one-man State Department, a fact which has not always endeared him to Secretaries of State. They have resented his unsolicited and publicly given advice, not only on the grounds that they have access to information unavailable to him but also because he is responsible merely for opinions while they are responsible for actions.

In his approach to domestic problems Lippmann has shown the same flexibility of hope and judgment that he has brought to international affairs. His Presidential choices demonstrate this. They follow no party line. They have the independent's freedom, varying from election to election according to his diagnosis of the best interests of the country and the qualifications of the candidates. In 1912 he was for T.R.; in 1916, Wilson; in 1920 (as a protest), B. P. Christensen, the Farmer-Labor candidate; in 1924, Davis; 1928, Smith; 1932, Franklin D. Roosevelt; 1936, Landon; 1940, Willkie; 1944 FDR; 1948, Dewey; and in 1952 for Eisenhower.

Such a veering record, more than indicating the tug within him between conservative and liberal, would seem to support the charges of inconsistency often brought against him. These charges do not bother Lippmann. A genuine searcher after truth, he refuses to become the prisoner of consistency. As he wrote long ago when Vincent Sheean had taken him to task for reversing himself on the gold standard, "I do not wish to pretend that in all matters, or even in all aspects of this one matter, my articles have been consistent and unchanging. I have often changed my opinions, sometimes because they appeared later to be wrong, sometimes because I have lived and learned, and sometimes, as in the case of the gold standard, because events themselves had changed."

We have lived through times in which each decade has had its different climate of opinions. This climate has changed so markedly that wise readers, picking up a book written more than four years ago, look first at the date of publication to prepare themselves for the atmosphere of thought into which they are likely to be moving. If Lippmann's thinking had not changed with the times, it would not have kept pace with them. He is well aware that even the conclusions he states with the most seeming finality in his columns are subject to revision if the news of the day following their writing brings forth fresh evidence.

In his admirable and thorough *Walter Lippmann, A Study in Personal Journalism,* David Elliott Weingast cites many instances of Lippmann's fluctuations and contradictions. He makes a point, however, generally overlooked. This is how seldom Lippmann has succumbed to the columnist's temptation to turn prophet. No journalist who analyzes events and personalities in the headlines has to assume the risks of predicting the future in order to make mistakes. Having to form day-to-day opinions is a sufficient guarantee of errors.

Lippmann, though he would never stoop to the vulgarity of boasting how frequently he has been right, would be the first to admit how often he has been wrong. One of his verdicts which people will not let him forget is his estimate of Governor Roosevelt as a possible Presidential candidate—"Franklin D. Roosevelt is no crusader. He is no tribune of the people. He is no enemy of entrenched privilege. He is a pleasant man who, without any important qualifications for the office, would very much like to be President."

Collectors of the errors of others (especially of those we are asked to venerate as wise) recall this as gleefully as they remember that

Dorothy Thompson, after her first interview with Hitler, wrote, "When I walked in Adolf Hitler's room I was convinced that I was meeting the future dictator of Germany. In something less than fifty seconds I was quite sure that I was not. It took just about that time to measure the startling insignificance of this man who has set the world agog."

History was to prove both Lippmann and Miss Thompson shamefacedly wrong. Even so, historians ought not to err as Quincy Howe does, in *The World Between the Wars,* when he accuses Lippmann of writing his dismissal of Roosevelt at the time of the Chicago convention. The convention was held in June, 1932, and Lippmann's column had been published on January 8 of that year. Lippmann was judging FDR entirely on the basis of his performance as governor and had no way of foreseeing how he would rise to meet the tests ahead. Although he concedes he was wrong in the light of what was to come, he still thinks he was not so wrong on the basis of the evidence then at hand.

"The Great Elucidator"

All men have perfect vision when it comes to hindsight. Lippmann has never sought to conceal how wide the gaps have sometimes been between his insight and his hindsight. There are those who think his manner oracular. There are those who believe he fancies himself as an oracle. But an oracle is neither what Lippmann strives to be nor pretends he is. The philosopher, so strong in his make-up, has stated with unaffected humility the dilemmas which have confronted him as journalist. "For more than twenty years," he acknowledged in 1937 in *The Good Society,* "I have found myself writing about critical events with no better guide to their meaning than the hastily improvised generalizations of a rather bewildered man. Many a time I have wanted to stop and find out what I really believed."

Unfortunately, the contemporary world has refused to grant the pause that refreshes to those intrepid enough to face its problems. Although the questions which bewildered Lippmann in 1937 have since multiplied, they were overwhelming enough then to bewilder any honest observer. Rightly or wrongly, the New Deal (which on the whole he had supported in its first years) had by that time come to represent for him an alarming, if "gradualist," version of centralization. In *The Good Society* he, therefore, bracketed it with other forms of centralization—Fascism, Nazism, Communism—which were imperiling the individual.

Not as a conservative but as a student of history aware of the needs and virtues of certain basic continuities, he regretted that "everywhere the movements which bid for men's allegiance are hostile to the movements in which men struggled to be free. The programs of reform are everywhere at odds with the liberal tradition. Men are asked to choose between security and liberty. To improve their fortunes they are told that they must renounce their rights. To escape from want they must enter a prison. To regularize their work they must be regimented. To obtain greater equality they must have less freedom. To have national solidarity they must oppress the dissenters. To enhance their dignity they must lick the boots of tyrants. To realize the promise of science they must destroy free inquiry. To promote the truth they must not let it be examined."

Valid or invalid as Lippmann's statement of them may have been so far as the New Deal was concerned, these "intolerable" choices were already in 1937 a tragic reality in large portions of the outside world. Instead of disappearing, they present themselves today in greater areas and are, therefore, the more intolerable.

Santayana once said he thought it would have depressed William James if he had had to confess that any important question was finally answered, so anxious would he have been that something might turn up on the other side. Lippmann would have understood, if not shared, this depression, because he has enjoyed exercising his mind on questions which, even when they have bewildered him, he has stated with unbewildered clarity.

The world's problems, the current ones dealt with in his columns or the most lasting ones considered in many of his books, have been at once his hobby and vocation, his diversion and absorption. Not only has he lived with them professionally far longer than most, but no one over the decades has sought more earnestly to think them through. Nonetheless, he has never deluded himself into believing that he has had a final solution to offer or indeed that there was one.

Soon after he left college he had achieved the wisdom to realize that all the philosophical systems, though thought of by their authors as true and binding, are inadequate; that the biggest systems of theory are much more "like village lamp posts than they are like the sun"; that in the greatest philosophical work only an individual is speaking; that the search for the philosopher's stone, worse than being a quest for something not to be found, represents "the old indolence of believing that somebody [has] done the world's thinking once and for all."

Far from claiming he has done the world's thinking, Lippmann is conscious of the difficulties of doing his own. Even in his books he has been careful to point out that, if he is writing about government, he is not offering a legislative program; that, when he uses the word "preface" in a title, he does so to indicate what he has written is a beginning, not a conclusion; and that, instead of offering solutions, his hope is he may be supplying someone else with clues.

"God twist my tripes if I string out the obvious for the delectation of fools," wrote Mr. Justice Holmes when criticized for the brevity of some of his opinions and the speed with which he dashed them off. An elucidator always runs the risk of turning on the lights at high noon for those already in the know. Lippmann is not unaware that his readers include men and women who, by training or because of the public positions they hold, are experts on the topics he discusses. It is not for them, however, that he writes, and certainly not for them alone. Instead, it is for the millions who lack his background, who have little inclination and less time to give painstaking consideration to the subjects he analyzes, and whose search is for the illumination he endeavors to supply. His uncompromising premise is that, though his readers may not know, they either think or want to think, or they would not turn to him. He proceeds, therefore, to think out loud for them.

There are those who contend his writing is sometimes too clear to be true. Others, already in agreement with the point he is developing or familiar with the topic he has chosen, complain as a certain Twisden, C.J., did to a Mr. Saunders when, according to Holmes, he asked, "Why do you labor so for the Court is clearly with you?" Not many, however, whether they agree or disagree with him, question that in his writing he draws on an immense reservoir of knowledge; that he sees his task as a high one and tries to perform it in such a fashion; that thinking is for him an adventure which he trusts others will approach in the same spirit; or that, in the terms of his own definition of the true teacher, his chief concern is not persuasion but "the rationalization of the process by which conclusions are reached."

Few, even among those who oppose his beliefs violently, who scorn or mourn him as a liberal gone astray, or condemn his shifts in opinions as repudiations instead of reversals, deny his skill with words. Among his admirers many have themselves been distinguished writers. One is Van Wyck Brooks, who in *The Confident Years* saluted his career as "the most brilliant [that has] ever been devoted, in America, to political thinking." Another was Holmes (Sir Hubert indeed!), who during their long friendship seldom delivered a dissenting opinion on Lippmann's mastery of language. Holmes's letters to Pollock and Laski bubble over with such praise as "monstrous clever lad, W. L."; "he is a born writer"; "his writing is fly paper for me—if I touch it I am stuck till I finish it"; and "perhaps he doesn't get anywhere in particular (in *Public Opinion*) but there are few living I think who so discern and articulate the nuances of the human mind."

Harold Laski, that virtuoso among letter writers and Little Corporal of conversationalists, whose gift for fantasy and fiction was sometimes too urgent for him to keep under control, was one of those (there have been several) who, though once the intimates of Lippmann, have either cooled toward him or broken with him, even as he has broken with them. In the early thirties Laski [3] wrote about him to Holmes in whittling or jeering terms, saying, "he has arrived at the stage when he is eager not to take intellectual risks," or describing him as his "main American disappointment," a man who seemed "to have worn terribly thin, and to be pontifical and dogmatic in realms where his knowledge and insight were lacking." During the twenties, and just before them, Laski sang a very different song. In spite of reservations, he admired Lippmann's thinking for being "real, agile, quick, incisive"; expressed his gratitude in an introduction to one of his own books by admitting "there is little that can repay such friendship as he gives"; wished he had Lippmann's pen because "he makes words talk of themselves"; said "of all the *New Republic* bunch his mind [is] the wisest and most profound"; and applauded the "sparse, nervous strength in his style that obviously reflects great mental power."

[3] *Holmes-Laski Letters.*

Sacco-Vanzetti and Heywood Broun

Most of us are overtaken, without being aware of it, by testing moments to which we respond in a fashion symptomatic of our reactions in general. We react instinctively because of what we are predominantly, behaving at the direction of the controlling majority of our qualities. There is no hope of anticipating these moments. They steal upon us and, before we know it, we are revealed and self-summarized.

The Sacco-Vanzetti case was such a moment for thousands when, after dragging along for seven years, it reached the climax of its final phase and tragic ending in the summer of 1927. To many, here and abroad, then and even now, justice seemed at the time to have died in Massachusetts along with the shoemaker and the fish peddler who in its name were condemned to death.

Among those publicly tested were Walter Lippmann and Heywood Broun, both on the *World,* the one as the editor, the other as a deservedly popular columnist. On most of the fundamental points they were in full agreement. Both disapproved of Judge Webster Thayer's conduct of this trial in which two Italian-born anarchists were accused of murdering the paymaster of a shoe factory in South Braintree and his guard. Both felt the evidence, admittedly circumstantial, was contradictory, inconclusive, and confused. Both believed that, far from establishing guilt beyond reasonable doubt, it created sizable doubts of the most reasonable kind. Both were dissatisfied with and exposed the flaws in the report written at Governor Alvin T. Fuller's request by a three-man advisory committee headed by Harvard's president, the venerable A. Lawrence Lowell. And both hoped the execution would be stayed and a new trial held.

Seldom, however, have two men who agreed on so much reacted in ways so drastically different. This was inevitable since each in his response was true to his character, and their characters were poles apart. Broun, that great, stooping, kind-faced giant with the twinkling eyes, who managed to make whatever clothes he wore (including a dinner jacket) look like a mangy raccoon coat, was a man widely loved and widely loving. He was a grab bag of gifts supposedly contradictory. A sentimentalist (in his phrase "an easy weeper") at the same time he was a wit and humorist, he was also an extravagant champion, a formidable foe, and a crusader whose indignation blazed forth with passion and without restraint. He had only contempt for commentators whose search was for the right word rather than the just cause. He never had to search for either. Lazy as he was until forced by a deadline to face a typewriter at the last moment, there was nothing lazy about his conscience. It was as outsized as he.

Inescapably, Broun and Lippmann did not see eye to eye on many things, and had not even at Harvard. In his second novel, *The Sun Field* (1923), Broun had his classmate in mind when he wrote about an editor who was so overeducated that "there wasn't room to put any more education on him," and added, "That is one of the things there ought to be a law about. A city statute should lay down the principle that nobody should be educated above the twenty-third story." Broun always took pains to make it clear he was not an intellectual; Lippmann has never taken any to disguise the fact that he is.

Broun approached the Sacco-Vanzetti case frankly as an emotionalist, Lippmann no less frankly as a logician. They battled with equal courage, but where the one thought with his heart (a huge and tender heart) the other felt with his mind (an excellent and incisive mind). Broun was as personal as Lippmann was impersonal, and as torrid as he was temperate. Broun was fighting mad and pulled no punches in the two unforgotten columns he published before the *World* refused to print other columns by him on the subject and he left the paper.

He was ashamed of the public because of its apathy; enraged with the entrenched order because, in his view, it was more interested in setting an example which would reinforce its own security than in guaranteeing justice; and no less infuriated with Fuller, Thayer, and Lowell. Accordingly, he went in swinging, thumping heads or groins with all the wit, sarcasm, passion, and eloquence at his command. The *World* accused him of stating his opinions "with the utmost extravagance" and taking a "witch's Sabbatical." But to this day the heat of the controversy is so flaming in his words that they burn like fagots.

Lippmann was as disturbed by Broun's violence as Broun was amazed at Lippmann's calm. Lippmann felt that such unrestrained invective was more an individual indulgence than a public service, since it was bound to anger Governor Fuller and stiffen his resolve not to stay the execution. As Lippmann saw it, it was all very well for Broun, who did not face the electric chair, to insist out of the most sincere high-mindedness that nothing less than a pardon or a new trial was satisfactory to him. To Lippmann, however, the saving of the lives of Sacco and Vanzetti was more important than the airing of anyone's views.

American journalism, so often charged with irresponsibility, was never more responsible than in the full-page editorial by him which appeared in the *World* on August 19, 1927. It remains a model of cool reasoning and detailed exposition. Facts, not fury, were Lippmann's concern, and he marshaled them with masterly logic as he reviewed the case, stressed the doubts it had raised, and pleaded for a stay of execution and a new trial. On the day following the execution Lippmann carried moderation to a point which outraged Broun. He wrote an editorial in which he praised such valiant defenders of Sacco and Vanzetti as Felix Frankfurter at the same time that he paid his respects to the members of the Lowell committee for having bravely done a disagreeable duty. Broun held that such "sportsmanship," while desirable at a Harvard-Yale game, was shocking when, as it seemed to him, two innocent men had been murdered.

He did not share Lippmann's willingness to recognize that there are two sides to almost every question. Once he accused Lippmann of being the greatest carrier of water on both shoulders since Rebecca at the well. Another time he condemned him as a specialist in safeties, "quite apt to score a field goal for Harvard and a touchdown for Yale in one and the same play."

Broun is not the only one in Lippmann's long career to have misinterpreted his eagerness to be fair as timidity. His enemies rejoice in quoting Mabel Dodge's "Walter was never never going to lose an eye in a fight." Such a verdict is a glaring untruth, as any openminded reader of Lippmann's columns or books must acknowledge. More accurately, it is no more true of him than of most other writers, including Broun, who frankly confessed that physically he was an elephant who could be frightened by nearly any mouse.

A writer fights in his own way. Words and ideas are his fists. Shaw, one of the most dauntless of intellectual combatants, knew this. When the Fabians had once become involved rather ludicrously in a street brawl, he decided that martyrdom was "the only way that a man can become famous without ability." Shaw valued his own intellectual abilities far too much to have a relish for physical martyrdom. "I am a thinker, not a fighter," said he. "When the shooting begins I shall get under the bed, and not emerge until we come to real constructive business."

Lippmann would not have the opponents he has, or have laid himself open to being proved incorrect, if he had ducked the risks of commitment. For that matter, he would never have been accused of reversing himself if he had not taken definite positions. His convictions are firm, and always have been. But there are those unable or unwilling to recognize this, because the tolerance with which he states them is intolerable to them.

Champion of Reason

Nowhere are prejudices more mistaken for truth, passion for reason, and invective for documentation than in politics. That is a realm, peopled only by villains or heroes, in which everything is black or white, and gray a forbidden color. Lippmann is aware of the disfavor he invites by appealing "to thought which is pale rather than to lusts which are strong." He realizes there are readers who find qualifications obnoxious and balance repellent—and disregards them. His hope is to weigh, not sway. He knows that the so-called "strong" position (with its overstatement and unquestioning partisanship) is often the "weak" one both morally and intellectually, since it refuses to face the intricacy of issues and the complexity of truth. He faces both, no matter how "mugwumpish" or "academic" his doing so may make him appear, and this in itself requires courage of a very real, if special, kind.

In *Man's Unconquerable Mind* Gilbert Highet tells how a wise man of our own time, when asked what was the single greatest contribution of Greece to the world's welfare, replied that beyond question it was the words meaning "on the one hand" and "on the other," since without these balances we cannot think. No political writer in our day has been more mindful of these balances or the need for them than Walter Lippmann. The right for him has never been the exclusive or abiding possession of any party or individual. Neither a hero-worshiper nor a debunker, he has been quick to praise our leaders from Theodore Roosevelt and Wilson down to Truman and Eisenhower for what he considers their good qualities and achievements, and no less quick to condemn them for their defects and errors.

Because he has refused to concede that an uninformed majority has any mystical guarantee of always being right, some have accused him of not believing in democracy. The best answer to such a charge is his own career, which has been a long and distinguished fight in the interest of democracy against ignorance, indifference, and bigotry. Keenly conscious that the democratic process is healthy only when defended from its weaknesses by an enlightened electorate, he has made it his life work to provide this enlightenment to the utmost of his ability.

As journalists must, he has written too much, turning out thousands of words bound to be dead almost as soon as they appear. Inevitably, he has had his good days and his bad, his lean years and his full. His recent years have been among his best, as demonstrated (to choose at random from his columns) in his wonderfully clear and clarifying article on the Brownell-McCarthy controversy; his vigorous exposure of Langer's abuse of Senatorial privileges when he tried to block Warren's confirmation as Chief Justice; his eloquent pleas for Eisenhower to abandon a Vice-Presidential concept of the Presidency as a presiding officer and assert his full authority and leadership as Chief Executive; his admirable analysis of the issues presented by Formosa; and his searching discussion of the problems raised by publication of the Yalta records. Indeed, Lippmann's recent writing has even caused Dean Acheson, a cooled friend of whom Lippmann has long been fiercely critical, to say, according to one of their mutual acquaintances, "I begin to think something must be wrong with me. I find myself agreeing a lot with Walter."

Readers are apt to believe political commentators, like all other critics, are at their best when they agree with them. Agreement with Lippmann may add to the pleasure of reading him, but one does not have to agree to be interested in his writing. The processes of his thought, the whys and wherefores of his thinking, the steps in logic by means of which he moves forward to his conclusions or supports a thesis, have an interest and a value of their own, both uncommon. In the Emersonian sense Lippmann is Man Thinking, a scholar in his own field and therefore a person with a "delegated intellect," but Man Thinking nonetheless, and a man who has been thinking hard these many years about political and governmental problems as current as any day's headline or as old as Plato's *Republic*.

Politically, his search has been for an outward order that would guarantee the dignity and freedom of the individual by protecting him from the encroachments of the state. Philosophically, he has sought for a faith that would restore serenity to those "perplexed by the consequences of their own irreligion." He has endeavored to define not only the Good Society but the good man in that society, and in the process has made a unique contribution to our own society. He has not shut his eyes on the horrors of the altered world in which he finds himself. No one has stated the dangers of present-day democracy in more uncompromising terms than he did in *The Public Philosophy* (1955). Though his despair has grown, Lippmann continues to hope, in this age of democratic "decay" and as he sees it "the misrule of the people" by themselves and their governors, that "liberty and democracy can be preserved before the one destroys the other."

Both as a journalist and philosopher, he has been more significant as an elucidator than an originator. As both, he has fought for and against many things and the fairness of his fighting method has set a notable example.

Lippmann's most important fight has been his long battle against the darkness in men's minds. He has pleaded for sanity in a period of hysteria, moderation in the place of intemperance, and the rigors of thought instead of easy surrenders to partisanship. In spite of other inconsistencies, he has never failed in these respects to practice what he has preached. Even now in an age of unreason, when slurs, lies, innuendoes, and rumors have been widely accepted as facts, Lippmann still speaks with the quiet voice of reason. Always valuable, in these times when fear has reduced so many to irrationality, he has become invaluable.

X

IN THE MATTER OF J. ROBERT OPPENHEIMER

The Case Gets Under Way

For twenty-nine and a half days Joseph N. Welch, the quiet-spoken counsel for the Army, had endured McCarthy unruffled. To the millions following the Army-McCarthy hearings on television the patience of the "gentle man" from Boston had seemed inexhaustible. With his wry humor, his old-fashioned, almost quaint courtesy, and his winning mixture of city sophistication and country innocence, Welch had disregarded the bellowings, the self-pitying sighs, and the droning interruptions of McCarthy. On this particular afternoon, however, the older man could restrain himself no longer. His moral sense was outraged. He turned on the junior senator from Wisconsin, his voice quivering with emotion.

Before the huge television audience McCarthy had tried to brand as a Communist a respected young member of Welch's firm. The young lawyer he attacked was not working on the hearings, but, according to McCarthy's ethics, it was fair to drag him in and besmirch him because he had once, and briefly, belonged to the Lawyers' Guild. Such conscienceless tactics were more than Welch could stomach. "Until this moment, Senator," he cried, "I think I never gauged your cruelty or your recklessness. . . . Let us not assassinate this lad further. You have done enough. Have you no sense of decency, sir? At long last, have you left no sense of decency?"

Among the watching millions sickened in Welch's manner by McCarthy's methods was a thirteen-year-old boy living in Princeton. He walked away from the television set, his face white with indignation, went upstairs, and on the blackboard in his bedroom wrote:

The Amican Govermerant is unfair to Acuse Certain People that I know, of being unfair to them. Since this true, I think that Certain

228

People, and may I say, only Certain People in the U.S. govermeant, should go to HELL.

Yours truly,
CERTAIN PEOPLE.

The boy's spelling was shaky but his emotions were understandably strong. When he printed these words on the afternoon of June 9, 1954, his father, J. Robert Oppenheimer, was going through hell. From April 12 through May 6 he had faced the ordeal of appearing before the Personnel Security Board, better known as the Gray Board because its chairman was Gordon Gray. At this hearing he had been badgered about his present, had his motives doubted, his patriotism questioned, his memory subjected to merciless and impossible demands, and his public and private life left naked. Having at last learned the Gray Board's vote after nearly a month of tormenting anxiety, he had been dwelling for more than a week with the wounds to his pride, his reputation, and his career inflicted by its recommendation that in the "interest of the United States" his security clearance should not be reinstated. For another three weeks he was to live under the tension of waiting for the decision of the Atomic Energy Commission. His foreboding that the verdict would be against him cannot have eased his nights and days.

Oppenheimer's world, a most distinguished one on the highest level of government service and international recognition, had exploded on December 21 of the previous year. Admiral Lewis L. Strauss, Chairman of the AEC, had asked to see him on that day and Oppenheimer had gone to Washington, not knowing why he was summoned. The note he wrote Strauss the next day reveals the reason and gives his version of the meeting. For the first time he was told that his clearance by the Atomic Energy Commission was about to be suspended. Strauss offered an alternative, though it was more like a gun in the ribs than a choice. It was, in fact, an ultimatum. Either within twenty-four hours Oppenheimer would request the termination of his contract as a consultant to the Commission or the Commission would begin proceedings against him as a security risk. He was shown a draft of a letter signed by General K. D. Nichols, the Commission's general manager, and assured that if he accepted Strauss's offer the stale allegations regarding his veracity, his conduct, and even his loyalty would not be explored.

No self-respecting person could have entered into this agreement. To do so would have been at once a denial of competence and an admission of guilt. The more one tries to understand Strauss's offer, the more probable it seems that, in spite of its air of clemency, it was never intended to be accepted at all. In the light of what lay behind it and the climate of Washington at the time, it is otherwise inexplicable.

As Oppenheimer wrote Strauss, such a course would mean that "I accept and concur in the view that I am not fit to serve this Government that I have now served for some twelve years. This I cannot do." Accordingly, on December 23 Nichols sent Oppenheimer at the Institute for Advanced Study in Princeton the fateful letter informing him that "to protect the common defense and security" his work for the Commission was terminated, his clearance suspended, and his access to restricted data denied as of that moment, pending final determination of his status.

The letter was marked "Confidential," it said, so as "to maintain the privacy of this matter" between Oppenheimer and the Atomic Energy Commission. How private this was apt to be can be guessed from the fact that all American Army, Navy, Air Force, and atomic installations were notified immediately of Oppenheimer's suspension as a routine security measure, and that, by accident or design, before the hearing started, copies of the letter got into the hands of more and more people not involved in the proceedings.

The sending of the Nichols letter marked the official opening of the Oppenheimer case. A month and a half before, another letter played its decisive and unhappy part behind the scenes. The original went to J. Edgar Hoover at the FBI, a copy to the Joint Committee on Atomic Energy.

Almost anyone unacquainted with its author, William Liscum Borden, might be justified in guessing from a mere reading of his letter that it must be the work of a zealot. It vibrates with an overcharge of conviction in which objectivity is victimized by allegations made without restraint. Borden meant well, as his friends attest. Then thirty-two, from a fine family, happily married, intelligent, a prodigious worker, and austere in his self-discipline, he was a Democrat who thought of himself as a liberal of a moderate variety.

He had stood high in the class of '42 at Yale, served with distinction in Europe as a pilot in the Eighth Air Force, and acquitted himself creditably at the Law School on his return to New Haven. In 1946 he had written *There Will Be No Time,* a remarkably lucid book about the revolutionized pattern of atomic warfare. After this he had been executive secretary in Washington to the late Senator Brien McMahon, and subsequently worked well for more than four years as executive director of the Joint Committee on Atomic Energy to which he now wrote and from which he had resigned in June, 1953.

Love of country, like all other forms of love, can dim judgment. That love of his country induced Borden to write is as clear in his letter about Oppenheimer as that he wrote as a man carried away by emotion. Oppenheimer had come to haunt him. During his years on the Committee, Borden had met him only occasionally but he had lived with Oppenheimer's file. He had brooded over it with such ever-mounting alarm that, "detestable" as he found doing so, he finally persuaded himself it was his patriotic duty to inform those in key positions of the conclusions he had reached. He wrote from agony rather than anger, and not in haste but after years of deliberation. Yet seldom has a sincere sense of responsibility led to a more unfortunate action.

That he had convinced himself by no means meant that Borden had taken a position which was convincing. Had he had the facts to justify his conclusions, the course he chose, more than being commendable, would have been mandatory. What prompted him to act, however, was chiefly his horrified assumptions. On the basis of charges long cleared and mainly familiar (except in the instance of Oppenheimer's opposition to an all-out program for the H-bomb) he leaped to new deductions, and advanced these as reasons for dismissal.

The conclusions Borden had come to were terrible ones which no official later judging the case ever even hinted at. They were that "more probably than not" from 1929 until 1941 Oppenheimer had been a Communist volunteering espionage, and that, again "more probably than not," since then he had been functioning as a Soviet agent under a Soviet directive. Such assertions were of so grave a character that J. Edgar Hoover felt compelled to call them, along with a summary of Oppenheimer's file, to Eisenhower's attention; that the President discussed them with Secretary of Defense Wilson, Admiral Strauss, and other high officials; that the AEC voted unanimously to investigate them; that Oppenheimer was summoned to Washington by Strauss; and that, with the sending of the Nichols letter, the machinery was set in motion which resulted in perhaps the major, and beyond question the most complicated, loyalty-security case to have darkened our times.

Certainly no other such modern procedure in this country has centered in a figure of equal eminence, included a cast of higher distinction, caused stormier controversy, or left wounds so abiding on most of those involved. None has raised more fundamental questions and supplied sorrier answers. None in the interest of clarifying confusing issues has created greater confusion, and while attempting to fortify our security has made clearer the defects in our security system.

The case, as handled, can have made few happy, fewer proud, and no one wiser. Had it followed a straight line as it progressed from one stage in its unfolding to another, it would itself have been easier to follow and perhaps to excuse. But the road it traveled, as it moved from Borden's letter to Nichols's, and from the findings of the Gray Board, through Nichols's recommendation to the AEC, to the Commission's final decision, was a crooked path. Down this it zigzagged, shifting positions, making contradictory charges, abandoning previous issues, and introducing new ones.

That one of the three men on the Gray Board (Dr. Ward V. Evans) and one of the five on the Atomic Energy Commission (Dr. Henry D. Smyth), with the same evidence before them, reached opposite conclusions from their fellow members and voted to restore Oppenheimer's clearance is not surprising. Jurors disagree daily in this fashion; so do judges; so do friends. What was surprising and remains confusing is that, even in their majority opinions, the Board and the Commission could not agree on why they agreed that Oppenheimer should not be reinstated. In these opinions the same case often seemed two separate cases, the same man two different men. The Gray Board's negative recommendation was of a rueful, it-hurts-me-more-than-it-does-you tone; the Commission's verdict almost gleeful in its harshness. The former commended in order to condemn; the latter was so bent upon destroying that it had no room for regrets. The result was that the one was as bewildering in its kindness as the other was in its cruelty.

Where the Board paid tribute to Oppenheimer's "loyal and mag-

nificent service," applauded his "undoubted and unparalleled contributions" to the atomic energy program, spoke of his "love of
[and] deep devotion to his country," discovered no "attachment to
the Soviet Union" behind his stand on the H-bomb, and praised his
"high degree of discretion" and his "unusual ability to keep to himself vital secrets," the Commission in a single sentence made the
most reluctant mention of his achievements.

To the Board's majority Oppenheimer was no saint. It found he
had not been "blameless in conduct, character, and associations"
and thought in several instances he had been "less than candid"
in his testimony, though he impressed Dr. Evans, the sturdy dis-
senter, as being "extremely honest." Nonetheless, the Board wrote
of Oppenheimer with unconcealed admiration as a loyal citizen of
"brilliant capabilities" and proven worth. Not so the Commission.
To its majority he was practically a villain. He had "fallen far short
of acceptable standards." He had "repeatedly exhibited a willful
disregard of the normal and proper obligations of security." He was
given to "falsehoods, evasions, and misrepresentations." His associations with Communists had "lasted too long to be justified as merely
the intermittent and accidental revival of earlier friendships." In
short, he suffered from such "fundamental defects in his 'character' " that the concurring Commissioners must have wondered, even
as they wrote, how the man they pictured could ever have conjured
Los Alamos from the desert, fathered the A-bomb, won the Medal
for Merit (the highest award a President can make to a civilian),
ably directed the Institute for Advanced Study, and gained the
respect and confidence of the nation's outstanding scientists and
pivotal people in its government.

One Commissioner, Dr. Smyth, found nothing in Oppenheimer's
record or behavior to support the AEC's serious charges or justify
its abusive language. He was as positive in stating that Oppenheimer's further employment would "continue to strengthen the
United States" as he was in disapproving the intemperance of the
verdict's phrasing and judgments. As he saw it, Oppenheimer was
no threat to our security, but the conclusion his fellow Commissioners drew from the evidence was "so extreme as to endanger the
security system."

Beyond these intramural disagreements, there was another difference between the majority findings of the Board and the Commis-

sion. At least there was on the surface. In spite of denying that it did so, the Board in effect punished Oppenheimer for having opposed an all-out or crash program for the H-bomb in 1949 when he was chairman of the General Advisory Committee. The Commission, on the other hand (perhaps due to the adverse press which had greeted the Board's recommendation), insisted that Oppenheimer "was, of course, entitled to his opinion," an opinion by the way then shared by such of his distinguished confreres as Conant, Fermi, and DuBridge. Though one welcomes this sudden intrusion of tolerance in the Commission's verdict, and would think that expressing an honest opinion—right or wrong—was an adviser's duty, the near certainty remains that, had Oppenheimer not temporarily opposed the H-bomb program, he would never have faced a hearing or had his clearance challenged.

As the case progressed, its contradictions and confusions multiplied and in the process its paradoxes proved the more disturbing because they pushed irony to the point of tragedy. The service it supposedly performed for the nation proved mainly a disservice. To add to our safety, it subtracted from our strength not only by depriving us of the knowledge of one outstanding man of science but by frightening other much-needed scientists away from government work. The attention it gained throughout the world was equaled by the prestige it cost us. Worse by far than the face we lost abroad because of it was the faith temporarily lost at home by many Americans in the fairness, wisdom, and gratitude of their government.

Even those convinced that Oppenheimer was too complicated a character to make an ideal public servant or those not sorry to see him go had their misgivings about the way in which his services were dispensed with. Though men of the highest integrity, Gordon Gray and Thomas A. Morgan, the two Board members who voted against him, were as much the victims of the criteria by which they were asked to judge him as Oppenheimer was himself.

No case, it would seem, could be more serious or demand maturer consideration than this one in which not only the good name, life work, and character of such a citizen were at stake but also, as the Board clearly saw, "the security system of the United States" was put on trial. But, in expressing its own doubts in its adverse finding, the Board destroyed the confidence of others when it wrote, "It seemed to us that an alternative recommendation would be possible, if we were allowed to exercise mature practical judgment without the rigid circumscription of regulations and criteria established for us." This amounted to admitting that, though wrong was being done, it was being done in the right way.

The Board's honest desire was to conduct an inquiry, not a trial, and its repeated insistence was that it was doing so. Yet one of the most upsetting aspects of the hearing was the way in which it was often allowed to turn into a trial, and a criminal trial at that. This was due to Gray's strange tolerance of the ruthless tactics of the Board's counsel, Roger Robb, who again and again behaved as if he were a district attorney out for blood. Of all the paradoxes, however, in which the investigation and discrediting of Oppenheimer abounded, perhaps the most disconcerting was that in the opinion of many wise lawyers and laymen this, one of our major security-loyalty cases, was in the ideal sense also the most unnecessary. I say "in the ideal sense" because in the political atmosphere of Washington both ideals and sense frequently wither away.

Political Weather Report

Ideally, had Admiral Strauss and the AEC left well enough alone, everything would have been better. Ideally, had they done nothing, time would have done for them what they elected to do. Oppenheimer's contract as one of their consultants was to expire on June 30, 1954. This was a little more than six months after Strauss had summoned him to Washington and Nichols had sent his letter. It was less than three months after the hearing started and exactly one day after the AEC released its savage verdict. To deprive Oppenheimer of his "Q" clearance (the highest type of clearance, guaranteeing access to any material needed for one's work), ideally Strauss and the Commission did not have to take public action. They had only to let his contract lapse and he would have lost this clearance automatically. They had employed him as a consultant for a mere six days after he had ceased being the General Advisory Committee's chairman in 1952. While waiting for June 30 to come around, they could easily have not employed him at all.

When Strauss delivered his December ultimatum, he unwittingly made two revelations by his assurance that if Oppenheimer resigned within twenty-four hours the "derogatory information" in his file would not be explored. One was a strong feeling of urgency; the other that he did not consider the allegations serious enough to require a hearing if a bargain could be reached.

If it had not been for other, and outside, influences, the alarmed speed of Strauss's action would seem as strange as his bothering to move at all, in view of the vintage of most of the charges. Pease porridge hot is one thing, cold another, but this pease porridge was far more than nine days old. Of the twenty-four "derogatory" items listed in the Nichols letter twenty-three concerned Oppenheimer's left-wing associations at Berkeley before the war and mainly in the late 1930's when, as a scholar unbelievably isolated from the actualities of life, his interest in politics and world affairs was tardily awakened. The twenty-fourth had to do with his opposition in 1949 to a full-scale program for the hydrogen bomb. This accusation he protested with vigor, explaining that previously he had favored the superbomb as an idea and that his attitude toward it would have been different in 1949, had Edward Teller then come up with the same brilliant inventions or discoveries that he did in early 1951.

Most of the remaining "derogatory" items—except for the lie which ten years earlier Oppenheimer had confessed telling to protect his friend, Haakon Chevalier, from being thought of as a Soviet go-between—went far back into his past. They charged that he had given his name to Communist-front organizations, contributed money through a Communist to the Loyalist cause in Spain, counted Communists among his friends and been engaged to one; that his brother and sister-in-law had been party members; and that his wife, Kitty, was a Communist when she was married to her first husband Joseph Dallet, a Communist. (She testified later this was only from 1934 until 1936, when she was separated from Dallet because she could no longer tolerate the party.) Oppenheimer conceded the correctness of these charges. Never a Communist himself, as he said under oath, he had never denied, nor was it a secret, that he had had a fellow traveler's interest in left-wing causes ("very brief and very intense") which began in 1936, tapered off after 1939, and practically died out by 1942.

No life story was better known to those "in the know" in Washington than Oppenheimer's, and no one "in the know" knew it better than Strauss. Oppenheimer had long lived under the microscope of government scrutiny. During the previous eleven years he had been under actual surveillance. His movements had been followed, his conversations noted, his mail opened, and his telephone calls checked. Even under this unrelenting observation his loyalty had always been cleared.

In 1950 Richard M. Nixon, at that time a ranking member of the House Un-American Activities Committee and associated in the public mind with the conviction of Hiss, had come to Oppenheimer's defense when in California he had been charged with entertaining Communists at a party in his Berkeley home. Nixon expressed his "complete confidence" in Oppenheimer's loyalty, described him as "on all occasions a cooperative witness," and saluted him as "one to whom the people of the United States owe a great debt of gratitude for his tireless and magnificent job in atomic research."

Informally, Oppenheimer had been cleared that same year by Gordon Dean, then chairman of the AEC. As late as July, 1953, his reappointment as a consultant had been "unqualifiedly" recommended by Dr. Walter Whitman, the retiring chairman of the Research and Development Board of the Department of Defense. Because of the derogatory information in Oppenheimer's file, Dr. Whitman had been instructed to go over it to comply with Eisenhower's Executive Order 10450 of April 27 of that year. Officially, Oppenheimer had been cleared in 1943 by General Leslie Groves, the head of the Manhattan Project, and again in 1947 by the full Atomic Energy Commission of which Admiral Strauss was a member.

On the surface Strauss's sudden and drastic move against Oppenheimer may appear preposterous, in spite of his claims that the hearing produced important new evidence and that old allegations became facts because for the first time they were stated under oath. Beneath the surface of this seeming irrationality there were reasons for the urgency which involved personalities, opposite policies, external compulsions, and political considerations.

Assuredly at that late date Oppenheimer confronted the government with no emergency question of security, but he did present the administration with a problem in expediency. This may provide a key to the otherwise inexplicable inconsistency of Strauss's being able to vote for Oppenheimer's re-election as director of the Institute for Advanced Study in Princeton (a post for which he had nominated him in 1947) some three months after making the most shattering charges against his character and veracity in the AEC verdict. Whether it was Strauss or Oppenheimer who in this case was cast as Dr. Jekyll and Mr. Hyde it was hard to tell, but one of the two, on the basis of Strauss's action, obviously had a double personality. Apparently to Strauss, Oppenheimer out of a responsible position in government was not the same man that he was in a responsible position out of government, or to be judged by the same standards. All this seems to point to the fact that, quite aside from divergences in policy or clashes of temperament, Oppenheimer in an important job in the Washington of 1953 and 1954 could have been a source of embarrassment to the administration.

When the hearing began in the spring of 1954, Strauss was to claim that on July 7 of the previous year, four days after Eisenhower appointed him chairman of the AEC, he had initiated steps in the national interest which led to the removal from Princeton of Oppenheimer's classified documents. What he did, no one has disclosed. Inasmuch as the documents were not removed until late December after Oppenheimer had declined Strauss's bargain, his steps must have been at best lackadaisical. But by the time November, 1953, had come to an end, with its mounting tensions that concerned the administration as much as they affected Oppenheimer, the tempo of Strauss's actions suddenly changed.

Borden's letter was sent to J. Edgar Hoover on the 7th of November. By the 30th, when Hoover forwarded it to the White House along with a summary of Oppenheimer's file, so much had happened which had to do with politics rather than science or security that new justifications for sacrificing Oppenheimer could be advanced. Although, as was well known, Strauss and Oppenheimer had had their sharp differences, by then events had placed Strauss in a situation where he could feel committed to act by his sense of duty. In his Pooh-Bah position as chairman of the AEC and the President's adviser on atomic matters, the nation's security was very much his province. Yet, as a good Republican and an Eisenhower appointee, Strauss was also interested in the security of the administration and its leader. From the viewpoint of party loyalty it could be thought he was obliged to see to it that a person such as J. Robert Oppenheimer, vulnerable to attack because of his past associations, would never plague Eisenhower as Harry Dexter White during this November had plagued Truman.

On the very day the Borden letter was sent, the White case broke in the headlines of every newspaper. Attorney General Herbert Brownell, Jr., was responsible for this. In an astounding speech to the Executives Club in Chicago the previous day Brownell implied Truman knew from two detailed reports sent him by the FBI that White was a Soviet spy when in 1946 Truman promoted White to a higher position in the Treasury. Immediately Harry Dexter White, though dead for five years, became a living symbol and a very live issue. Truman denied the charges to reporters and later on the air; Eisenhower at a press conference said he thought it "inconceivable" that a President would "knowingly damage the United States"; and Brownell was roundly criticized for making such assertions about a former President, especially before a luncheon club instead of the proper authorities.

In the ensuing tumult certain things stood out. Truman had been the victim of incredibly sloppy staff work. Brownell had embarrassed Eisenhower. Those serving Eisenhower must try not to have him embarrassed in the same way again or placed in a predicament similar to the one in which Truman had been trapped. Moreover, having created the impression that the Democrats were soft on Communists, the administration must make it plain that it was living up to its campaign promises and taking bold steps to rid the government of security risks.

Since his two reports to Truman on Harry Dexter White had been misplaced or ignored, Hoover was no doubt determined to have his FBI summary of the derogatory information against Oppenheimer brought to Eisenhower's attention. His determination may have been strengthened by his having appeared before a Senate subcommittee during the White case after he had received Borden's letter, and by his stated dissatisfaction with certain details of the Chevalier incident in Oppenheimer's file when the AEC had cleared Oppenheimer in 1947.

Six days before Hoover forwarded Borden's letter along with a report on Oppenheimer to the President and interested government agencies, both Hoover and Strauss had a storm warning as to the danger Eisenhower might invite if nothing were done about Oppenheimer. On the 24th of this November, in a speech that rocked the nation, McCarthy butted into the White case as he was butting into everything else. As usual, he burst in as a whimperer but also with a bang. Supposedly he took to the networks to answer the broadsides at "McCarthyism" that Truman had released eight days before in his reply to Brownell. To do this, the senator demanded and was given, as a measure of the importance which was then his, the same time on the air as the ex-President.

As expected, McCarthy's speech began with an attack in which he accused Truman of coddling Communists at home and abroad. As was not expected, his speech soon turned into an attack on Eisenhower on the same grounds. If the senator slugged the former with insults, he stabbed the latter with innuendoes. The few kind words he had for Eisenhower led to many harsh ones, the faint praise to indirect condemnation. In past speeches McCarthy had sniped at the President; in this one, as Lippmann said, he declared war. Those close to Eisenhower who, from his campaign trip to Wisconsin on, had advised him to placate the junior senator were now forced to realize that he could not be placated. Unmistakably his purpose was as much to snatch Eisenhower's leadership as to smear Truman's. No less unmistakably, when McCarthy charged the Republican party with breaking its campaign promises by being soft to Communists and added, "It is up to us now to deliver," he was thinking neither of Eisenhower nor his administration but of himself as the one and only deliverer.

How much McCarthy's speech influenced Eisenhower and his advisers in the position they took on Oppenheimer, no outsider has any way of knowing. But in the first days of December, 1953, before the President left for the Bermuda Conference, Strauss (in his capacity of adviser on atomic matters) did confer with him on the problem Oppenheimer might present. Secretary Charles E. Wilson and Arthur S. Flemming, director of the Office of Defense Mobilization, were also at this meeting. Clearly all of them, as was later disclosed, were in a mood to avoid such a problem and all must have seen the political wisdom of the administration's moving against Oppenheimer before McCarthy could do so. At any rate, when Strauss met with the Commission after his talk at the White House, he had instructions from Eisenhower to place "a blank wall" between Oppenheimer and any secret data until a security review of his file had been made.

To this extent Eisenhower was involved in the Oppenheimer case. He had known Oppenheimer. Indeed, Oppenheimer had flown to Paris in December, 1951, to discuss at SHAPE the plan (contained in the Vista Project) for using small atomic weapons for tactical purposes, and Eisenhower had been "particularly interested in the views as to what the developments might be and how they could be employed in his mission." When he issued his "blank wall" order two years later, he could maintain that, as Commander in Chief, he was in a position above politics and had no choice except to guarantee the security of the United States by letting Strauss go ahead, if there were any doubts. Eisenhower did not play a direct part in what followed. He did, however, turn on the green light. Among those who blame him for doing this, and think that Strauss has been overblamed, are some who feel they have not reached too far for an analogy when they point out that the Spanish Inquisition would have been impossible without the consent of Ferdinand and Isabella.

At a press conference held when the Oppenheimer hearing was in its third day, Secretary Wilson said that during the previous July, in order to get rid of Oppenheimer on the Research and Development Board, they "dropped the whole Board." With more candor than felicity the Secretary added, "That was a real smooth way of doing that one as far as the Defense Department was concerned." Eisenhower's "blank wall" order and Strauss's plan to press for a hearing may also have seemed a "real smooth way" of handling Oppenheimer.

Actually, they added still another paradox to the case by proving to be unintentional acts of mercy, since they saved Oppenheimer from McCarthy, the Klieg lights, the cameras, the microphones, and the cruel and tawdry circusdom of a Congressional hearing as conducted by him. In the same paradoxical fashion the Gray Board's and the AEC's decisions against Oppenheimer, however wounding or unjust, turned out to be acts of involuntary kindness. Had the votes been the other way around (two to one on the Board, four to one on the Commission) to clear Oppenheimer, or even if both had been unanimously for him, the probabilities are close to certainties that McCarthy would have tried to take over. If he had, the Joint Committee on Atomic Energy, as the appropriate and responsible Congressional agent, would in all likelihood have acted to protect its prerogatives, and the result would again have been a public hearing, even though one uncontaminated by McCarthy's methods.

"McCarthywasm"

McCarthy had been eying Oppenheimer hungrily for some time. Guessing when he would strike had long been a popular game among insiders in Washington. A threat of his interest, enough to frighten those who lived in the fear of him that chickens feel at the mere sight of the shadow of a hawk, was thundered on the air a week before Oppenheimer first faced the Gray Board. Then, when answering an attack on him broadcast by Edward R. Murrow, McCarthy had cried, "If there were no Communists in our government, why did we delay for eighteen months—delay our research on the hydrogen bomb, even though our intelligence agencies were reporting, day after day, that the Russians were feverishly pushing their development of the hydrogen bomb? Our nation may well die because of that eighteen-month deliberate delay. And I ask who caused it? Was it loyal Americans—or was it traitors in our government?"

On the day the hearing opened McCarthy, who, as the guest of his friend Westbrook Pegler, was in Phoenix, Arizona, recovering from a virus infection, tried to make the best of having had such big game snatched from him. "Oppenheimer's suspension," he told a reporter, "was long overdue—it should have taken place years ago." With condescension as his substitute for praise, he said, "I think it took considerable courage to suspend the so-called untouchable scientist," carefully giving "credit" to Strauss rather than Eisenhower for this courage. At the same time the senator created the impression that the Gray Board hearing was being held not only with his knowledge but with his blessing. He confessed his own investigation of the delay in the H-bomb program had been begun the year before and that he would have taken action himself if he had not "arranged a dinner meeting with two White House aides," who convinced him that "it would not be wise to hold public hearings at that time because of the security measures involved." He also was careful to stress that later he and some other senators received assurances from "top administration officials that this matter would be gone into in detail." In his own mind McCarthy was in the driver's seat. So was he at that moment in the minds of all too many.

That "McCarthyism has become McCarthywasm" is widely repeated nowadays. More than a hope, it is so nearly a fact, at least as far as the senator's domination is concerned, that it is almost impossible to recall why the hope a short two years ago should have been so fervent and seemed so desperate. For the McCarthy who once bullied the country as a Paul Bunyan of bluff and bluster is no more. As a threat, he has shrunk to a minor nuisance of Tom Thumb size and is about as menacing as the blurred recollection of a nightmare.

When the Gray Board in its recommendation spoke of "the present peril," it could have included McCarthy in it. As surely as he contributed to that peril, it was the source of his power. America was afraid, and his public actions were the most frightening form its fear took. The reasons for alarm were obvious enough. In Adlai Stevenson's swift summary they resulted from an unprecedented "coincidence of crises . . . that brought together the flames of war, the atom's unlocking, and the emergence of aggressive Communism that created dangers—at first imperfectly perceived—of insidiously organized disloyalty." These fears, all of them based on realities, were the diet on which McCarthy fed and thrived, and it is not without irony that Oppenheimer was in part responsible for them because of the notable role he played in ushering in the atomic age.

When McCarthy stepped onto a stage in Wheeling, West Virginia, on the 9th of February, 1950, he walked into history, making an entrance very much in character. He is reported to have said that he had in his hand "a list of 205" known Communists who were still working in the State Department. In Denver the next day these "Communists" became "bad security risks," and in Salt Lake City the day after that the 205 dwindled to "57 card-carrying Communists." In other words, the pattern of adjustable statistics was set even at the start of the long and loud campaign which was to follow.

As a new senator, McCarthy had been searching for an issue that would win him attention. In charging the government with harboring Communists he stumbled on one that made him notorious. Though he approached it as a Johnny-come-lately, he struck pay dirt in headlines by choosing a subject which was everyone's concern. The big fish had already been caught. Minnows were to be his catch. Yet one of the triumphs of his technique was to persuade many Americans that he was their dauntless and rather lonely defender against a Communist conspiracy in this country.

Facts were never the preoccupation of either McCarthy or his followers; emotions were, and at arousing these he was a master. Abuse was his weapon, the creation of distrust his questionable service, fright his most effective ammunition. He was one of the greatest headline snatchers in American history. His energy was stupendous, his ingenuity inexhaustible. What he began he seldom finished, because he was frequently racing ahead of yesterday's unproven accusations to make new ones equally unproven. Ridding the government of Communists was his proper objective, but he made even this indecent by employing improper means to achieve it.

During the years that he huffed and puffed to the delight of many and the dread of more, some feared he would blow the house of the United States down. Although "point of order" is a phrase associated with him, he was the high point of America's disorder. Unlike such of our other demagogues as Townsend and Huey Long, who became menaces by trading on poverty and hope, he built his fame by appealing only to fear. Daily he supplied the excitements of the man hunt; daily he provided bad news. But from the point of view of reader interest the fact that he was bad news was good.

McCarthy was no more hampered by consistency than he was by any instinct to be fair. In 1947, before he had hit his stride, he said on the *Town Meeting of the Air,* "I think a tremendous amount of damage has been done by calling a lot of good, serious liberals Communists. The word 'Communism' is such a libelous phrase that I think it should be reserved only for those who should receive that type of defamation." After Wheeling, he turned out such attacks on a gargantuan assembly line. On his lips even the Fifth Amendment (still in the Constitution as a guarantee of rights, regardless of how wrongly used by many witnesses) became a dirty word.

He had skill, intelligence, daring, and a certain genius, this American who could be so like Vishinsky in his tactics. No enemy of

Communism, while attacking it, was ever more adept than he at such tricks, so often employed by Communists, as the multiple untruth, the manipulation of documents, insinuation and innuendo, overstressing the insignificant, or diversionary tactics. By these reprehensible means he traded on justifiable fears which made the years of his ascendancy possible.

He added to these fears by the fear which he himself created. Plenty of Americans were unafraid of McCarthy, some were reeds before his wind, but none were unaware of him. The newspapers, though misled into playing him up until he got beyond their control in the news, were for the most part courageous in berating him editorially. Because of him, schools and colleges suffered most, though our libraries here and particularly abroad, the theatre and the movies, and adult forums for the exchange of ideas also suffered. Teachers who depended upon freedom of inquiry to teach became aware that they were not free to inquire. Most films and plays retreated from controversial themes to the security of subjects that were innocuous.

Discussion sank until it became something to avoid rather than encourage. Conformity or, better still, a protective silence which pretended to be indifference emerged as a guarantee of safety. The old who might have had ideas and the young whose healthy consciences would have expressed themselves in protest became allergic to convictions in the interest of holding jobs or getting them. Apathy was the new golden rule. The average citizen proved his wisdom by not talking out of turn because, as Senator Fulbright said, it had got so that "you could be arrested for unlawful assembly if you stopped to collect your thoughts in public."

The damage McCarthy did to us abroad was, if anything, greater than the consternation he caused at home. So reliable an observer as the late Anne O'Hare McCormick could report that his "grandstand plays for publicity [had] succeeded in making him almost the best known American in the foreign press," a figure used by our enemies as a "scarecrow" to frighten our friends and make them wonder if we were trustworthy as champions of freedom.

Though taken less seriously here, he was taken too seriously for the country's well-being. So powerful was he as a menace that the Army, more than courting his favor, gave in to him to such an extent that at one point the London *Times* commented, "Senator

McCarthy this afternoon achieved what General Burgoyne and General Cornwallis never achieved—the surrender of the American Army." Those in the government, in high places as well as low, were conscious of him, though not all of them by any means were intimidated by him.

Even Eisenhower, as previously noted, had been persuaded by his advisers of the wisdom of making no open break with McCarthy and, when he campaigned with him in Wisconsin, cut from a speech a planned tribute to General Marshall, his close friend and the sponsor of his career, so as not to offend the junior senator who had shamelessly attacked Marshall. In the White House, Eisenhower at first tried to pursue the same policy. This became impossible when McCarthy, in his answer to Murrow, declared war on the President, and later when the senator as a supposed Republican changed his tune during the Army hearings from his familiar "twenty years of treason" to "twenty-one," thus including his own party and its leader in his outrageous charge.

The Gray Board inadvertently saved Oppenheimer from Mc-Carthy. The country was saved from him by a combination of factors. Among these can be counted our regaining as a nation the self-confidence we had temporarily mislaid, Eisenhower's ultimate recognition of the battle the senator had forced on him, the Senate's motion to condemn McCarthy, and television, which day after day showed McCarthy for what he was and how he operated, and finally did to him the damage it does to all comedians who appear on it too often. We are a people easily bored; a good thing at times, too, because as a cure for excesses boredom can be the most potent of wonder drugs. America became fed up with this badgerer who got too big for his own breeches and was too small for Uncle Sam's. Yet it was in the smog of fear McCarthy had created that the Oppenheimer hearing was held.

An Opinion That Exploded

As far as the case is concerned, the senator was a potential rather than an actual antagonist. There were many others eager to attack Oppenheimer and mobilized against him, among whom were politicians not of the species found on the Hill but of the equally adept variety that swarms in the Pentagon. As a lobbyist, Oppenheimer is widely reported to have been no amateur himself.

Many insist he was among the most adroit molders of opinion on the national scene.

That physically he bore no resemblance to the cartoonist's notion of a politician, that intellectually he abhorred the obviousness of their methods, and that in his frail person he seemed the embodiment of pure science, almost an idea rather than a mortal, only made him the more effective as the champion of a cause. Few have heard him lecture or talk at a board meeting, few have seen him on television, and hardly anyone has written about him without being forced to fall back in resentment or approval on such words as "mesmerizing" or "mesmerist" to describe the impact of his personality, the conquering charm that is his when he wishes to release it, the aura of sagelike wisdom he creates, and his incredible eloquence, mystical in its feeling yet precise in its phrasing, as he says things easy to listen to but hard to remember.

The pressure Oppenheimer exerted on government circles was the harder to combat not only because he was a brilliant technician speaking, for the most part, to those without technical knowledge, but because his opponents claim that to win a point he often ignored the disciplines of the chain of command. He worked quietly, not noisily, and some swear with a subtlety that was hard to combat. He could "pull science" as easily as a general or an admiral can pull rank, and he could not have been unaware of the advantage he enjoyed by being able to do so. More than a teacher who had placed admiring and grateful pupils, he was recognized by many scientists as the leader of a school and, as such, had disciples where his opponents had defenders. His influence was so formidable that, in spite of his way with words, he did not have to speak to achieve the results he desired; he had only to keep silent.

Dr. Smyth of the AEC noted in his minority report that over several years the professional check on Oppenheimer's actions was "supplemented by enthusiastic amateur help from powerful personal enemies." Though such behavior is a sorry comment on human nature, Oppenheimer's having enemies was inevitable. A formidable opponent himself, a man of strength, he was bound with his uncompromising superiority of intellect, and with the great power which he did not hesitate to exert, to win more than friends in Washington.

To interfere with military plans as a civilian, to back measures which subtract from the authority of a department, or to champion a theory which will result in a reduced appropriation is not to ask for trouble in the capital but to be a mendicant for misfortune. Oppenheimer did all of these things and, as the Alsops observed,[1] one of the outstanding features of his story was the "cool courage" he showed "in challenging the greatest power groups of the government with [the] knowledge of his own vulnerability always in his mind."

Intellectual humility was not one of Oppenheimer's restraints. He knew he knew, and did not always bother to mask this knowledge, though plenty contended hotly that he thought he knew more than he did. He was not alone among scientists in laying himself open to such criticism. A common complaint against them, all-important as they have become in the new and terrifying age they brought into being, has been that, since they are masters of a mysterious wisdom, they think they are wise in all things.

The question of how far a specialist should depart from his specialty and try to shape policy outside of his area is a real one which the Gray Board recognized. It was not a question that troubled Oppenheimer. He had not asked to work on the A-bomb or to concentrate all his gifts and energies on war and destruction. The government had sought his services in a period of acute emergency. Once the new weapon was created which contributed notably to resolving that emergency, he no doubt felt that the same knowledge which aided him in the creation of this weapon made him an authority on its use. As a theoretical physicist, he did not shrink from having theories about the basic concept of our national strategy. Inevitably this antagonized those, in or out of uniform, who were responsible for our military planning when he opposed or endangered their concepts.

The Soviets detonated their first A-bomb in September, 1949, but the biggest explosion caused by that bomb occurred in Washington. In Moscow Russia's bomb was a threat of future war; in Washington it was the beginning of a fierce battle within the government. In time the person most hurt by that Soviet A-bomb was Oppenheimer, the producer of our own. That it should almost destroy him by the decision it forced on him and the struggle in

[1] *We Accuse! The Story of the Miscarriage of American Justice in the Case of J. Robert Oppenheimer*, by Joseph and Stewart Alsop, New York, Simon and Schuster, 1954.

which it embroiled him is one more irony in his career. Still another is that we learned of this Soviet bomb only because of Strauss. Fortunately, he had had the foresight, in spite of the indifference of the Defense Department and the AEC, to insist on a detection system, which had just been installed when the explosion took place.

Prior to that explosion America had been complacent in its confidence that it had, and would have for several years to come, a monopoly of atomic power. Oppenheimer along with the vast majority had been overoptimistic in thinking it would take the Russians longer than it did to catch up with us. After "Joe I" our complacency was shattered, the whole picture was changed, and an appalling new national emergency created. The question thrust upon us was how we could regain our lost supremacy.

The answer to many was an all-out attempt to produce an H-bomb, a project upon which Teller had been experimenting on a modest scale since 1942. Among Teller's early converts to such a crash program were Strauss and Senator McMahon. Although the AEC was indifferent to this idea and its chairman, David Lilienthal, opposed it, Strauss had requested that a meeting of the General Advisory Committee be called to consider the problem presented by the Russians' having the A-bomb.

When Oppenheimer presided over the historic sessions which opened on October 29, 1949, he, like his fellow members, had his technical objections to the new bomb. He did not doubt such a bomb would be developed in time, but he believed it was still "a weapon of unknown design, cost, deliverability, and military value." His conviction was that the plans which Teller then presented were not sufficiently advanced to justify committing us to an uncertain program at the expense of building up and diversifying our proven atomic weapons.

Like most of his eminent associates on the committee, Oppenheimer also had his ethical objections. Like them he was distressed at the idea of America's taking the lead in creating still more terrible means of destroying cities and civilizations. This distress was "part of the freight" he took with him into these meetings. His moral concern was deep and understandable, and shared by other scientists who had helped to make the A-bomb possible. The responsibility they felt was "peculiarly intimate." As he had said two years before at the Massachusetts Institute of Technology, "In some sort of crude sense which no vulgarity, no humor, no overstatement can quite extinguish, the physicists have known sin; and this is a knowledge which they cannot lose."

Although Strauss apparently had expected that the GAC would not favor the H-bomb program, he is reported to have been surprised and irritated to have the vote against it unanimous among those present. Senator McMahon was "disgusted" with the outcome. The two were not alone in being unhappy but determined. The minority forces which favored giving the thermonuclear experiment a high priority were, in spite of a temporary setback, already on the march. These included Teller and other prominent scientists, and military and governmental figures of prominence. Among the champions of such a program, working for it as a stage manager, was William Liscum Borden, the executive director of the Joint Congressional Committee on Atomic Energy, who was later to send J. Edgar Hoover the letter which initiated the proceedings against Oppenheimer.

Even as a dubious possibility, the hydrogen bomb had divided military, scientific, and governmental Washington into Montagues and Capulets. They were then indulging only in thumb-biting at their opponents. The real, the wounding clashes lay ahead. Without being aware of it, by taking the adverse stand he did in 1949 Oppenheimer had given in all good faith what was to prove the costliest advice he ever gave. He was to be cruelly penalized for it, his career almost blighted, his life changed, and humiliation and agony heaped upon him.

News as upsetting in its way as that the Russians had exploded an A-bomb caused a GAC meeting to be held in Washington on the 30th of the following January. Three days before, high officials had learned to their consternation that Klaus Fuchs, a member of the British Mission at Los Alamos, had confessed to handing over atomic secrets to the Soviets. The GAC was asked how much Fuchs knew, and by the meeting's end it became frighteningly clear that he knew far too much. The aid he could have given the Russians did not stop with atomic secrets. Fuchs had also attended a revealing seminar on the H-bomb at Los Alamos in 1945. Regardless of how other members of the AEC felt, this was enough to convince Strauss that he had been right in wanting our H-bomb program accelerated. It was enough for Truman, too. The next day, with the support of Dean Acheson and Louis Johnson, he issued his order for a crash program to produce the superbomb.

In the light of subsequent events this was the right, the realistic, the inevitable answer, however regrettable. As Truman summed it up beforehand with incisive simplicity, "Can the Russians make this thing? And if so, how can we help making it?" Oppenheimer himself, because of these events, later admitted he thought that the GAC's negative recommendation had been a mistake, though he continued to have his misgivings about the plans for the bomb until June, 1951, when Teller proved by a "brilliant" new invention that he had conquered the thermonuclear problem. Oppenheimer, according to Teller, then said that if anything of this kind had been suggested right away he never would have opposed it.

The H-bomb program had been a long time getting under way. But this delay was generally forgotten the next year when, on November 16, a fortnight after the test at Eniwetok, America learned to its intense relief that it had regained its supremacy in destructive weapons. Both the supremacy and the relief were short-lived. Nine months later, on August 8, 1953, Malenkov in a speech to the Supreme Soviet announced that "the United States of America has long since ceased to have the monopoly in the matter of the production of atomic bombs. . . . The Soviet government deems it necessary to report that the United States has no monopoly in the production of the hydrogen bomb either."

By the time we learned of this lost monopoly and realized the short while the advantage had been ours, the temper of America had changed drastically. The fever of McCarthyism was raging, the unpopular and draining Korean war had dragged on to an inconclusive truce just signed, Red China was becoming an ever-increasing menace, war with the Soviets seemed a dismal probability, and talk was not of doom but of a new doomsday. In Bertrand Russell's phrase it appeared more and more difficult to persuade man to acquiesce in his own survival.

Three months after Malenkov's announcement Borden sent his letter; four and a half months after that announcement Oppenheimer was called to Washington by Strauss and shown a draft of Nichols's letter. When the GAC had opposed a crash program for the H-bomb, no one had questioned the patriotism of the committee. Its recommendation, right or wrong, was accepted as an honest one, even by those who disagreed with it. But, four years later, things were very different not only in the world but in the world in Washington that Oppenheimer touched. He had had time to make new enemies, and his old ones had had time to move against him. His influence continued just as he, the civilian-scientist, continued to invite trouble by being duty bound to have opinions on military matters.

Before the Soviets exploded their A-bomb, his fear had been that we were relying too much in our over-all planning on the monopoly we then had and on the atomic striking power of the Strategic Air Command. As early as 1948 he saw clearly that, while we must be ready "to engage in total war" and "to carry the war to the enemy and attempt to destroy him," we must also be "prepared in planning, in logistics, and in development for more than one kind of war." In the same way he had been troubled in 1949 by the likelihood that we would depend too much on the new monopoly the H-bomb would give us. In advance of the GAC meeting, he wrote Conant, he was afraid that the H-bomb, if and when developed, would "even further . . . worsen the unbalance of our present war plans" by persuading us to depend all the more on one kind of weapon, one branch of the service, and one kind of warfare.

Within the next two years he became the more concerned that we were overstressing our offensive strength and underplaying our defensive needs. In his opinion the defense of the capitals and factories of our European allies was as neglected as that of our own cities and industries. Furthermore, he could not bring himself to believe, if we struck at the Soviets first or waited to make a retaliatory air attack on them, that a modern war would stop there. He still thought, in spite of the enormous strategic and tactical importance of aviation, that the air was not all and that ground forces should have atomic weapons of their own.

When in 1951 he submitted to NATO in Paris the Vista report, in which it was suggested that we divide our stock pile of atomic weapons roughly into three parts—one to be held in reserve, one assigned to the Strategic Air Command, and the third to the tactical defense of Europe—Oppenheimer may have won the interest of such Army men as Eisenhower and Gruenther, but he could scarcely be accused of courting the favor of the Air Force and particularly the SAC. Knowing Washington and its jealousies well, Oppenheimer was almost certain this recommendation would not be accepted in full, though he did think it was "in a healthy direction."

He was aware that the SAC had fought a hard and long battle to acquire and retain a monopoly of our atomic stock pile. What he proposed, more than being a radical divergence from existing policy, was a serious threat to established power. The opposition Oppenheimer had anticipated soon showed itself. The SAC and many high officials in the Air Force combined to bury the recommendation, but they did not forget it or Oppenheimer's part in it. The next year he worked with the Lincoln Summer Study Group that favored an elaborate continental defense system which would also have threatened the SAC. By cosponsoring such a plan Oppenheimer gained no new friends among those dedicated to strategic bombing.

His enemies, evidently considering that war between him and them had been declared, were neither slow to attack nor unskilled in taking the offensive. The ammunition they used was largely blank, but in their hands it seemed live and did almost the same damage. Because his thinking threatened what was dear to them, they answered by imperiling him.

If political stresses in Washington and the sudden unhappy turn in the arms race with Russia played into their hands, so did Oppenheimer by his unshakable independence. In Edward Teller they had found the means they needed to combat him—another genius. Because of Teller they were able to fight science with science. Forgetting Oppenheimer's contribution to the A-bomb, they concentrated on Teller's contribution to the H-bomb. In spite of creating dangerous divisions in the ranks of our scientists, they encouraged these divisions. Teller became not only their hero but their spearhead, and they rallied around him even as he had turned to them for help in getting his thermonuclear program started. An article in *Fortune* of May, 1953, pointed the way the wind was blowing by presenting the case for Teller in such a way that it seemed to be a case against Oppenheimer.

Alone among the members of the GAC who had opposed a crash H-bomb program in 1949, Oppenheimer came to have his vote held against him as a punishable offense. In the witch-hunting days of the early fifties the easiest way to cast doubts on his opinions was to raise suspicions about his loyalty. If Russia's interests had really been Oppenheimer's, as Borden concluded that they were when he charged him with being "more probably than not" a Soviet agent, one would think that Oppenheimer would not have waited to oppose a crash program for the H-bomb. He would have seen to it that the A-bomb's development was delayed so that the Soviets, who got into the war in the Pacific only one day before Nagasaki and six days before V-J Day, would have had time to contribute substantially to victory in that theatre and hence would have been entitled to make greedier grabs after Japan's surrender.

But battle slogans do not depend on logic for their appeal, and *Fortune* accurately described what was happening in Washington as "a life-and-death struggle over national military policy." To create the impression that everybody against Oppenheimer resorted to rumor to destroy him would be to tell a lie. There were plenty lined up against him who, without denying his patriotism, thought that he had outlasted his usefulness, resented his influence, disliked his temperament, and, since they believed strongly they were right, felt that he must be wrong and therefore ought to go.

Nonetheless there were some, like Borden, sincere in their fanaticism, and others, for whom this was a convenient way of getting rid of him, who began to reconsider Oppenheimer's record and question it. His old Communist associations made him an easy target, he knew as well as they. Starting with this advantage, they sought to impose a damaging pattern on his whole career by combining innocent single instances from his recent past with his earlier activities. In this way they achieved a sinister design which to them justified their opposition to Oppenheimer and explained his attitude both toward the H-bomb and the SAC.

Among the least reluctant to dispense with him was Strauss, considered by many the chief architect of Oppenheimer's undoing. When Strauss confronted Oppenheimer with Nichols's letter, he had much more power than he commanded as an early and fierce defender of Teller and the H-bomb. In 1949 and until the next year, when he resigned from the AEC, Strauss had been only one of the commissioners. In 1953 under Eisenhower he doubled in brass, as it were, being both chairman of the Commission and the President's adviser on atomic matters. That he and Oppenheimer had no fondness for each other was not a secret. The differences between them at the time of the hearing were many and fundamental, but none was more important than that Strauss then occupied a position of greater authority.

The Hearing as Drama

The animosities Oppenheimer ignited, counterbalanced by the friendships he inspired, add to the fascination of the 992-page volume, printed by the government in retina-detaching type, which is known as *In the Matter of J. Robert Oppenheimer*. The recommendations sent by the Gray Board and General Nichols to the AEC and the Commission's final decision with its withering language are not included in this monumental transcript of the hearing. They came later. Missing, too, are the briefs which Oppenheimer's counsel filed with the Board and the Commission. Even so, there is far more than enough in this volume to make it one of the most remarkable publications of its year, an invaluable source book of American history, and a commentary on our time unsurpassed in its tragic and irresistible interest.

Though it has its unavoidable interludes of dullness, for the most part it is engrossing. Reading it, rereading it, and living with its complexities, more than being a job, is almost a profession. But it has its rewards. For *In the Matter of* (to give it a title) does not have to resort to fiction for suspense or contrived drama for conflict. For plot and counterplot, for a theme which involves individuals by concerning a nation, and for characters, weak or strong, likable or repugnant, large or small, with their agonies and confusions, their decisions and indecisions, their follies and their wisdom revealed by the test of events, it has only to rely on reality.

As the bookish have pointed out, it is as long as *Gone With the Wind* or *War and Peace*. It includes as many characters, seen or unseen, as they do, or as *Remembrance of Things Past*, or as can be found in the wide stretches of Balzac's *Comédie Humaine*. Yet, lengthy and unwieldy as it is, it also brings the stage to mind. It has the cumulative tension of such a play as *The Caine Mutiny Court Martial*, the taut interest of the theatre's better trial scenes, and, if *In the Matter of* were not a tragedy, it could at times claim the excitement of a courtroom melodrama.

It needs no help from scenery to be dramatic, and it got none.

The hearing was held in Room 2022 in Building T-3 of the Atomic Energy Commission, one of those dreary structures which, though meant to be temporary when built for the Navy in World War I, have proved lasting. The room itself was an office, not large, not impressive, and properly bureaucratic in being without individuality. Like kitchen silver, it had only usefulness to recommend it. Yet those present do say that, with the Board seated at a table at one end, with Oppenheimer or whoever was testifying at the other, and opposing counsel at facing tables along the walls in between, it did create a sense of confrontation. As a setting, however, it was undesigned, except for the chance mockery of having the windows behind Roger Robb its one source of natural light.

By common consent drama, even the slightest comedy with its tempests scaled to teapot dimensions, is conflict. The tempest that raged in this smallish room for the almost four weeks of the hearing was many conflicts, and the tempest not one but a bewildering accumulation of many sullen storms. Some of these conflicts, forced at last into the open, were petty, others noble or mean, but all involved large issues since they centered not only on one man's fate but on the essentials of our survival as a free people.

Bitter as the struggle was between professional or personal antagonists, between scientific camps or great governmental agencies, one of the fiercest fights was the battle which individual after individual had plainly fought within himself. The final fascination of this transcript, which can be read like a script, is the insights it provides into the hearts and minds of men whose words, without their being aware of it or wishing it, at moments beyond prediction disclose their innermost selves as fully as if the secrets of the confessional had been violated. What good dialogue does by design, their speech does by hazard. They are characters self-delineated and self-betrayed.

Take the members of the Personnel Security or Gray Board, for example. They were high-minded citizens, distinguished in their professions, who at true inconvenience to themselves performed a difficult and thankless public service. Although there were three of them, in the transcript there might as well have been only two because Thomas A. Morgan, ex-president of the Sperry Gyroscope Company and admired by those who have served with him on the boards of many large corporations, appears to have taken the vow of silence. He gives his name to the majority recommendation against Oppenheimer, and may have given the Board the benefit of his advice at their secret sessions, but his resolute muteness gives no hint of the quality of his mind or what is going on in it. He is absent, though present, and when at one point Gray asks him, "Is that correct?" and he answers, "That is correct," it comes as a great relief to learn that he can speak.

If Morgan remains by choice a cipher throughout *In the Matter of*, Dr. Ward V. Evans leaps by nature from its pages very much alive. An outstanding chemist, now at Loyola and until his retirement on the faculty of Northwestern, he establishes himself as an idiosyncratic figure, gruff though kindly, with a broadsword of a mind. His thinking does not show its deep cutting power until he writes his dissent. Then he knocks beclouding subtleties and legal trickeries aside and stabs straight to the heart of the case. Twice in his dissent he uses the phrase "we don't have to go out of our way" to make a point, and he never does. No one has been more concise in showing up the charges against Oppenheimer or presenting the reasons for his clearance.

The jabbing directness of Dr. Evans's dissent comes as a surprise, for in the transcript his questions are irrelevant or rudderless, and there is something about him of the character actor at work. Partly, one suspects, this is because as a veteran professor he knows the value on a campus of being different, but mainly it is because as a person he *is* different. He turns eccentricity into an asset by making it an honest and endearing expression of nonconformity. His sincerity is intense and unmistakable, and he a man profoundly troubled as he considers his task and the criteria which bind the Board as the three figures in the Laocoön group were bound by the serpents.

Without disclosing his sympathies, he several times makes plain his distress and never more clearly than when he says, "This is not a job that any of us sought. . . . We didn't want it . . . I don't want it today. We all know Dr. Oppenheimer's ability. Nobody knows better than I do. This act mentions certain things—character, associations, and loyalty. It doesn't say anything about ability which is mentioned here so much. Perhaps the act ought to be rewritten. I don't know. I just want you to understand the position we are in. It is not a pleasant position."

Gordon Gray was no happier and his fondness for the criteria no greater. As chairman, he had an assignment frightening in its responsibility, heavy in its difficulties, and full of pitfalls. Widely respected, the chancellor of North Carolina University, an intelligent and thoughtful man who had graduated from the Yale Law School, published newspapers, been Secretary of the Army and a special assistant to Truman, he seemed in advance an ideal choice. That he meant well is clear, that he did well another matter. His ignorance of Malraux's place in literature and his unawareness that Malraux, long since disenchanted with Communism, had become one of the most anti-Communist of De Gaulle's close associates only show how strange the gaps can be in the education of any educated person.

The dignity of Gray's spirit is real and makes itself felt again and again in the transcript with the same balance and sensitivity that distinguish the regretful pages of the Board's negative findings. Yet, if he has the liberal's strength, which is genuine moderation, Gray also is the victim of the liberal's self-destroying weakness, an excess of tolerance. He emerges as gentle rather than forceful, meticulous instead of bright, and more patient than penetrating. A diligent observer of trees, he does not seem to see the forest. He is a perfect front man but inadequate and spotty as a performer, setting a model for the entire hearing in his questioning of Oppenheimer and then permitting others to behave, and occasionally behaving himself, as if he were unaware of the model he had set.

Almost at once it is plain in *In the Matter of* that something has gone wrong and that, though Gray thinks he is doing one thing which his high-mindedness tells him he should do, he is doing another which is neither his wish nor in accord with his frequently stated ideal of what he ought to do. In no time the sound of a dropped monkey wrench is heard, and one becomes aware that it is through Roger Robb's fingers that the wrench has been allowed to slip, not in spite of Gray's protests but with his bewildered approval.

Robb's concept of his role as the AEC's counsel is in direct opposition to Gray's desire to conduct the hearing as an inquiry rather than a trial. The adversary tactics used in a murder case to win a conviction are alien to a hearing such as Oppenheimer's, which was an inquiry. A hearing of this kind employs the inquisitorial process, which, instead of having any relation to the Inquisition, has only investigation as its purpose. Robb's tactics were adversary through-out and he was the prosecutor, brilliant, resourceful, and merciless, with the manner of a man more intent upon springing the trap than discovering the truth. Whenever Gray weakens or is indecisive, Robb moves in and, if possible, takes over by default. Such are the strength and aggressiveness of this courtroom duelist, who had grad-uated from Yale in 1928 and later from its Law School, who had long practiced in Washington, and knew his way around in a Congressional investigating committee, that he often imposes his will on Gray and the Board without their seeming to be aware of it, and all too frequently he turns the inquiry into a trial.

Robb versus Garrison

The prosecutor's by obligation is a special mind, mon-goose-quick, bullying, devious, unrelenting, and forever baited to ensnare. It is almost duty bound to mislead, and by instinct dotes on confusing and flourishes on weakness. Its search is for blemishes it can present as scars, its obligation to raise doubts or sour with suspicion. It asks questions not to learn but to convict, and can read guilt into the most innocent answers. Its hope, its aim, its triumph is to addle a witness into confession by tricking, exhausting, or irritating him into a verbal indiscretion which sounds like a damaging admission. To natural lapses of memory it gives the appearance either of stratagems for hiding misdeeds or, worse still, of lies, dark and deliberate. Feigned and wheedling politeness, sarcasm that scalds, intimidation, surprise, and besmirchment by innuendo, association, or suggestion, at the same time that any intention to besmirch is denied—all these as methods and devices are such staples in the prosecutor's repertory that his mind turns to them by rote. To all of these Robb resorted.

Lawyers, connoisseurs in such things, differ in their estimates of his handling of the case. Some describe it as able, others as routine district attorney stuff. To the layman, however, even if he abhors it, Robb's performance seems dazzling. His mastery (files or no files) of a hugely complicated case is extraordinary, his vigilance unflag-ging, and his an agile mind which is tirelessly at work, questioning with a remorselessness more like the drive of a pneumatic drill than the drumming of a woodpecker.

The manner in which Robb operates at the hearing may perhaps best be suggested by recalling a speech he delivered at Amherst nearly a year after the hearing was over. There, when speaking about security in general and Oppenheimer in particular, he said, "Security is not new, it is as old as our government. You will recall that George Washington had security difficulties with one of his best and most trusted generals—Benedict Arnold." Eight paragraphs later, with the bad seed carefully planted, Robb referred again to Benedict Arnold, this time as a man whose downfall had been brought about by two things, "his lack of character," and "the blandishments of the fellow travelers of his day, the Tories." In the next sentence Robb was quick to add, "Lest anyone misunderstand me, let me make it plain that I am using Arnold merely as an illustration; I am *not* comparing him to Dr. Oppenheimer." But the damage had been painstakingly done.

It is precisely this soiling, squidlike technique with which Robb concludes his cross-examination of so pre-eminent a contributor to the theory of thermonuclear fusion as the German-born Dr. Hans Bethe, whose faith in Oppenheimer's loyalty is "absolute." Robb: "Doctor, how many divisions were there at Los Alamos?" Bethe: "It changed somewhat in the course of time. As far as I could count the other day, there were seven, but there may have been eight or nine at some time." Robb: "Which division was Klaus Fuchs in?" Bethe: "He was in my division, which was the Theoretical Division." Robb: "Thank you. That is all."

Those who heard him report that the word "doctor," as Robb said it sneeringly when addressing Oppenheimer, became almost a term of disparagement. Those who read him in *In the Matter of* are forced to suspect that he has no liking for intellectuals and to know that as an interrogator he is thwarted neither by civility nor awe. He can be snide as when he says to Oppenheimer, "You attempted to establish your whereabouts and with the assistance of counsel had found you were in New Mexico, is that correct?" He can be insulting as when he asks Colonel John Lansdale, Jr., "You would not say that lying was one of the manifestations of the scientific mind, would you?" He can be threatening as when, after trying to get Oppenheimer to deny some completely forgotten detail in a conversation of almost eleven years before, he says, "Doctor, for your information, I might say we have a record of your voice." And he can be tasteless as when he turns to Teller with, "In your opinion, if Dr. Oppenheimer should go fishing for the rest of his life what would the effect be on the atomic energy and thermonuclear programs?"

Such samples are not ingratiating. Yet it is absurd and unfair to be too horrified at Robb's tactics and to condemn them as improper when they are the stock in trade of many prosecutors. Robb is playing the prosecutor's part and playing it with vigor. The real impropriety is Gray's for permitting him to play it at all; Gray's because, though he knew and believed "the purpose of the inquiry is not entrapment," he allows himself, along with Oppenheimer and many of the witnesses, to be entrapped by Robb again and again.

Oppenheimer's counsel, Lloyd K. Garrison, was at first unprepared for Robb's technique, due not to lack of knowledge of how the prosecutor works by convention but to a correct assumption that such a technique was out of place in a hearing of this sort. The surprise felt by his able cocounsel, Herbert S. Marks, Samuel J. Silverman and Allan B. Ecker, at the tactics permitted soon manifests itself, and later turns to understandable distress. In his opening statement Garrison touches upon a major source of future difficulties. In front of the Board was a large file, the Pandora's box of the hearing. To it by existing FBI rules Oppenheimer's lawyers had had, and were permitted to have, no access, but from it for a week Robb had been briefing the Board. Garrison was confident that, in spite of the knowledge thus gained which was unavailable to him and his associates, the members would receive with open minds the testimony he submitted to them.

What Garrison in his decency did not foresee was the uses to which Robb would put the file, how he would suddenly declassify at the moment of cross-examination materials which until then had been classified, how he would read from transcripts without providing Oppenheimer's lawyers with a copy which they could follow, and how he would use fragments from documents to startle and confuse witnesses or create the appearance of conflicts in their testimony when they had no way of refreshing their memories about forgotten details from the past. Early in the hearing Garrison was to rise, and often thereafter, though always calmly and courteously, to protest such a mockery of justice in the name of safeguarding freedom. Every time he and his associates did so, as Diana Trilling [2] observed, "they were made to seem unfriendly, even petulant and unreasonable," and were reminded "repeatedly and humiliatingly . . . of the many courtesies to which they were responding with an insufficient gratitude."

At the end of the long four weeks Oppenheimer and Garrison, with the conviction of children "making company manners," did thank the Board, and wisely too since it had not voted. Oppenheimer, with customary precision, qualified his gratitude by saying he hoped he was "properly appreciative of the patience and consideration" shown him. Garrison, with his politeness perhaps tinctured with irony, also expressed his appreciation of the Board's "having borne so patiently" with him and for its "great consideration." In its finding the Board noted proudly Oppenheimer's approval, adding "courteous" to "consideration," no doubt out of hope or misunderstanding. It mentioned Garrison's praise, too, converting his "patiently" and "great consideration" into "fairness." But Oppenheimer knew better. So did Garrison, who, with marvelous moderation in the brief he filed with Strauss and the AEC, called attention to the "disturbing aspects" of the hearing. He also pointed out that "had this in fact been recognized as an adversary case, procedures would have been open to us to secure documents which were used in cross-examination (except perhaps a very few which were classified and remained classified)."

That Garrison did not anticipate Robb's methods is not surprising. It would have been surprising if he had because, as *In the Matter of* makes unmistakable, he and Robb are not only opposing counsel, they are opposites in almost every way. In his photographs Robb looks the shrewd trial lawyer. His is an astute face, foxlike, more given to calculation than contemplation, rooted in the present, thin-lipped, and with eyes which, though sharp, would never see visions. Garrison, on the other hand, has the appearance of a statesman. His face, with its phosphorescent, tender dark eyes, its broad, giving mouth, its faun ears, its spread of chin and height of forehead, has nobility and reflects spaciousness of mind and spirit. It has a portraitlike quality, suggesting a Romney or a Raeburn. But, though it could come from the past, it is decidedly forward-looking.

[2] "The Oppenheimer Case: A Reading of the Testimony," by Diana Trilling, *Partisan Review*, November–December, 1954.

Such differences, written in their faces, are no less marked in the behavior of the two men during the hearing. Both are able but in ways which, instead of having anything in common, are constantly in contrast. Where Robb is smart, ingenious, and driving, Garrison is thoughtful, straightforward, and patient. The one scores by discarding courtesy, the other by maintaining manners. Robb can be angered, Garrison outraged. The chill severity of the former is matched by the warm tolerance of the latter. Robb's concern is making a point, Garrison's guarding a principle. Once when Oppenheimer is on the stand and Garrison complains about Robb's handling of him by saying, "I think he ought to try as much as possible not to put words into the witness's mouth," Robb's answer, given as an explanation, is "I am cross-examining him."

Garrison's record is an indication of the pitch of mind which he brought to the trial and which compelled him to give his services. A great-grandson of the abolitionist William Lloyd Garrison, a graduate of Harvard (1919), for ten years dean of Wisconsin's Law School, chairman of the War Labor Board, a past president of the National Urban League, a former overseer of Harvard, a trustee of Sarah Lawrence College, Howard University, and, since 1953, of the Institute for Advanced Study in Princeton, he is an intellectual, widely read, interested in education, generous in his thinking, and passionate in his decency, with the kind of conscience that rises to a cause.

Some have contended that Oppenheimer would have been better served had Garrison hit harder and combated Robb's adversary methods by adopting them himself. Had he tried to use them, had he by temperament been equipped to do so, it seems certain that he would only have antagonized the Board. There is no lack of strength in Garrison's conduct of the defense. Instead, there is a sturdy majesty which is impressive. Taken off guard at the start and at a disadvantage throughout because of the documents denied him, he remains unperturbed by the Board's polite hostility and unrattled by Robb. He gains his procedural points with quiet force and in his summation speaks with moving eloquence.

The hearing owes him much. A layman who feels this strongly is encouraged to have his impression backed by the judgment of so knowledgeable a lawyer as Charles P. Curtis. In his admirable legal

analysis [3] of the case, Curtis says, "Garrison's unswerving service
to an inquiry helped rather than hurt his client's cause. It was good
strategy against Robb's bad tactics. . . . Robb's trial tactics very
nearly turned the proceedings into a criminal trial. The Board could
have prevented it, but the Board owes its survival as an inquiry to
Garrison."

"The New Men"

In spite of its disquieting dips, the hearing has its admirable stretches when wise and fine and fearless things are said.
At its best when strong minds are beyond confusing, as it is worst
when small jealousies are beyond hiding, it never loses its one
consistency—the ceaseless disclosure of character.

The cast of *In the Matter of* is not only large; it is star-studded.
Not counting Oppenheimer, thirty-nine witnesses take the stand.
Of these by far the more distinguished are the thirty-one who volun-
teer to testify for Oppenheimer. They represent a considerable raid
on *Who's Who in America*, including as they do such leaders in
government, business, education, and science as Gordon Dean,
David Lilienthal, John J. McCloy, Sumner T. Pike, Hartley Rowe,
Mervin J. Kelly, George F. Kennan, James B. Conant, Vannevar
Bush, K. T. Compton, Enrico Fermi, Lee A. DuBridge, Jerrold R.
Zacharias, Hans Bethe, and I. I. Rabi. Though their voices are very
different, they all sing one song and sing it lustily when it comes to
the value of Oppenheimer's contribution, their belief in his loyalty,
and their denial of his being a security risk.

"We speak of ourselves every time we have not the strength to
remain silent," wrote Anatole France. All these witnesses, for or
against Oppenheimer, speak volumes about themselves when they
summon their strength (and the strength of many of them is great)
to speak about Oppenheimer. They reveal themselves the more
fully because each has been assured by Gray that what he says is
"confidential" between him and the AEC. It would have remained
so had not Strauss suddenly decided to make it public. He would
have rushed the transcript into print without informing Oppen-

[3] *The Oppenheimer Case, The Trial of a Security System,* by Charles P.
Curtis, New York, Simon and Schuster, 1955.

heimer, had not McCloy refused to release his testimony unless
Oppenheimer were notified.

Conant, an intrepid man, broad-gauged of spirit, all mind and
spine, and as New England as Plymouth Rock, may seem exact to
the point of caution, yet he stands firm by the letter he wrote in
1947 at Lilienthal's request in which he said, "I had no knowledge
of Dr. Oppenheimer previous to the summer of 1941, but I say
unhesitatingly that whatever the record might show as to his
political sympathies at that time or his associations, I would not
deviate from my present opinion, namely, that a more loyal
and sound American citizen cannot be found in the whole United
States."

Is Vannevar Bush too explosive to be a prudent witness? As a foil
to Conant he is excellent and, it seems to me, excellent in his own
right too. Surely it would be a poor world inhabited by a poorer
breed that had no indignation in it, and, after all, righteous indignation has Biblical sanction. There is something heartening and
splendid about Bush when, finding his principles threatened, he
roars like a wounded bear, "I think this Board or no board should
ever sit on a question in this country of whether a man should serve
his country or not because he expressed strong opinions. If you want
to try that case, you can try me. I have expressed strong opinions
many times, and I intend to do so. They have been unpopular
opinions at times. When a man is pilloried for doing that, this
country is in a severe state."

The folk image, the cracker-barrel touch, the family phrase that
belongs to the hearth is always dear to Americans. In *In the Matter
of*, with all its technical military terms, its blur of code names
(Charles, Vista, Super, The Maniac, etc.), and its new vocabulary
for a new age (tritium, bevatron, meson, megaton, implosion
weapon, linear accelerator, and the befuddling rest), it is with joy
that one finds such a scientist as Dr. Rabi, Oppenheimer's successor
as chairman of the GAC, stating his belief in Oppenheimer's patriotism by saying, "I am in possession of long experience with this
man, going back to 1929, and there is a kind of seat of the pants
feeling [on] which I myself lay great weight." What exactly such a
feeling is we may not know, yet we understand it and somehow

think we have grown up with it. It is as humanizing as learning from Oppenheimer that Gregory Breit, in charge of the work on "fast fission" in Chicago after Pearl Harbor, had the wonderful code name of "Coordinator of Rapid Rupture."

Of the eight witnesses to testify against Oppenheimer, one is Borden; one is Colonel Boris T. Pash, a conscientious security officer rightly trained to think in Alfred Hitchcock terms, who had met Oppenheimer only once and long considered him a security risk; two are devoutly air-minded men who distrust Oppenheimer because his ideas run counter to the policies and dreams of the Air Force; and three are scientists from Berkeley who, apparently on the basis that anyone who likes tea must hate coffee, are in varying degrees opposed to Oppenheimer because they feel he has opposed Teller. The eighth, and by far the most important and no doubt the most distressed, is Edward Teller himself.

Of the two air-minded witnesses Major General Roscoe C. Wilson, former commandant of the Air War College and by his own admission "first of all a big-bomb man," is the more interesting. His right to his opinions and his honesty are evident, though both seem irrelevant if only because it is not Oppenheimer's loyalty to the United States he questions but his lack of loyalty to the Air Force program. Hell hath no fury greater than a woman scorned except that of the partisan of a government agency who thinks his department is being slighted. When General Wilson talks, as the Alsops say, he sounds almost like an aroused institution. In fairness, however, it must be pointed out that, if he is a voluble special pleader, Wilson is a witness appearing, as he quickly establishes, by military orders and not of his own volition. Much less can be said for the testimony of David Tressel Griggs, chief scientist of the Air Force from 1951 to 1952. In a controversy, he is a self-confessed motive hunter, who is as busy in relaying yarns as a messenger in a Greek drama. He is a willing reporter of rumor and hearsay, but his belief in what he repeats is not always a guarantee of its soundness.

A person, pitiable and disturbing, big and small, in *In the Matter of* is Teller; Teller because he is the rival giant thrown into the ring by circumstance and both glad and sorry to be there; Teller because he is the genius singled out to combat genius; Teller because, driven by his own obsession, his first frustrating experiences at Los Alamos, his ultimate triumph with the H-bomb, and the use others have made of him, he has been beguiled into leading one of the two opposing armies in a disastrous civil war between America's scientists. Nearly a year later, when he had suffered unfairly from the ostracism of some scientists as a result of his battle with Oppenheimer even as Oppenheimer had suffered unfairly and cruelly because of Teller's fight against him, Teller saw the light. In a magazine called *Science*, in a chastened and conciliatory mood, as if ashamed of the victory he had scored, Teller was to write, "Disunity among the scientists is one of the greatest dangers for our country."

It was too late. This was the wisdom of twilight, not noon. For the moment the harm had been done. Like Soviet Russia and the United States if ever they fight with the new weapons, the two men in the minds of many, especially in the minds of many scientists, had been compelled to face each other almost in the manner of the two scorpions in a bottle—in Oppenheimer's unforgettable image. They had been forced to do this against sense, against decency, against our national security, and certainly against Oppenheimer's wishes or acceptance of their personal disagreements on any such terms.

What Teller is like, except for being brilliant and having made as major a contribution to the H-bomb as Oppenheimer did the A-bomb, it is hard to say from reading the transcript. In it he is of two minds, forgiving and resentful, generous and grudging, elated and depressed, clear and muddied. Plainly he is a man with a mission, whose zeal can be blinding and exasperating. As is true of all strong enough to care more about getting something done than about being liked while getting it done, he has his detractors and his admirers.

One scientist, with him at Los Alamos, has described him to me as being petulant, intellectually jumpy, and bursting with ideas only some of which are good. Another has said he was charming and unfailingly invigorating. Still another, while not denying his genius, has likened him to an overgrown baby and accused him of being difficult to work with. Wendell M. Latimer, denying the last charge at the hearing, says that he can think of hardly anything "further from the truth." Yet Latimer is quick to qualify this by adding, "I am sure that Dr. Teller would be a hard man to work with if the man above him were trying to stop his program and to put an obstacle in his path. Then he would be a very hard man to work with because he would fight fiercely for what he thought was right. But in any friendly climate Dr. Teller is a perfect colleague, scientifically and personally."

An individualist, a leader not a follower, and like Oppenheimer able to induce other scientists to become members of his orchestra, Teller struggles to be fair as a witness. At one point he can say, "Oppenheimer and I did not always agree at Los Alamos and I believe that it is quite possible, probably, that this was my fault." At another he observes, "I believe that Dr. Oppenheimer was wrong. Of course, it is quite possible that his advice was right and mine wrong."

Unfortunately, there are also times when Teller, the large man, shrinks and becomes very small indeed. There is the embarrassing moment when he agrees with Robb that the postwar Oppenheimer could just as well go fishing for the rest of his life. Even more distressing is his answer when Gray asks him if Oppenheimer's clearance would endanger the common defense and security. Teller, who has already said, "I have always assumed, and I now assume, that he is loyal to the United States," again supports Oppenheimer on the grounds of character. But, apparently unable to forgive him for their differences in opinion, he adds, "If it is a question of wisdom and judgment, as demonstrated by actions since 1945, then I would say one would be wiser not to grant clearance. I must say I am a little confused on this issue." He was not alone.

"Confused" is the adjective Teller also uses to describe Oppenheimer. "Complicated" is another. In this respect, at least, the two men are average in spite of being exceptional. If to the nonscientific reader of *In the Matter of* they seem more complicated than most, no doubt it is because they think, and are equipped to think, along lines beyond our grasp. Perhaps the right word for them is "difficult," that word we so often reach for to console us for not being artists when we speak of the artistic temperament.

In the sense that artists are complicated and can be difficult, Teller and Oppenheimer are both of these because they, and their comasters of the new science, have much of the artist in them. They, however, are artists who, instead of intending to fashion beauty or give pleasure, have stumbled onto the control of forces which have contributed to the more abundant death and can contribute to the more abundant life. The mystery of creation is theirs, though their creation best known to the rest of us is so far a phallus-shaped column which fathers only destruction. Like many artists they are gloriously endowed children who live in a world of their own. Yet theirs is not a world of their imagining but of their making and possible unmaking, and they are no more adjusted to it than we are.

Forced into a loneliness they resent, chagrined because theirs is a knowledge incomprehensible to the most knowing in other fields, and compelled for security reasons to lead lives as restricted as if they were on a sealed ship, they are "The New Men," [4] as C. P. Snow called them, so set apart by mind and gifts, by profession and vocabulary, that he says in England even the British-born scientists are referred to as "the new foreigners." They are individualists, not unconscious of their powers, and discipline is not their dish. In their pursuit of knowledge and still more knowledge, they find it hard and unhealthy to think scientifically in nationalist terms. Like Catholic priests, they feel their faith is a universal religion; like many Jews, they believe they belong to a people apart that stands together regardless of frontiers. By training, instinct, and need they are often at odds with security officers. The struggle between them is the fundamental one noted by Arthur M. Schlesinger, Jr.[5]—"the struggle between those whose business it is to discover and propagate truth, and those whose business it is to conceal it."

The Exceptional Man as a Problem

At M.I.T. Oppenheimer had spoken of the "traditional fraternity of scientists." It was over this order of decidedly odd fellows, close-knit only in their absorption in science, that General Leslie R. Groves was called upon to preside as head of the Manhattan Project with full responsibility for the Los Alamos laboratory and the completion of the A-bomb. He and Colonel John Lansdale, Jr., a Cleveland lawyer and a graduate of V.M.I. and the Harvard Law School, who was accountable to General Groves for the over-all security and intelligence of the atomic project, did not have enviable assignments. They could not have been harder had the men been asked to serve titans as baby-sitters. And both of them showed remarkable insight and patience.

[4] *The New Men*, by C. P. Snow, New York, Charles Scribner's Sons, 1955.

[5] "The Oppenheimer Case," by Arthur M. Schlesinger, Jr., *The Atlantic Monthly*, October, 1954.

In the Matter of boasts no character more likable than General Groves, who appointed Oppenheimer as director at Los Alamos and was to be the one who ordered him to tell the truth about Chevalier and Eltenton. As self-revealed, the General is a kindly, garrulous military type, somewhat of an American Colonel Blimp. Soon in his testimony he proves disarming by saying, "If I talk too long, Mr. Gray, if you will just tell me to stop, it is your time and not mine." Twice he boasts about such a small thing as having a signature that "nobody has been able to forge yet, and they have tried many times." But he has big things to be proud of, too, such as his selection of Oppenheimer and the job done. And no one has better explained the lie Oppenheimer told to protect Chevalier than General Groves, who thinks Oppenheimer had "a typical American schoolboy attitude that there is something wicked about telling on a friend."

As a soldier, the General must have been disturbed by the organization under his command. He knew it was not military; indeed, he described it as being "peculiar." Nonetheless, he had the wisdom to let it be just that, realizing that "the academic scientists . . . were not in sympathy with compartmentalization [or] with security requirements." While he was "always on the other side of the fence," he was "never surprised when one of them broke rules." He was aware that he was "put in positions where he had to approve of things, things people knew he did not want to approve." But as he says in one of the finest statements made at the hearing, "they were the kind of men I wanted, and they were the kind of men that made the project a success. If I had a group of yes-men we never would have gotten anywhere."

We have all been told that the exception proves the rule. The Oppenheimer case should have taught us how disastrous the rule can be when applied to the exception. At the heart of the hearing is the problem presented to the government by the extraordinary man, sorely needed and immensely contributive but difficult because different in temperament and endowment. It is not a simple problem, though General Groves solved it by his very simplicity. He expected the scientists under him to be different and got his results by putting up with the difficulties they caused him. The General, however, was free to take responsibility and use horse sense; the Gray Board's majority felt fettered by the criteria supplied it for judging Oppenheimer and did not presume to use its "mature practical judgment."

The extraordinary man is not apt to reach the full ripening of his talent in average ways. Nor does he become extraordinary merely by being born so or by remaining static. His past, whatever it may have been, is part of his present, not as he once knew it but as he has assimilated it and it has changed him. His wisdom is not the result of his having always acted wisely. It can be the product of former follies which, when recognized as such, have deepened his judgment. Once he may have been irresponsible, but his sense of responsibility grows with increased responsibilities just as one gets sunburned by staying in the sun.

The process of the exceptional man's development is admirably comprehended and expounded by George F. Kennan, former Ambassador to Russia, and himself an extraordinary man. "I sometimes think," says he in an interlude in the hearing in which all of us can take pride, "that the higher types of knowledge and wisdom do not often come without very considerable anguish and often a very considerable road of error. I think the Church has known that. Had the Church applied to St. Francis the criteria relating solely to his youth, it would not have been able for him to be what he was later. . . . I have often said it is the people who have come to their views through the questioning of other things who have the highest and firmest type of understanding in the interests of the government. . . . The exceptional people are often apt not to fit into any categories of requirements that it is easy to write into an act or a series of loyalty regulations."

Acknowledging the problem is real, Kennan hopes the government will consider in the people "who have greater capacities" the whole man and not merely portions of their personality. Of course, Oppenheimer is human enough to have made his mistakes, but he thinks Oppenheimer is the kind of man who, because he has made them, is not apt to make them again. To Kennan, as to many, Oppenheimer's is "one of the great minds of this generation of Americans," and integrity is one of its scientific compulsions.

Asked if Oppenheimer could possibly have been dissembling when he gave opinions contrary to Soviet interests at some very high government policy meetings, Kennan says, "I would suppose that you might just as well have asked Leonardo da Vinci to distort an anatomical drawing as that you should ask Robert Oppenheimer to speak responsibly to the sort of questions we were talking about, and speak dishonestly." Immediately and instinctively Kennan thinks of the scientist in terms of the artist, recognizing that one basis of their kinship is professional integrity.

Some Tantalizing Ifs

Both art and science become creative because of impulses which neither the artist nor the scientist can explain. Both are to this extent chancy affairs, in spite of the order they superimpose on the orderless by selection, arrangement, and calculation. This element of chance, which science and art share with life, is more than ordinarily present in the tangled tale of how at the time of their marriage in 1940 the Oppenheimers became close friends of Haakon Chevalier, that flamboyant member of the French Department of the University of California and translator of Malraux, who looms large in the charges against Oppenheimer, in the testimony at the hearing, and in the unfavorable findings.

Lord Dunsany once wrote a play called *If* in which he showed how different the life of his central character would have been if only he had taken another train. The "ifs" which bring the Oppenheimers and Chevalier together are many and far-reaching. They go back twenty-one years before the hearing; roam two continents; start in the time frame of a different world of thought and sympathies; involve youth, young love, and disenchantment; snatched, hungry happiness; death, loneliness, more sorrow, and confusion; and love found again, love lasting and sustaining which has been made the richer and the fiercer by the new and terrible sorrow that has engulfed it.

These particular "ifs," added to the countless other overlapping twists, complications, conflicting motives, and personalities, explain why Judge Simon H. Rifkind, one of Garrison's partners, said to Oppenheimer, "What you really need in this case is a novelist rather than a lawyer." At moments during her two brief, touching, and dignified appearances as a witness, when Katherine Puening Oppenheimer is talking about the young lovers' Paris that once she knew or about the Civil War in Spain, it almost sounds as if the novelist had been found and his name was Ernest Hemingway.

Kitty Oppenheimer is a small, pretty brunette, forceful, earnest, trained in science, and widely cultivated, who is able intellectually to keep up with Oppenheimer. She was born and raised in Germany of a conservative and well-to-do family, and an irrelevant, though tantalizing "if" in her story is that her mother was once engaged to her distant relative General Keitel of Hitlerian and Nuremberg trial fame. Although Kitty's face is stamped with the agony she and her husband have been through, her figure is as slim as a college girl's.

It is at college that the long trail of "ifs" begins which leads to the Oppenheimers' friendship with Chevalier. If Kitty, when she left the University of Wisconsin for her Christmas vacation in 1933, had not spent it in Pittsburgh; if she had not gone to a party there at the prompting of a friend to meet a Communist just for the fun of seeing what one would be like; if she had not fallen in love with him and married him early the next year; if she had not separated from him in 1936 because, though still in love with him, she could not stand the Communist party which he had persuaded her to join; if he had not gone to fight in Spain with the Loyalists and been killed (after he and Kitty had had a blissful two weeks' reunion in Paris); if, when lost and trying to find life again, she had not drifted into a marriage with an English doctor who was interning in Berkeley; if she had not met Oppenheimer there in 1939, and had they not fallen so tumultuously and uncheckably in love that Kitty got a swift divorce and Oppenheimer broke away from the young girl, a Communist and the daughter of a noted professor of English at Berkeley, to whom he twice thought of himself as engaged; if Kitty's divorce and their marriage had not rocked and bitterly divided the campus community; and if, at a time when the Oppenheimers needed friends, Chevalier had not won Oppenheimer's loyalty by warmly befriending them, things might have been different for the Oppenheimers in the storm that lay ahead, though not better since they would not have each other.

Strauss as an Antagonist

Nonetheless this friendship and this loyalty were to prove costly. And of them no one was to take a dimmer view or to put them to more damaging use against Oppenheimer than Admiral Strauss. His part in the abasement of Oppenheimer is a major one. As chairman of the AEC, he does not, of course, appear at the hearing. He does not have to; the hearing appears because of him. He is its producer, Eisenhower a backer. Although absent in *In the Matter of*, Strauss does make an appearance after its close which is more personal than he may have wanted it to be. For it is then, by writing the final verdict for the AEC, that he, as it were, speaks the merciless epilogue.

Even so, it is regrettable that Strauss, along with Roosevelt, Senator McMahon, General Vandenberg, General Doolittle, Finletter, Acheson, and Bernard Baruch, as Mrs. Trilling notes, is not heard from. All of these men could have made interesting additions to a story, overcopious though still strangely incomplete. None, however, could have made a contribution more interesting than Strauss, if only he had revealed why his feelings about Oppenheimer were so strong that they drove him to write about him as he did.

These words and actions of his are my only way of judging (or misjudging) Strauss directly. Since he did not speak for himself at the hearing and would not be interviewed about the case, I have no choice except to rely on what others have said or written about him for a more complete picture. On one point the friends and enemies of Lewis Lichtenstein Strauss (pronounced "Straws" because this is the way his family's name has long been pronounced in Virginia) are forced by his record to agree. He is exceptionally able, exceptionally cultivated, and has been exceptionally lucky. A candied apple could not be shinier in its sugar coating than his career in its success.

Fortune is the proper magazine to run an article on Strauss's latter-day version of an Horatio Alger story. And *Fortune* [6] did. Eight months after the hearing it chronicled his fabulous rise from being a shoe drummer on the back roads of the South for his family's jobbing firm in Richmond to his present position of frightening power and responsibility in Washington. *Fortune* says that Strauss made the most important of his many profitable investments when at twenty-one he took the $5,000 he had saved from three years of selling shoes and went to Washington in 1917 to work for Herbert Hoover as a volunteer with the Commission for Relief in Belgium. At the end of the next three years of frugal living Strauss had caught

[6] "The Controversial Mr. Strauss," by Duncan Norton-Taylor, *Fortune*, January, 1955.

Hoover's attention, become his "invaluable secretary," gone to Europe with him for the second time, been observed there by Mortimer Schiff, and received a letter from Schiff in 1919 offering him a high-salaried job with Kuhn, Loeb and Company in New York which he accepted. Four years later he had married Alice Hanauer, a daughter of one of the partners, and in 1929 at thirty-three had been made a full partner, a position which, according to *Fortune,* Wall Street then rated as worth a million dollars a year.

Intensely religious, a past president of Manhattan's Temple Emanu-El Congregation, a scholarly friend of scholars, an active philanthropist, since boyhood interested in science, a diplomatic negotiator, a tireless operator, a gifted public servant, an early and staunch advocate of the H-bomb, ever able to be important to important people whether Hoover, Schiff, the elder Morgan, the Rockefellers, Truman, or Eisenhower, and always a scrapper—these are the terms in which *Fortune* sketches Strauss. No wonder as a reservist in the Navy, ordered to report early in 1941 as lieutenant commander to work in ordnance, he retired four years later as a rear admiral. Or that his "rather owlish face," which used to be "caught by the camera's eye on the edge of events," has "now moved into the center of the picture."

But what about the man behind the owlish face, "the Old World manners, and the gentle, luminous brown eyes?" Though to his friends "dynamic, possessed of a brilliant mind, warm-hearted and loyal," *Fortune* admits that to his critics Strauss appears "thin-skinned, intellectually arrogant, and rough in battle." As one said, "he has more elbows than an octopus."

The Alsops, vigorous and skilled polemicists, are less gentle with him. He is the villain of their Zolaesque account of the Oppenheimer case. According to them, "With his chiefs, like Forrestal and Eisenhower, [Strauss] is all pliability. But from equals and subordinates, he likes no argument." They quote one of his fellow commissioners as saying, "If you disagree with Lewis about anything, he assumes you're just a fool. But if you go on disagreeing, he concludes you must be a traitor."

Oppenheimer disagreed with Strauss violently, openly, and not always tactfully. The Alsops cite an incident in the long-brewing trouble between the two men. It occurred when they clashed while giving their views to the Joint Congressional Committee on Atomic Energy on the question of exporting radioactive isotopes to Norway. Apparently Oppenheimer, who favored such an action, took undisguised delight in attacking Strauss's stand. The Alsops say that Joseph Volpe, who was present as counsel for the AEC at that time, saw Strauss's face "darken with fury" during the testimony, and that Volpe recalls Oppenheimer's asking at the meeting's end, "Joe, how did I do?" and his answering, after another look at Strauss, "Robert, you did much too well for your own good." This was five years before Strauss, then a commissioner, returned to the AEC as its chairman.

By some miracle of civilized control the two men are said to accomplish courtesy even now when they meet, as at the Institute for Advanced Study. Though this courtesy is strained and puts a strain on others, the tension between them is not new. Those who worked with them before Strauss called Oppenheimer to Washington to make his unacceptable offer report their behavior, though correct, has long been prickly and that their good manners, though studiously maintained, have been unequal to masking the fact that their personalities are incompatible. Perhaps another source of friction has been that, whereas both enjoy power, Strauss has had to struggle to achieve authority and Oppenheimer, with his very special intellect, has grown up assuming that he had it.

The suffering Oppenheimer underwent because of the hearing is public knowledge. What is surprising, though light-shedding, is that Strauss is surprised he should have suffered, too. *Fortune* notes that "this man who has lived by making friends" has said "for the first time in my life I have enemies." After pointing out, quite rightly, that he was only one of a number of high officials who, in effect, decided it was good policy to have Oppenheimer written off as expendable, Strauss, with more self-interest than generosity, refers to the case as "a tragic thing—I shall live with it as long as I live." To this he adds that he does not see how the administration (not the government) could have pursued any other course, and flatly denies that any exception should have been made because of Oppenheimer's eminence (not because of his past services or future value) in the world of science. Strauss does this on the grounds that "the whole of democracy breaks down unless you apply the same rules to all men equally."

Regardless of the reasons, noble, high-minded, or even politically expedient, that Strauss may have advanced to justify the hearing, there is nothing noble, high-minded, or even politically expedient that he could come up with to excuse the tone of the decision at the hearing's end.

It would be difficult to find a sorrier example of an ungenerous judgment. The decision may seem to show moderation in granting Oppenheimer the right to his opinion on the H-bomb. Yet the opinion it states of Oppenheimer's defects in character is devoid of tolerance. So brutal is it as a condemnation that it sounds like outrage turned into cruelty. As Harry Kalven, Jr., has succinctly suggested,[7] since the Gray Board had been unable to prove Oppenheimer a traitor, the majority of the Commission, under the leadership of Strauss, endeavors to condemn him as a liar, and a habitual one at that.

The Six Examples

Strauss's decision cites six examples which by accretion are supposed to establish that Oppenheimer and the truth are not on speaking terms. Considered singly or jointly, these samples are more preposterous than persuasive, based as they are on instances of a sort that a friend would understand and only a prosecutor misinterpret. Four of the six go back to 1943 and were known to Strauss in 1947 when he voted for Oppenheimer's clearance; two date from 1949 (the year of the fight about the crash program for the H-bomb) ; and all are made public nine years after Oppenheimer had shortened the war by the A-bomb, one day before his contract with the AEC would have expired, and three months before Strauss (who may not dislike having the power to give no less than to take away) was to vote for Oppenheimer's re-election as director of the Institute for Advanced Study.

Three (concerning Lomanitz, Lambert, and Weinberg) have to do with contradictions and confusions in recall or total lapses of

[7] "The Case of J. Robert Oppenheimer before the Atomic Energy Commission," by Harry Kalven, Jr., *Bulletin of the Atomic Scientists*, September, 1954.

memory such as anyone would—not might—be guilty of eleven or five years later, when it comes to remembering having met or even twice lunched with one stranger, having written at a friend's request an endorsement (carefully qualified) about another, or recalling the exact time or manner of learning that still another was known to be a Communist. One instance centers in the fact that Oppenheimer, having said before a Congressional committee words perhaps too unkind about the political background of a man named Peters, later changed the emphasis of his opinion by writing to a newspaper words perhaps too kind upon hearing that his previous statement had imperiled Peters's job.

The final instance attempts to show that Oppenheimer was a liar because in the hearing he said that at the GAC meeting in 1949 the vote against the H-bomb program had been "surprisingly unanimous." (The eight present had voted that way.) He had forgotten that from Sweden before this meeting he had received from Dr. Glenn T. Seaborg, the one absent member, a letter so meandering and noncommittal until it reached the negative sentence in which it approved the program that not many people would have been able to remember it two weeks, much less five years, later. The only lie beyond question in the six instances is the lie Oppenheimer had admitted to telling in 1943 to protect Chevalier and about which Strauss had long known.

Perhaps because of recognizing that, as proofs of Oppenheimer's addiction to untruth, these instances are inconclusive when not slightly ludicrous, the AEC verdict adds, "The catalogue does not end with [them]. . . . The work of the Military Intelligence, the Federal Bureau of Investigation, and the Atomic Energy Commission—all, at one time or another, have felt the effect of his falsehoods, evasions, and misrepresentations." This is a statement of the most terrible seriousness which cannot be taken seriously, except as a blow below the belt, since the evidence offered to support it, if not nonexistent, is certainly unproduced.

To the six instances intended to destroy Oppenheimer's "character," a section is added about his "associations." In this the visit Chevalier paid the Oppenheimers in Princeton in 1950 and their two meetings in Paris in 1953, like Oppenheimer's slight assistance to Chevalier in his attempts to get a passport in those years, are pounced upon by Strauss almost with relief, because they are nearer to the present than the other dusty exhumations submitted as accusations.

The Paris meetings could not, as is clear in testimony given under oath, have been more innocent. Chevalier had heard that the Oppenheimers were coming to France. He made the first move by letter and Kitty replied by phone in Paris. The Oppenheimers dined one night with Chevalier and his new wife, who impressed Oppenheimer as being "an extremely sensible, non-Communistic girl." To give this a conspiratorial sound, the AEC decision says they "visited privately," which in everyday language means they had dinner at the Chevaliers' home. The talk was "personal" and "diffuse." Among other things it dealt with how the two couples were living and at one point with Chevalier's continued employment at UNESCO. The next morning Chevalier picked up the Oppenheimers and took them to call on the, by now, vehemently anti-Communist Malraux, with whom for an hour they discussed "his philosophical and literary work." Then Chevalier drove them back to their hotel and left them there. The whole much-publicized and criticized affair was as subversive as that.

Many have doubted the wisdom of these meetings. Even Dr. Evans in his dissent says he does not like them but cannot condemn Oppenheimer because of them. To Gray and Morgan, however, they take on "a high degree of significance" as being inconsistent with the strictest interpretation of security interests. By this they mean that, regardless of the topics discussed and notwithstanding his "strong, strong guess" that Chevalier was not then active in Communist circles, Oppenheimer, because of his access to top-secret information, should not have continued to see Chevalier at all. To Strauss, in his AEC verdict, these reunions in Paris are additional proofs of Oppenheimer's "persistent and willful disregard for the obligations of security" and part of a sinister pattern. To Dr. Smyth "there is no evidence that they had any security significance."

They would, and could, have had none had it not been for the far more important earlier instance of the admitted lie, or the so-called Chevalier incident. Of all the information against Oppenheimer this alone comes close to being derogatory, and then only because of the false impression it can be used to create. Though decent in its motives, it is beyond dispute a blunder which might have been merely regrettable had it not been disastrous in its results.

Because of it the Paris meetings acquire guilt by association, Strauss is able to speak of a pattern, and Oppenheimer comes close to wounding his reputation mortally.

In its essentials the Chevalier incident is very simple and would have remained so if Oppenheimer had not distressed his friends and delighted his foes by making it very complicated. Early in 1943 or late in 1942, Chevalier and his wife had come to the Oppenheimer home, "Eagle Hill" in Berkeley, for cocktails or for dinner. Oppenheimer was aware that Chevalier was mixed up in left-wing activities, and in 1946 was to tell the FBI that he was a fellow traveler, but at the time of the "incident" and afterward he did not think that Chevalier was a Communist.

When Oppenheimer went into the pantry to make drinks, Chevalier followed him and said, "I saw George Eltenton recently." Oppenheimer believes Chevalier asked him if he remembered Eltenton, a British scientist he had met a few times. In any case Chevalier did say that Eltenton had told him he had a way of getting scientific information to Soviet scientists. Oppenheimer thinks he replied, "But that is treason." He knows he said, "This is a terrible thing to do," or "made some strong remark to the effect that this sounded terribly wrong." The brief interchange ended there. According to Oppenheimer, nothing in their friendship would have led him to believe that Chevalier was actually seeking information, and he is certain that Chevalier had no notion of the kind of work on which Oppenheimer was engaged.

Thinking he had handled the situation and in his own way taken care of security, Oppenheimer did nothing more about this interchange until he learned that Colonel Lansdale was worried about the security situation in Berkeley because of a forceful Communist union there. Then he remembered that Eltenton was a member and promoter of this union. Of his own accord he went to Colonel Pash late in August, 1943, to warn him that "Eltenton would bear watching." When pressed for details, out of his anxiety to shield Chevalier and his reluctance to mention himself, he was foolish enough to invent "a cock and bull story" about Eltenton's having attempted to approach three members of the project through an intermediary. He refused to disclose the identity of the intermediary or the three men, but to give the illusion of truth to his lie added some details about microfilm and a man at the Russian Consulate.

With a few variations he remained faithful to this falsehood when he talked with Colonel Lansdale in September, but in December, when ordered by General Groves to do so, he named Chevalier, told the full truth, and confessed his lie.

No one can defend the lie Oppenheimer told. The world's sorry state has forced us to come (or decline) a long way in our acquiescence to security measures, yet it is hard to see even now how any decent person can fail to understand the dilemma Oppenheimer faced or the impulse that led him to protect a friend rather than turn him in, especially when he thought the incident closed. Certainly the motive that prompted him was decent though misguided, just as the motive that led him of his own free will to warn Colonel Pash about Eltenton was decent. In obeying the first of these motives, however, Oppenheimer was guilty of an error in judgment of which no one has been more unreservedly critical than Oppenheimer himself in *In the Matter of*.

Oppenheimer's story about Chevalier was one lie told with different trimmings, as Dr. Evans had the wit to see, and not the string of lies it is represented as being by the majority of the Gray Board, the AEC, and General Nichols. Oppenheimer is himself to blame for providing an excuse for such a misrepresentation. It is his dazed and unexpected cooperation as a witness which makes it possible— and fair—for Robb to create this impression.

No passage in the transcript is more sickening to read, and none can have been more discouraging for Oppenheimer's counsel to hear, than the one in which Oppenheimer not only walks into Robb's trap but sets it for him. Instead of explaining his error by giving the good reasons he presents many days later, for once he gets hopelessly rattled.

Out of shame or remorse, due to fatigue, confusion, or anger at his past stupidity, when Robb asks him why he lied he replies, "Because I was an idiot." Still speaking of the lie as one lie and still being questioned about it as such, he describes "the whole thing" as "a fabrication" and "a piece of pure idiocy." Then Robb, immediately after referring to it as "the story," sees his chance. "Isn't it a fair statement today, Dr. Oppenheimer," he asks, "that, according to your own testimony now, you told not one lie to Pash but a whole fabrication and tissue of lies?" Oppenheimer's unthinking and fatal answer is "Yes." The damage is done.

Both the Chevalier incident and the Paris meetings raise vital questions about security; about loyalty, too, as it was once and is now understood. Both touch upon the problem of the exceptional man, and the extent to which someone in a very sensitive government position has the right to exercise his own judgment, regardless of regulations, in handling a special case or seeing old friends, however casually, if seeing them can be misinterpreted or lead to danger.

That in both instances Oppenheimer should have felt himself equipped to cope with the situation, holding himself above regulations, is no cause for astonishment to those who have known or worked with him, though it is a reason for questioning a security system which, after seeking to defame him, exiles from the nation's service a man of such extraordinary and proven abilities. Nothing in a democracy is more needed or intolerable than a person whose mental superiority is such that it cannot be disguised. Oppenheimer's intellectual prowess is neither a fabrication nor a secret. It is a fact admitted by others of which he cannot himself be unaware.

Oppenheimer, Then and Now

Charming, friendly, capable of the most winning and considerate manners, Oppenheimer can seem humility itself. Yet it is impossible not to suspect that, though he may believe his humility is genuine, it is a garment he wears much as Garbo wears those dark glasses which are not the convincing proofs of modesty they are meant to be, since they make her the more, not the less, conspicuous.

Immodest Oppenheimer is not, though he is above the mockery of pretending that he does not recognize his worth. Arrogant as he may at times be, what in his case is often mistaken for arrogance is in the truest sense honesty. He does not boast about being exceptional, and does not have to. His talk, his writing, and his professional record prove that he is. Being exceptional is a condition which he accepts, doubtless gaining a sense of protection from realizing his superiority.

When at the hearing he says, "it seems to me and other knowledgeable people," or "radar is not the subject of my expertness," or, when he tells Ed Murrow on *See It Now* that "at the Institute they won't let me teach, they are afraid I will confuse the students," he is not being egotistical. He is only telling the truth and facing the evidence as a scientist. He is no less candid and equally exact in his reply to Robb's question, "Doctor, is it true that from 1943 until recently you were the most influential scientist in the country?" At first he spars by answering, "I think that is a question you will have to ask the people influenced." Then, when pressed, he adds, "I think with some people I was very influential, with others not at all. I was certainly an influential physicist and put it anywhere you want."

By some of his fellow physicists Oppenheimer is said when young to have been more impatient with the slower witted than he now is, and always to have been more respectful to experts in other fields than to those in his own. A little of this impatience seeps into his testimony, as when he says to Robb, "To questions that are badly phrased, categorical answers are not always possible." The miracle is that under the strain of days of cross-examination, especially Robb's cross-examining, his impatience does not show itself more often.

Oppenheimer's impatience is not a display of unkindness or of rudeness, except when he has cause to be rude. Instead it is the expression of a mind that runs while other minds walk, a mind that cannot be held in check, that values time too much to waste it, that interrupts only because it anticipates what is coming long before it comes, and that has a passion for precision. He is not being a slippery witness; he is being true to this passion when he gives such answers as, "I don't say I believe his denial. I just say he denied it," or "That is part of the answer. The rest of it is that I also didn't attend such a meeting at any time."

As is entirely understandable, he has his fun fencing with Robb and enjoys irritating him by this very insistence on exactitude. What is beyond understanding is how, with such a precise mind, he fails to note that Robb has tricked him into saying that the one lie he told about Chevalier is many lies.

In *In the Matter of,* what Oppenheimer forgets is natural, what he remembers is phenomenal. Although his command of his own subject is to be expected, his comprehension of military problems is amazing. One of the most precise of mortals in his choice of words, he is also one of the most fluent employers of the language, having a talent for articulateness equaled only by the many uncommon gifts he has brought to the service of science.

Dr. Evans, who is for him, may agree with those who are against him in maintaining that he is still naïve. If he is, naïveté has seldom taken so sophisticated a form or simplicity been more intricate. He has had to master, and (being Oppenheimer) did master quickly, the tough realities of governmental politics. Nonetheless he continues to have an artlessness of manner which suggests a man wise in the ways of the world, yet uncontaminated, and above its worldliness. In adult, intellectual, and tortured terms, a Billy Budd-like quality of purity persists in him, despite his dexterity as a manipulator, the disenchantment he must have experienced in Washington, or the sadness which now furrows his face.

Those who resent the range of his mind and the sweep of his sensibilities insist that his only remaining naïveté (and a sure betrayal of his arrogance) can be found in his readiness to discuss art, painting, music, books, the theatre, or strategy with the same authority that he talks about theoretical physics. The truth is that he is a strong believer in "convertible talents" and his knowledge by no means stops with science. Unlike many men who have contented themselves with hitching their wagons to a star, Oppenheimer has hitched his to a constellation.

The rounded knowledge which is his today he came by tardily. The slow process of his education is described in his autobiographical answer to Nichols which serves as a prologue to *In the Matter of*. Though the self-portrait of an exceptional man, it is surprisingly familiar in its basic lines. At least it is to those of us who lived through the anguishing depression and postdepression years and, much as we hated Communism, understood how many people, especially intellectuals, were then drawn to it in this country, not because their impulses were bad but because they were good.

Oppenheimer was one of these. Born in New York in 1904, the son of protectively well-off parents, he had a prodigy's lonely youth and growing up. Even after 1929, when he had started teaching at the University of California and the California Institute of Technology, he lived in a kind of scientific Cuckoo-Borough-on-Clouds until 1936. Then he came to feel "a smoldering fury about the treatment of the Jews in Germany," and realized that a decisive struggle was being fought by the Loyalists in Spain. He expressed his belated concern with politics by becoming interested in and contributing to left-wing causes. His political awakening occurred during the same year that Kitty, fed up with the party, was separated from her Communist first husband.

By his own confession, he never read a newspaper or such a current magazine as *Time* and *Harper's* (his bracketing), never had a radio or telephone, did not learn of the 1929 crash until long afterward, and did not vote until he was thirty-two. The word he selects to summarize his career up to this point is "bizarre," which is something of an understatement. He did, however, read Sanskrit. He did know Greek. French was his second language. He was widely read in the classics. He had tried his hand at painting and doted on music. The comments of two of his professors at Harvard, from which he was graduated in 1925, give some notion of what he was then like. One of them remarked, when Oppenheimer submitted a formidable bibliography at examination time, "Anyone who says he has read all these books is a liar, but anyone who knows their names deserves to be a graduate student." The other said, "You have so much talent, it is too bad you have no interest in learning what has happened."

He did learn, first, by his mastery of science; next, by his disillusionment with Communism at the beginning of World War II; and finally, by playing a vital part in great events. The twenties, that supposedly frivolous decade, were for Oppenheimer "a heroic time." After Harvard he had studied abroad at Cambridge and Göttingen, and in collaboration with scores of scientists from many lands had come to know the "terror" and "exaltation" of the new insight into atomic physics. As a pioneer in this field, he began teaching at Berkeley, having only one graduate student his first year, but in time building up the largest school in this country devoted to the study of quantum theory, nuclear physics, relativity, and other modern physics.

The Oppenheimer of those days was apparently quite different from the Oppenheimer of *In the Matter of* or the Oppenheimer of today. Already he had the mesmerizing touch, already the actor's knowledge of how to make a point by underplaying. In California before his marriage he was very much the Bohemian, long-haired, and a night owl who expected his students to be night owls, too. Looking like a peripatetic philosopher of old, he would take his classes on long walks and lecture to them under trees. One visitor to his ranch in New Mexico remembers that the guest who wanted to eat was wise if he arrived with some ham sandwiches, because Oppenheimer often forgot about meals. When he remembered, he was apt to breakfast on sour wine and hard toast, lunch on chile, skip dinner, and have a snack at 2 A.M. before going to sleep.

Today his pork-pie hat is his last outward vestige of unconventionality. In the quiet of the Institute grounds at Princeton, he, Kitty, and their son and daughter live in a smoothly run and charming home, built around a house dating back to 1696. It is the perfect mirror of their cultivation, with its square piano, excellent collection of records, its many books (especially French ones), with a fine Van Gogh and a Vuillard in one of the three living rooms, and a Derain in the dining room.

Except for his mud-colored pork-pie hat, Oppenheimer is now decidedly Ivy League in his clothes, often wearing a dark gray suit, well cut and pressed, a light gray shirt, and a greenish gray tie. He is thin and small and frail to the point of transparency, yet singularly impressive. The power of his personality is the stronger because of the fragility of his person. When he speaks he seems to grow, since the largeness of his mind so affirms itself that the smallness of his body is forgotten. His tiny hands and fingers are birdlike, and as he talks, when not gesturing with his horn-rimmed glasses, he emphasizes his leanness by being apt to encircle his right elbow or forearm with his left hand, or stroke his scrawny, gobbler neck with it.

His head is the head of a Rameses, small, flattish on top, and so fine, though firm, in its bony structure that it appears carved. His face is a mind openly at work, at once a reflector and a light. Though in no ordinary sense handsome, it nonetheless has a strange beauty, the beauty of intensity, of awareness, of sensitivity and wisdom, and that grief can bestow like a decoration. His light blue eyes, extraordinary in their brightness, darken to a Mediterranean hue when he laughs, feels strongly, or concentrates.

There is now much sorrow in them and heavy sorrow in his expression, for the hearing is a wound with which he lives and it has aged him. The close-knit thatch of hair remains black at the base, though it has whitened above. The wrinkles on his throat, high on his forehead, and in the wishbone cornering his mouth are more plentiful and have stabbed deeper. His enunciation is as meticulously word-loving as ever, but his low, rich voice, with its slight scratch of gravel, has increased in melancholy. Although he continues to suck his pipe with elaborate deliberation, when not chain-smoking cigarettes, the restlessness within him churns as it did not before the agony.

When he learned of the majority findings, first of the Gray Board, then of the AEC, Oppenheimer doubtless felt a reeling of the mind and a cracking of the heart almost beyond endurance. Aware of the course the hearing had taken, he may have foreseen the outcome. Anticipating it was bad enough; living with it, when it had ceased to be a dread and become a fact, far worse. He must have been tempted to borrow George Herbert's words and cry, "No more; I will abroad!" The questions asked in Herbert's poem (a favorite of his) are questions he could well have asked himself, "Have I no harvest but a thorn? . . . Have I no bay leaves to crown it, No flowers, no garlands gay? all blasted, All wasted?"

Publicly discredited, pictured as a habitual liar, confused in the minds of many with a traitor because of having been branded a security risk, and declared by two groups of distinguished men for different but equally poor reasons unfit to continue to serve a government he had served brilliantly, he seemed through. The outlook was black, very black. If his enemies were pleased, it was for the same reason that his friends were dejected. One friend, in the desolation of those first months, said, "There are only three things you can do about Robert—clear him (which would be very complicated and demand a courage lacking in most administrations), let him go through life with a bleeding wound, or out of kindness kill him."

He was still director of the Institute for Advanced Study, which he had helped to make a sanctuary for scholars and a mecca for physicists. Strauss had voted to leave him that, and his vote, if he really believed the devastating charges to which as chairman of the AEC he had subscribed a short four months before, could be said not to prove his clemency but to cast doubts on his responsibility as a trustee.

In the serenity of Princeton, among the questing, away from telephones, committee meetings, and classes, and "where deep thoughts are duty," Oppenheimer has been able to pursue his studies and aid others in pursuing theirs. "Most people," he told Ed Murrow, "depend on being interrupted in order to live." He depends upon not being interrupted in order to think, and thinking is his life. The Institute by design takes away from men "the cares, the pleasures that are their normal excuse for not following the rugged road of their own life and need and destiny." Oppenheimer is able now "to guess in the night and correct in the daytime." Immersed in the action which he holds research to be, he can again devote himself to pure science, spared the impurities of government and politics.

Nonetheless, the hearing abides in the Oppenheimer home as a permanent resident. In Kitty's blood it continues to boil, an understandable source of indignation. Oppenheimer has tried to put it behind him, explaining, in a phrase large in spirit and Biblical in phrasing, "I cannot sit with anger." But the hurt is there and always will be, and the scars are deeper than the deep ones which show. Nearly a half year after the verdict I remember telling him of my shame as an American because of the dry crucifixion to which he had been subjected, and I cannot forget his reply. Smiling the unhappiest of smiles, he said, "You know, it wasn't so very dry. I can still feel the warm blood on my hands."

Aftermath

The final irony of the Oppenheimer case is its aftermath. At its conclusion, to his enemies he may have seemed disposed of, to his friends and to himself destroyed. Yet, due to the mutability of his creative talent, to the quickly altered temper of the times, and to three salvaging occurrences, his career, apparently ruined, has already entered upon another of its contributive phases.

The rewards of martyrdom are real but posthumous. Oppenheimer, always the exceptional man, has survived his martyrdom. Though he will never outlive its pains, some of its rewards even now are his. The nimbus of the cruelly sacrificed is about his head, and his reputation and following have grown accordingly. He has lost much because of the injustice done to him, and because of it the government has lost the benefit of his counsel. Yet in one respect he has gained along with the public and the community of scientists. Denied one release for his creative power, he has been forced to find another, and become the spokesman for science and its interpreter, its voice and philosopher.

In different professions the peak is reached at different times, early or late, in the spring, the summer, the fall, or even in the winter. Scientists say that, unlike the experimental physicist who blooms later, the theoretical physicist flowers in the spring. His need is not for experience, hence time, but for the audacity and inspiration which belong to youth.

Einstein blossomed in this fashion, reaching his greatest creative period between 1905 and 1915 during the decade after he was twenty-five. In the same way, according to some scientists, Oppenheimer's years of highest personal "creativity" as a theoretical physicist came in his early and middle twenties when he was abroad, publishing in English or German a large number of distinguished papers on various subjects related to the quantum theory. These same scientists point out that after this productive outburst Oppenheimer did not cease to be a creator. His creative gift merely expressed itself in different ways, as a teacher at Berkeley where it was transferred to his students, as an excellent and evocative administrator at Los Alamos, as an adviser and consultant to the government on many commissions and committees of the utmost importance, as an inspirational developer of the whole field of theoretical physics at the Institute, and since the hearing more than ever as the statesman and symbol of science, or, to repeat, as at once its spokesman and philosopher.

As a major contributor to the giddying and frightening new world in which we live, Oppenheimer is acutely aware of the "changes which have unmoored us from the past." "We have changed the face of the earth," he said at Princeton four months before the hearing. "We have changed the way men live. We may not change the condition of man's life, but we have changed all the modes in which that condition occurs." Seven months after the hearing, he said at Columbia, "One thing that is new is the prevalence of newness, the changing scale and scope of change itself, so that the world alters as we walk in it, so that the years of a man's life measure not some small growth or development or rearrangement or moderation of what he learned in childhood but a great upheaval."

Like everyone else Oppenheimer had changed with the altering years. The change in his function, so marked after the hearing, was clear even before his government, by discarding him in the shabby way it did, demonstrated that for the time being fear, folly, or vindictiveness had changed its understanding of the American concept of gratitude, courage, and justice. The totally dissimilar subjects which interested him with the passing decades are the surest guide to the shift in Oppenheimer's concerns. Where in 1926 he was writing about "Quantum Theory and Intensity Distribution in Continuous Spectra" and in 1928 "On the Quantum Theory of the Autoelectric Field Currents," in 1953 he was writing in *Foreign Affairs* about "Atomic Weapons and American Policy" and talking the next year at Columbia about "Prospects in the Arts and Sciences." He had moved from the specific to the universal, from the single problem in science to the general problem presented by the new science, and from one area of investigation to the contemplation of the meaning of science to men.

On June 11, 1954, at the time when Strauss had rushed *In the Matter of* into print, a small-big volume by Oppenheimer was published in this country. It was called *Science and the Common Understanding*,[8] and consisted of reprints of the six Reith Lectures he had delivered over the home service of the British Broadcasting Company the previous November and December.

It is a fascinating but enormously difficult book, quite different in its tone from the colloquial Oppenheimer who at the hearing talks about getting more bang for a buck, keeping old ideas on the back burner, or a chairman's need to get everybody into the act. It is written in the prophet's style that Oppenheimer has come to employ in his latter-day addresses and articles. Easy enough to follow in most of its single sentences, it is easier still to get lost in it paragraph by paragraph and chapter by chapter. It is the work of a scientist who is an artist and an artist who is a poet.

The rhythms of the *Bhagavad-Gita* are in it at the same time that it sings the wonders of the great house of science in the manner of a psalmist. It is incantation, not exposition. Often it is the kind of prose, heavy with incense, that Robert Edmond Jones used to employ in his dithyrambs about the stage. Yet, lucidly murky or plain fancy as it sometimes is, it nonetheless possesses a glow, and has beauty in it, and greatness too. Inevitably one of its themes is loneliness or "the incommunicability of the scientific experience" since it speaks for a mind which, because of its singularity, dwells in solitude far above the timberline of average thoughts and insights.

Oppenheimer is no vulgarizer or popularizer, and would loathe being either. Yet it is his phenomenal gift with language and the

[8] *Science and the Common Understanding,* by J. Robert Oppenheimer, New York, Simon and Schuster, 1954.

unmistakable superiority of his mind which have enabled him to become the acknowledged spokesman for his profession since the hearing. The three occurrences which helped to rehabilitate him, when to Strauss and even to himself his reputation must have seemed beyond redeeming, were his eloquent broadcast address with which on December 26, 1954, he closed Columbia University's year-long bicentennial celebration; his memorable television appearance with Ed Murrow on January 4 of the next year; and the incredible decision of the University of Washington not to let him lecture there that spring. The first two introduced Oppenheimer to an audience of a size that he had never had before, making America aware of the man and his quality; the last was an instance of suppression which not only rallied the scientific and academic communities to his defense but outraged everyone interested in freedom.

What was done to Oppenheimer in the days of the recent terror was done to others, and in the future will undoubtedly be done to still more. In the hearts and minds of people of a certain kind the cruelty is always there which prompts them to bully, and maim, and slaughter, and do dark deeds in the bright name of liberty under the misapprehension that they are making it secure. Few ever believed Oppenheimer guilty of disloyalty, but more and more Americans have come to feel guilty themselves because of what he was forced to endure. Our shame for the injustice done him in our name and allegedly in our interest in part explains the wide esteem in which he is now held. In his presence it is not his mind alone which makes us uneasy. It is our consciences.

ACKNOWLEDGMENTS

Thanks are due, and gladly given, to *The Saturday Review* for permission to reprint certain chapters which first appeared in its pages, and to *Look,* which carried a condensation of "The Trumans Leave the White House."

My thanks and obligations do not stop here. In fact, I am indebted to so many people for their aid, stimulation, and patience that space will not permit me to mention them. I must, however, express my gratitude to those men discussed in these pages who gave generously of their help and were kind enough to submit to the bothersome process of being interviewed at length. I must also thank their friends, and those who are not their friends, for being no less generous with their time and knowledge. Since all were candid in stating their opinions, I cannot for obvious reasons reveal their names, though I do want them to know how sincerely I appreciate their help.

I am, however, free to name, and am more than happy to do so, Norman Cousins, Gardner Cowles, Dan Mich, and Edward C. Aswell for their encouragement, and, above all, Cass Canfield for his invaluable suggestions and for his faith and friendship.

I also want to thank Charles P. Curtis for his wise advice while I was writing the Oppenheimer chapter, Francis McCarthy for his unfailing helpfulness in supplying needed information immediately, and Howard M. Teichmann upon whose friendship I not only leaned heavily but imposed. A kind man and a brave one, he submitted to the ordeal of letting me read him most of these pages. There are others too numerous to list who have been exposed to this same ordeal. I only hope these coerced listeners know how much they helped and how grateful I am to them. Though words are supposedly my business, I cannot find any that are adequate to convey my appreciation to Elisabeth Sill, whose assistance has been so unfailing that I must thank her as a collaborator.

Finally, there is my family—my wife, Catherine, and my two sons, Preston and Meredith—who have my profound apologies and grateful love for putting up with me (not always an easy assignment) during the writing of this book, and for assisting in ways beyond counting or repaying.

J.M.B.

INDEX

295

Set in Intertype Baskerville
Format by Robert Cheney
Manufactured by The Haddon Craftsmen, Inc.
Published by HARPER & BROTHERS, *New York*